C000293411

CUDMORE
AND
THE AMERICA'S CUP

CUDMORE
AND
THE AMERICA'S CUP

A sailor's perspective

MALCOLM McKEAG

The Kingswood Press

The Kingswood Press
an imprint of William Heinemann Ltd
10 Upper Grosvenor Street, London W1X 9PA

LONDON MELBOURNE
JOHANNESBURG AUCKLAND

First published 1987

ISBN 0 434 98120 6

Printed and bound in Great Britain by
Richard Clay Ltd, Bungay, Suffolk

For Graham Walker, gentle giant of British yachting, without whom there would quite simply be no viable British America's Cup Twelve Metre effort today.

Harold Cudmore
April 1987

Malcolm McKeag
April 1987

Contents

Language Convention

The America's Cup was a trans-Atlantic and is now an International competition sometimes divided – as is so much else – by the common language of English. In discussing the Cup and its competition in general English spelling is used, but where a specifically American aspect of the Cup is concerned, American spelling is used where appropriate. In particular, the word 'defense' has been used throughout specifically to refer either individually or collectively to the twenty-three successive and successful American campaigns spread over 132 years to retain the Cup in American hands. Americans spell the name of the class in which the Cup is now raced 'Twelve Meter', but as the class is administered by the International Yacht Racing Union whose official language is English, the official name of the class – International Twelve Metre – is that used throughout the book.

Britain's Twelve Metre was first named *Crusader* in November, 1985 and re-named *White Crusader* in 1986 when the final sponsorship deal with White Horse Whisky was announced. The term 'the White Crusade' was thus subsequently coined by the author as a neat umbrella for Britain's 1984–87 America's Cup campaign and in this book for the sake of simple clarity is occasionally used in contexts which strictly speaking pre-date the signing of the White Horse sponsorship deal and the consequent bestowing on the yacht of her final name.

Acknowledgements

For any book on a sporting event so vast as the America's Cup an author must rely on at least some of the great store of already published literature as source material or as corroboration or denial of vaguely recalled prejudice. Among the sources I have frequently turned to are William Lawson's *History of the America's Cup*, a wonderful read and containing by Winfield M Thomas the most detailed, painstaking and apparently objective account of the first fifty years of the Cup's long history. No less well informed and equally helpful has been Hugh Somerville's *Sceptre*, still ranking as surely the best British book ever published on the America's Cup.

Also much appreciated have been Keith Wheatley's thoughtful *America's Cup '87; Keelhauled*, Doug Riggs' examination of the seamier side of the contest; the late John Illingworth's *Twenty Challenges for the America's Cup* and Chris Freer's authoritative technical book *The Twelve Metre Yacht*.

In compiling the racing record of *White Crusader* I have unashamedly and gratefully turned to Bob Fisher's day-by-day accounts of the Fremantle racing published in *Yachts and Yachting* as the most – if not only – reliable and complete factual record by a journalist who thoroughly understands yacht racing and all its nuances. I have re-read other magazine articles too numerous to list going back to the *Sceptre* challenge, but in particular have relied on the material published in *Yachts and Yachting* by the late Jack Knights, C A J Marchaj (in particular with reference to the genesis of the curved-top rig he developed for Ian Howlett and *Lionheart*) and by the aforementioned Bob Fisher. I have also been helped by W M Nixon's reminiscences of Cudmore, both published in *Yachting World* and more informally conveyed over many a pint and many a year.

I must thank, too, all those who gave me their time when the decision was made to write this book, in particular Admiral Sir Ian Easton, Ian Howlett, Stephen Wallis, David Hollom and Philip Tolhurst along with Paul Antrobus of White Horse Whisky. And finally I have to thank both Peter de Savary and Graham Walker for many individual acts of kindness and hospitality dispensed over several years of both the *Victory* and White Horse challenges.

Malcolm McKeag

CHAPTER ONE

Another day, another dollar

It was over. Like a crowd leaving a football stadium the spectator boats began to stream away from the race course and back to Fremantle's sprawling harbour. David Hill, vice-president (sports) of Channel 9, Australia's major television sports network, his system suddenly drained of the adrenalin which had sustained him while directing the previous five hours of live television broadcast, half hopped and half slumped from his high stool in his control room, turned his back on the banks of monitors which had engaged his attention since noon and made for the door.

In the narrow corridor of the two-storey temporary studio complex built on one of the many arms of the harbour's interlocking walls he met Geoff Mason, executive producer of ESPN's US coast-to-coast cable sports network. As befits a refugee from an American television control room where directing any programme, however live, is akin to running the Third World War, Mason was coming down off an even bigger high. He had just completed a five-hour telecast back to the States, beaming his pictures up to a satellite which had beamed them back down to his company's receiving station at Bristol, Connecticut, on the opposite side of the globe for onward transmission to upwards of 100 million homes.

In a room immediately below the corridor the director of SailVision, a real-time computer graphics display invented specially for this America's Cup to show the race course and the changing positions of the two yachts even while they were racing, cleared his data screen and typed a final message upstairs to his counterparts in the two control rooms:

'Thank You For Your Kind Attention: See You In Hawaii.'

He was already wasting his time. No one in either control room was looking any more. Behind him the Sony editing machines were already whirring, the speaker from the dubbing studio already relaying the voice-over for the first of the evening's news stories. Big bad Dennis Conner, the big, big man of international sailing, had just finished his methodical demolition of Australia's Iain Murray four-zip in as monotonous and one-sided a sporting contest as has ever claimed a nation's attention and had put the America's Cup back in American hands yet again. In its 135-year existence, the Cup had been out of American custody for just three years, four months and a few days. One might have been forgiven for thinking that three and a half years of hype and spurious excitement had just crashed out in three and a half days of yawning anti-climax. One would have been wrong.

Hill and Mason climbed not a little wearily on to the rooftop verandah of the temporary building to join a fast-growing gathering of engineers, technicians and production assistants who for the past quarter of a year had worked, eaten, worked again and virtually lived inside the cramped, link-wire compound that housed the studios. 'The Great America's Cup Hostage Crisis' had joked an earlier sweatshirt slogan in an attempt to see the funny side of three months of eighteen-hour days and seven-day weeks, a joke that had by now begun to wear a little thin. Mason was off duty now but Hill took one look at the scene unfolding before him and ran back downstairs. 'Get a camera up on the roof, quick' he told his floor manager and went to find Mike Gibson, his link man and one of Australia's best-known sports presenters. 'We'll do the pay-off from the roof,' he told him. 'Have you seen what's happening in the harbour? Have you seen the people outside?'

Outside the crowd appeared as if from nowhere, welling up out of the ground in cheerful, good-humoured throng. Like ants invading a gardener's potting shed they poured along the roadway, carrying with them the mounted police who might in vain have tried to control them. They piled on the rocks that form the breakwater arms of the extended harbour complex, they swarmed up the scaffolding towers of the temporary buildings and they even climbed the lamp-posts.

One group of youngsters, in thongs, shorts and yellow and green singlets, found a way on to the roof of one of the low buildings overlooking the harbour. Within minutes the pale, corrugated asbestos shed was all but invisible beneath the seething mass of people which engulfed it. Within only minutes more, every other building was being taken over, invested, each an impromptu grandstand for the hundreds who could find no place on the people-blackened rocks.

Out in the harbour, the first of the spectator boats had begun to arrive but, instead of streaming as usual back to their berths and docks in the myriad alleyways of the haven, they were stopping, loitering in the gentle swell of the harbour's long entrance channel, backing and filling, waiting like the crowd for what they knew would soon appear. Every boat was laden with people, every person in happy, noisy mood. Every boat, were it speedboat or passenger ferry, was wildly waved and tooted at by the shore-bound crowd; and aboard every boat, the waterborne crowd waved and tooted back. There were klaxons and hunting horns, bugles and trumpets – even one of those fancy car horns that plays the first notes of some tune.

Now the multi-coloured teeming crowd was topped with a line of waving flags, the Stars and Stripes of America outnumbered five to one by the rich, royal blue of the Australian national flag with its Union emblem and the five silver stars of the Southern Cross. Fremantle's famed 'doctor', the brisk sea breeze that blows in every afternoon off the Indian Ocean to cool the land and town and provide blessed relief from the flies and the heat of an Australian summer, stretched the flags and the Kookaburra banners, the sun blazed down and still the crowd, afloat and ashore, grew and grew and grew.

A gold and green *Kookaburra* Taskforce support boat swept into the harbour, picked up some more supporters and swept out to sea again. Still the harbour entrance clogged with more and more and yet more boats. One of the several big 350-passenger catamarans normally used as tripper boats and for the past months re-assigned as yacht race spectator craft appeared with a jazz band on the top deck, stomping out The Saints and Dixie. Another Taskforce support boat appeared with a figure in a Disney-style foam and feathered Kookaburra suit, waving and bowing to the happy crowd which laughed and waved and bowed back. Tall and graceful yachts, the playthings of millionaires from Texas and Boston, Marseille and Sardinia slid into the throng. Speedboats, several having aboard them young ladies who to the delight of both crowd and television cameras were not wearing tops to their bikinis, bobbed around in the wash and general melée.

Then into this swarming, seething thicket of boats swept *Kookaburra* under full sail, her huge Foster's spinnaker swelling aloft and her gold hull foaming along at a good nine knots. She roared in mere yards from the boulders of the harbour wall, hardly more than an arm's length away and the crowd went wild, the noise became a cacophony. White water churned under transoms as those in her way cleared a path for her; a crewman leaned out and patted her topsides; Iain Murray, Peter Gilmour, Derek

Clark – young men who in the past weeks had become household names – waved and the crowd waved back.

She shot past a big cat, threaded the needle's eye of two others, swept her long boom over the heads of the ladies in the speedboats and gybed all-standing to disappear round into the inner harbour. Her spinnaker slithered down the forestay, she rounded into the wind's eye and her mainsail slid down the mast to the deck for the last time.

Then it was Conner's turn. Not to be outdone, his *Stars & Stripes* arrived under spinnaker, a huge US flag, the Stars and Stripes of her name, floating lazily from her standing backstay. From the coastguard lookout on the breakwater end came the steady *crumpfh crumpfh crumpfh* of a twenty-one maroon salute, each deep-throated explosion preceeded by a burst of grey-white smoke high overhead. The waves of sound swelled and rebounded from the crowds lining the two sides of the harbour entrance as the wash from the tenders and rubber-duckies bounced and splashed back and forth, back and forth, between the two arms of the breakwaters.

A yawning anti-climax? Hardly. The sun had dropped almost to the horizon, flaming the sky with pink and turning the Indian Ocean to molten silver before the Twelve Metres were finally put away and the crowds at last began to melt. Again and again *Kookaburra* and *Stars & Stripes* had been towed out and back past their supporters, round to the Royal Perth Yacht Club's waterside harbour clubhouse and back again, out again for one more lap of honour. Even then, the crowds had not gone home, but had instead laid seige to the compounds of their heroes, to congratulate, to commiserate, to hold out a hand in the hope that Murray or Conner or anyone might shake it.

At last the press conferences, the post-race appearances, were over and the town became quiet. The America's Cup had once more been won and lost and the longest-running competition in the whole of international sport was about to lie quiescent for another three years. Perhaps.

The America's Cup had brought an estimated $A1000 million to the economy of Western Australia, along with a circus that was said to represent an all-up expenditure of close on $US200 million. The circus included thirteen different teams from six nations to challenge for the Cup and four teams from Australia to defend it. There were seven new Australian Twelve Metres and at least twenty-one from overseas. Few were the syndicates whose personnel numbered less than 100 and several employed twice that number. One of the American syndicates had been working-up in Fremantle for more than two years before the racing started, most of the others for at least a year.

The America's Cup itself consisted of one single, best-of-seven series of races each between only two boats, but the preliminary racing – in the challengers' case for the Louis Vuitton Cup and in the defenders' case in the tightly-run and formal Defender's Selection Trials – had encompassed three months, over 450 individual formal match races and uncountable informal races and tuning sessions.

Over 3,300 journalists and assorted media personnel from cameramen and still photographers to production assistants and sprocket-wheel numberers' clerks had been accredited at the central media centre – and that number did not include those support staff working directly for the television and radio stations involved. One experienced sports producer rated his network's effort to be the equivalent of two Olympic Games and a World Cup all rolled into one.

The decaying and by-passed town of Fremantle was taken over, spruced up, smoothed down and laid seige to by hundreds of thousands of visitors. It acquired three new yacht clubs, acres of new harbour and a couple of dozen new restaurants, from bistro bars to stylish and elegant retreats where entrance was by recommendation and plastic security card only. When the Cup itself was on, Fremantle – once the port of Western Australia and before the days of popular air travel the only way for immigrants to the land to enter – had more passenger liners alongside its quays than it had ever seen, while no one ever bothered seriously to estimate the value of the fleet of private yachts which sailed or were shipped to its once-modest working harbour.

The America's Cup, in short, could fairly lay claim to being the biggest single sporting event the world had ever seen.

There were seven American Twelve Metre syndicates alone in Fremantle. The Twelve Metre is the biggest and most specialised inshore racing yacht in the world, the sailing equivalent of the Formula One Grand Prix car in terms of its specialisation and its unfittedness for anything other than the role for which it is designed. In absolute terms or in relation to the cost of other large yachts – or racing cars, for that matter – a Twelve Metre itself is relatively cheap: about £350,000 or $US500,000 to build and put afloat, fully rigged. It is the support and campaign costs which are so astronomical that no America's Cup Twelve Metre in the world today is owned and paid for by one man alone. All are owned and campaigned by syndicates – either wealthy patrons or commercial companies or charitable organisations or some combination of two or all of the above. A ludicrously too-small campaign budget for the 1987 America's Cup would have been £1m, a tight budget £4–5m and a realistic budget £10m or $US15m. When asked the size of his own budget, Arthur Wieslinger, manager of the New York Yacht Club's *America II* challenge, replied: 'Well, we don't really have a budget as such . . .'. *America II* and the New York Yacht Club spent two and a half years and an estimated $US20m in Fremantle, and failed to qualify for the semi-finals of the Louis Vuitton, leaving them three tiers away from the Cup the club lost in 1983.

And somewhere in the middle of all this were the British, representatives of the oldest yacht-racing nation in the world and the nation whose craftsmen had made, and whose yachtsmen had promptly lost, the America's Cup a century and a half earlier. By comparison with the big American and Australian campaigns, the British effort was a modest affair. The budget was £5m, helped at the eleventh hour by sponsorship reputedly of £1m but which in fact brought the campaign something closer to half that figure. Yet what they lacked in quantity the British could have made up in quality. They had started promisingly enough, with the apparent support of a distinguished and established yacht club with a respected reputation for a go-ahead and progressive approach to yacht-race management. They had scientific and technical resources at least the equal of anything in America and considerably in advance of facilities in many of the other nations participating. They had two design approaches, one through a much vaunted radical-thinking team which included the boffin responsible for the world's most innovative modern fighter aircraft. The other was through the designer who, if not universally admired in the yacht-racing world was at least the most experienced Twelve Metre designer in Britain. And they had a skipper whose reputation and stature were even higher and more widely respected outside of Britain than within it. His name was Harold Cudmore.

CHAPTER TWO

A match made in heaven

The Royal Lymington Cup is Britain's top match racing event, and Harold Cudmore is Britain's top match racer. In its thirteen-year history, Cudmore has won the Lymington Cup six times, four of them in succession, and of the three times he has been beaten in the event, only once has it been by a Briton – Phil Crebbin, in 1977.

The Lymington Cup of 1984 was one of Cudmore's Cups – in fact, it was the year he became what was jokingly called at the time a 'fifty-percent shareholder' for of the ten times a winner's name had had to be engraved on the Cup's silver surface, Cudmore's could now account for five. To win the event, Cudmore had beaten some of the best international match racers around including America's Gary Jobson, who had been in the crew of a successful defender of that most holy of all yachting's match race trophies – the America's Cup; Italy's Mauro Pellaschier, skipper of his country's 1983 America's Cup challenger *Azzurra;* New Zealander Brad Butterworth, fresh from a win in the Hong Kong Match Race Championship; and Chris Law, one of Britain's top Olympic sailors just returned from a devastating win at the Hyérès pre-Olympic regatta which had confirmed him as Britain's 1984 Olympic representative in the Soling class.

There was also a young, relatively unknown, Australian skipper: a many-times world champion in the 18ft skiff class and recently the helmsman of an ill-starred and spectacularly unsuccessful Australian contender in the campaign for the 1983 America's Cup, the one which John Bertrand and *Australia II* had finally won to change the face of the America's Cup for ever. His name was Iain Murray, and he was learning all there is to know about match racing, fast.

Waiting for Cudmore as he came ashore on the Saturday of the four-day event was a Southend-on-Sea lawyer and moderately successful Dragon sailor called Philip Tolhurst. Unlike Cudmore, Tolhurst had no claim to fame in the rarefied world of international sailing: he was not a match racer himself nor did he do that other thing which might have claimed Cudmore's immediate attention. He did not own a large and expensive race boat which might need a top-gun skipper to campaign her on the international circuit. But he did have something which interested Cudmore greatly, and something the two were keen to talk about: he had the reins of a British challenge for the 1987 America's Cup, to be sailed in Fremantle, Western Australia.

As is the way in these matters, Tolhurst himself was not the challenger, nor even a principal in the group of people who might fund such a challenge. 'The people I represent', he was able to tell Cudmore, using a lawyer's phrase which was to become a favourite in the months ahead, were really the people who held those reins, and they were keen to see Cudmore's hands enfold them. So was Cudmore.

Match racing is the most esoteric of all forms of what is to most people the already esoteric sport of yacht racing. A cross between ordinary sailing, mediaeval jousting and a sort of waterborne chess it requires consummate sailing skill, superb boat-handling ability and an intimate knowledge of yacht racing's complex right-of-way rules, combined with the sort of mentality that would stand a champion croquet player in good stead.

Its principal and obvious difference from the norm is that instead of a fleet of anything from half a dozen to half a hundred yachts taking part in the race, only two yachts compete. The successful match racer quickly learns that ensuring that one's opponent comes second is exactly the same as ensuring that oneself comes first, and is often the easier object to achieve.

It is also a relatively new type of yacht racing, at least in its present form. For almost one hundred years the America's Cup was the only match race competition of any note and for most of those hundred years only the Americans had even a shadowy grasp of the notion that match race tactics were any different from fleet racing tactics. After the War, when the America's Cup competition moved from the mighty Big Boats and J-Class to the comparatively diminutive but affordable Twelve Metre class, it was again only the Americans who appreciated the need to train potential defense helmsmen and tacticians in the special arts of this toe-to-toe contest.

So, in 1965 in California, a new event came into being: the Congressional Cup. The Congressional Cup was the world's first, and for many years its only, formal match race tournament, until in 1974 an expatriate Californian living, sailing and working in England's Solent called Bill Green persuaded the Royal Lymington Yacht Club to stage a copy-cat event and the Royal Lymington Cup was born.

Originally a locals-only affair, the Royal Lymington Cup began to attract both international interest (mindful always of the dangers of teaching the rest of the world anything that might be of use in the America's Cup itself, the Californians had adopted an Americans-only policy for their own event) and international imitation. By the end of the seventies a world-wide circuit of such events had been established, with championships in Hong Kong, New Zealand, and Australia as well as the English event and its American parent. Soon there followed other events – in France and in Bermuda – while in the sincerest form of flattery, the Americans had begun to extend invitations to their own event to yachtsmen from outside the States, as well as adopting some of the details of the English organisation.

Along with the international circuit of match races grew an international circus of performers. While each country was primarily interested in providing an arena for its own top yachtsmen, it was also keen to give its locals the very best of competition – as well as raise the status of its own event – by importing the top names from around the world. By a curious and fortuitous confluence of circumstance, talent and opportunity, Harold Cudmore had quickly become one of those top international performers, and by 1984 had at some stage in the previous decade won virtually every one of the match race events, except the Congressional Cup itself. At that time, the Congressional had only twice ever been won by a non-Californian ('by anyone' as the Americans themselves loved to phrase it 'from East of the San Diego Freeway') and never by a non-American. Soon, Cudmore would change that, too.

It was hardly surprising, then, that Tolhurst, charged by 'the people I represent' with the leg-work of putting together the apparatus for a British America's Cup challenge, should want to talk to Harold Cudmore. In some ways, it was more surprising that Harold Cudmore should want to talk to him.

CHAPTER THREE

What Cup?

The America's Cup is yachting's Holy Grail. In the almost 140 years of its existence it has come to represent the pinnacle of sailing achievement, the most difficult trophy to win in the whole and enormous array of trophies. Indeed, as virtually every newspaper sports writer or television commentator – even those who appeared to think a Twelve Metre yacht was one that was thirty-six feet long – incessantly told us as the 1983 contest began to push yacht racing to an unaccustomedly high public profile, it had become the most difficult trophy to win in the entire calendar of world sports. Until the Australians took it from the New York Yacht Club in 1983, no sporting trophy had even remained in continuing competition for so long, never mind remained in the custody of one holder.

From the moment Commodore J C Stevens, aboard the schooner *America* anchored in Cowes Roads in August, 1851, sat down to write to John Bates, Esq, Secretary of the Royal Yacht Squadron, to ask: 'Will you do me the favor to enter the *America* for the Royal Yacht Squadron regatta to come off on the 22nd inst . . .' the Cup has stood to represent the truth that its winner is the finest sailing yacht in the world of any type, bar none.

That this truth has not always been accepted as such by all is another matter, and that the nature of the competition for the symbol has not always lived up to so noble a truth cannot be denied – but the truth has remained, more or less intact.

The competition, rather than the prize, has been through many phases. Its latest represents merely another, but one which is remarkably close to bringing both trophy and competition back to where it started. It began with a nakedly commercial motive: the *America* was built with the express intention of using her to make money, particularly through wagers placed by her owners putting their money alongside their mouths in the belief that she was faster than anything the old world had to offer. Her cause, as Stevens' letters of challenge so ingenuously put it, was 'to test the relative merits of the different models of the schooners of the old and the new world'.

It became, as soon as Stevens and his fellow owners had presented to the New York Yacht Club the only trophy the old world had allowed them to win and which they subsequently named 'America's Cup', a private contest which soon took on nationalistic overtones. It remained a contest between the design-types of the old world and those of the new. To America the nation it quickly became a symbol of her still-new right and ability to face the old world as an equal. The New York Yacht Club after only eleven years and four defenses appealed to her sister clubs throughout the nation to come to the aid of the defence of the Cup, an appeal always answered if not without jealousy and ill-grace.

Yet on the other side of the Atlantic, pursuit of the Cup could garner no such nationalistic support and so the competition moved into an era that was to last until 1980, with a series of challengers taking on a combined defense more or less single-handed.

So came an era of private contest in the super-exclusive world of personal wealth and pride.

Gradually the Cup became the summer divertissement of the most ostentatious social set the world has ever seen. The Vanderbilts, the Pierpoint-Morgans, the Rockerfellers took the Cup like they took everything else about their lives, including their play. They took it very seriously indeed.

The competition took on new undertones with the arrival of Lipton. Although still played out in the arena of private wealth and public play, the canny grocer who liked to take his king boating was probably the first to discover the below-the-line benefits of an America's Cup campaign, and his sporting efforts made his grocery-store chain a household word on both sides of the Atlantic. If nothing else, it helped him make more money to build more America's Cup yachts.

Then came the Great War, and after it nothing was the same, including the America's Cup – although ironically the Cup enjoyed better fortune than many as it moved into an age at once of elegance and grace and of unlimited technical advance.

The Second World War brought an end to elegance and grace – and what looked to many the end of the America's Cup as well. Yet it revived and there came a brief Corinthian period that was in truth a different sort of test of the relative merits of an old world and a new – and the new world won hands down.

The arrival on the scene of a young(ish) Australian property developer Alan Bond brought a shudder of revulsion to many a Corinthian breast: the fellow was unashamedly using his involvement in the Cup as a method to promote his business activities. Yanchep Sun City, indeed.

But Bond not only knew how to manage his business, he also knew how to run Twelve Metre campaigns. Eventually, and at his third attempt, he beat the Americans at their own game. The Cup went to Fremantle.

And there, the story came full circle, but a circle in a spiral. The Cup was in one sense back where it started from, but on an altogether higher plane.

In 1851 Britain was at the zenith of a period of unchallenged military and economic supremacy in the world. The final defeat of her only serious military or economic rival on the continent of Europe had been accomplished at Waterloo and her next was yet to develop to maturity. The Great Exhibition was a festival to put the seal on that singular position and as a part of it the nations of the world were invited to send the best of everything they had to be put on display for comparison against the British Standard. One of the things sent was a sailing vessel.

The then Commodore of the Royal Yacht Squadron is usually credited with issuing the invitation that prompted the Americans to send over their finest craft to race against the best of the British, but in fact it was a merchant by the name of Sir H Buller who in August 1850 suggested to some New York business contacts that they send one of their famous pilot boats to compete at the World's Fair.

The idea was taken up, but in a way that has to this day made the America's Cup what it is. They would not, decided the Americans, send any old pilot boat; they would build a yacht to beat the fastest craft in America – and send her.

The schooner – to be called the *America* in honour of all that she represented – was from the beginning both a sporting and a commercial venture. At her builder's suggestion, a premium price was put upon her and when built she would take part in trials against all comers. Only if she could beat all those comers would her owners be required to accept and agree to pay for her.

For their part, the owners were to undertake – if she won the trials – to take her to England at their own expense and there race her against all comers – but if she were beaten, even once, they would not have to pay for her.

It was during this time that English yachtsmen got to hear of the venture, and one of their most noble, the Earl of Winton and Commodore of the Royal Yacht Squadron, wrote in February 1851 to invite the Americans 'to become visitors of the Club House in Cowes during their stay in England'. No mention was made then of a race, but the noble Earl 'in extending to your countrymen any civility that lies in my power' added that he should 'be very glad to avail myself of any improvements in shipbuilding that the industry of your nation have enabled you to elaborate'.

Commodore Stevens, replying in March (for there was then neither cable nor wireless, much less telex and fax, across the Atlantic and the mail was carried by fast packet) hedged his reply with reservation. If the yacht could 'answer the sanguine expectations of her builder' he would be delighted to accept the English hospitality and 'take with good grace the sound thrashing we are likely to get by venturing our longshorecraft on such rough waters'. It was not the last time that a proper humility would be seen as the most appropriate demeanour to adopt by a challenger in this particular enterprise.

The *America* won her trials and crossed the Atlantic – the first yacht ever to do so – in the early summer of 1851 and went first to Le Havre, arriving in The Solent late one evening to meet what generations of Solent yachtsmen, from home and from overseas, have met since: a foul tide and a falling breeze.

She anchored for the night and in the morning found an English cutter (for word of the Yankee's arrival had spread as fast as had word of her extraordinary, rakish appearance) 'come down to meet her'. Ostensibly the *Laverock* had come down to show the visitor the way in, but then as now the yachtsman is rare who, finding himself alongside another, can resist the temptation to tweak this and pull that to see whose yacht is the faster.

Stevens was far from ready for a speed trial, for the *America* was still laden with her trans-Atlantic stores and had only her working sails but with many a circle and dainty, curtseying tack the *Laverock* made it plain that her invitation was not to be rejected. With trepidation for the outcome in the hearts of those on board, *America* made sail and hauled her anchor and set off in the *Laverock*'s wake. Stevens' description of the emotions of those on board as the two yachts sailed together for the first time is vivid testimony that in sailing, there are some things that cannot change – the thumping hearts, the dry mouths, the whispered instructions, all eyes either on their own sails or on the other yacht. As easily imagine the *America* as

Columbia, Liberty or *Stars & Stripes*; the *Laverock* as *Sceptre, Australia II* or *Kookaburra* – or just two racers meeting in The Solent. The boats have changed, but the contest has not.

To Stevens' delight, he knew within minutes – as 136 years later Conner must have known within minutes – that at the very least he wasn't going to have to take that thrashing, with or without the good grace. *America* firmly worked up to weather of *Laverock*, pointing higher and going faster: still every racing sailor's dream.

With hindsight, Stevens might have done better to take a quick leaf out of later generations' books and do a bit of sandbagging. Thanks to that unequivocal demonstration, no British yacht was prepared to race against the American, and Stevens hopes of cashing in on his yacht's superiority by collecting wagers of anything from £100 to £10,000 were completely frustrated.

He did have some small commercial success however. In a reverse-sponsorship deal with the Cowes boatbuilder Ratsey, Stevens had a jib-boom and staysail made for *America*, betting the price of both spar and sail on the outcome of a race between *America* and any British yacht Ratsey cared to name. He named the *Beatrice* and when *America* beat her along with the rest in that famous regatta, Stevens got both spar and sail for free.

British yachting historians in particular have often rewritten *America*'s devastating display with handicaps, course changes and caveats which make the contest 'fairer' (and which, not unnaturally, in the process show how *America* was really no great winner at all). All of which is to miss the point completely. *America*, without dispute, was faster than the British craft and that is all that this particular test was about. That she was bigger than most and different to all is irrelevant. This was a one-day, one-race trial of types, and the American type was quicker on the day.

Subsequent contests continued the theme. Typical British types were sent to race against typical American types, and the American types always won. It was hardly anything to be surprised at. Early yachts were evolved from and consciously emulated the sailing working craft of their environment, and those craft themselves evolved for their own particular conditions. British yachtsmen and British working sailors did most of their work in deep water and short steep seas. The American types against whom they competed were evolved from craft designed to sail and work in shoal waters and often lighter winds. It was not surprising that, racing the

American types on their home waters, the American types held the general but by no means universal advantage.

The advantage lay not only in the type of American yacht but in the American attitude to the Cup races. By 1885, the New York Yacht Club had enlisted the aid of 'outside' help, by appealing to every yacht club in the land to enter yachts in the trials to select a defender, and by using the first non-New York defender, *Puritan* from Boston, as their champion in the races.

Yet while the Americans took the event more and more seriously, more and more regarding the defense as a matter of national pride, the challengers retained an altogether different attitude. To them the contest was one not between nations nor even yacht clubs, but between gentlemen. *America* herself had been denied entry to at least one yacht club regatta in England because she was owned by a syndicate, rather than a single owner, and in England still there persisted the feeling that gentlemen either owned their yachts independently or not at all. It was perhaps the serious end of the now jocularly-spoken old yachting saw: 'If you have to ask how much it costs, you can't afford it.'

That one side at least still looked upon taking part in a proper manner as being more important than winning is vividly demonstrated by one of the most famous incidents in all the tales of the America's Cup, of which there are many hundreds.

Genesta, owned by Sir Richard Sutton, was the challenger and the aforementioned *Puritan* the defender. In the pre-start manoeuvring (no less important then as now) *Puritan* on port tack tried to cross the starboard-tack *Genesta*'s bow and misjudged the distance. *Genesta's* bowsprit went clean through *Puritan*'s mainsail, ripping the sail and itself carrying away. With both yachts disabled the committee immediately disqualified *Puritan* and informed *Genesta* that she had only to sail the course and the race was hers. Sir Richard's refusal of the offer is well-known and is quoted (more often, misquoted) in virtually every America's Cup history book published, but the full significance of what happened is usually missed.

The committee (on the launch *Luckenbach*) found themselves conducting their negotiation with *Genesta* via the New York Yacht Club representative on board, Mr Roosevelt Schuyler, who when offered the opportunity to sail the course alone began to negotiate for time to effect repairs. It was only then, while the committee debated how much the scheduled start time would need to be delayed, that Sir Richard intervened with his now immortal:

'We are very much obliged to you, but we don't want it that way. We want a race; we don't want a walkover.'

There seems every likelihood that had it been left to the American, *Genesta* would have taken the sailover as a legitimate prize of war.

If a difference in attitude needed further demonstration, it came next year when *Galatea* was the challenger. No race boat she, she was nonetheless the finest of what the British felt a yacht should be. The permanent floating home of Lieutenant William Henn, a retired gentleman-officer from the Royal Navy, and Mrs Henn, her on-board equipment included not only lavish furnishings and weighty furniture including a full-on Victorian fireplace in the saloon but a menagerie of pets as well. One, the monkey, was said to run out along the bowsprit and perform tricks when the yacht got her nose in front.

Such laid-back sportin' activity was not what the New York Yacht Club wanted nor expected its America's Cup competition to be about, and a new era of seriousness descended upon the Cup from both sides.

After one more (by now annual) challenge the club in 1887 called a halt to review the situation. The result was a revision of the Deed of Gift (see Chapter 7, p. 61) and its publication caused an outcry, a six-year hiatus in challenges and brought an altogether more litigious atmosphere to the competition. The Earl of Dunraven was the last of the Sportin' Gentlemen to challenge the Americans. His first challenge gave the Cup one of the most magnificent races it can ever have seen before or since, but his second – and last – ended in such bitterness and recrimination (largely, as history now shows, the fault of the noble Earl) that the Cup became a by-word for everything that was opposed to good sportsmanship. Dunraven himself, having refused to resign from the New York Yacht Club, was actually expelled.

But then the Cup entered upon yet another era, an era of lavish expense both upon the yachts themselves and by those with whom it was associated. This was the turn of the century. In England the Victorian era ended with no diminution of the nation's industrial power and commercial success, while the Edwardians threw off the dour industriousness of the Victorians and learned to spend and enjoy themselves without the burden of doing so with a guilty conscience.

In America, the rough-readiness of life of a young emergent nation had been displaced by the supreme self-confidence that comes with self-made success. New York was the commercial capital of the nation and second only to London as a commercial centre for the world. J Pierpoint-Morgan, one of the richest men in the western world, had marked his Commodoreship of the New York Yacht Club by a gift of a quarter-million-dollar site in the heart of Manhattan for a new clubhouse – they built at West 44th Street the clubhouse they still use today.

Club members had taken to having little ten-, twenty- and thirty-bedroomed summer 'cottages' up at Newport, Rhode Island, to escape the sweltering city summer and thither they repaired in magnificent steam yachts which they used as both water taxis and as spectator craft to watch their magnificent sailing yachts race.

In a fuller history of the America's Cup Sir Thomas Lipton would deserve and receive a chapter or two to himself. In some ways he was a model for the Americans themselves – a self-made millionaire who had started life with naught. He had even in early life run away to America for a while, before returning home. He had made no fortune on his first visit to the States, but had learned at least one invaluable lesson of the value of advertising. As one of his oft-repeated stories used to say 'consider the hen and the duck. Both lay eggs and of the two the duck's is bigger, tastier and more nourishing. But while the duck sits quietly on her egg, the hen gets up and tells the whole farmyard about it: how many people buy duck eggs?'

Probably Lipton, who had no previous experience of or interest in yachting, lodged his first challenge – in 1899 – as much to restore the damage wrought between the two nations by the Dunraven affair as anything else, for he was genuinely fond of America. He realised very soon, however, that the publicity in America that his participation in the races brought did his businesses no harm at all and in quick succession he brought off three challenges round the turn of the century.

Each saw the America's Cup stretch out to new excesses of expenditure. For the first, the two sides spent an estimated $250,000 at current prices on their yachts alone. For the second, Lipton found himself up against a syndicate of no fewer than nine US millionaires. For the third, he found himself up against the biggest racing yacht the world had – or has – ever seen.

Reliance was 144ft overall on a waterline of 90ft. At that time the Deed of Gift stated – doubtless originally to keep Cup expenditure within some sort of sensible pale – a maximum waterline length (90ft) but no overall limit. It had doubtless been assumed that the waterline limit would impose its own sensible overall limit but, as is so often the case with the America's Cup, no one could foresee the technical developments which would take place – and that the protagonists would be prepared to pay for.

The yachts were by now quite useless for anything other than America's Cup racing. Most American defenders were scrapped within a few years of launching, sometimes to provide raw material for the next defender. The challengers were longer lived, not least because a clause of the Deed of Gift (and one which gave the home side an enormous in-built advantage) stated that the yachts must come to the races on their own bottoms – and of course that meant a trans-Atlantic voyage, whereas the furthest a defender had had to travel was a few miles down the coast from Boston or the Herreshoft yard at Bristol, Connecticut. One potential defender was so lightly built that even in the trial races her hull twisted so much as to lock the rudder stock within its tube and *Reliance* herself had such a cloud of sail as to heel to her rail in less than twenty knots of breeze.

It has been sometimes said that with Lipton, at last the challenger could match the defenders resources dollar for dollar, but it cannot have been so. Lipton was rich, but he was but one millionaire against many and as that consummate writer on America's Cup affairs Hugh Somerville has said, Lipton's sailing manager Duncan Neill repeatedly complained of his owner's tight control of the purse strings.

Such extravagance could not go on and after 1903 came one of the longest gaps in America's Cup history, while new rules were sorted out and a world war fought.

The new rule – the Universal Rule which gave the world the J-Class – heralded the Golden Age of the America's Cup. The yachts were magnificent. Aesthetically beautiful in repose, underway they were awe-inspiringly graceful. Aboard them in the few years of their existence – from 1930 to 1937 – were made such technical advances in construction, in rigging, in spar design and manufacture, in sail-handling techniques and equipment as had not been seen in the previous hundred years.

They brought, too, to the Cup a new breed of yachtsman, the owner-sailor who steered his own yacht, and a new breed of sailor, the amateur crewman. No fishermen nor longshore pilots steeped in the traditions of the sea, good and bad, but college graduates and technicians who approached sailing and yacht racing as a science. The Americans, in particular, perfected the use of this management group to bring method and precision to what had been the realm of instinct, cunning and experience and, as with *Reliance,* so with *Ranger,* the last of the Js. She stands for all time as the most perfect example of her type.

After the Second World War, there were those on both sides of the Atlantic

– even within the New York Yacht Club – who felt that yachting would best be served by letting the America's Cup die its natural death. Others wanted to see it resurrected but to be sailed for in ocean racers which after the Cup races were completed 'would still go on to give their owners pleasure and racing interest in other fields'. Not surprisingly this attitude prevailed most strongly among the British yachting establishment, where the spirit of the gallant Lieutenant Henn, his wife and monkey, still lived on and which, it must be said, had still after all these years not really cottoned on to what the America's Cup and its winning was all about.

Ultimately, the Twelve Metre was chosen as the yacht for America's Cup racing. Tiny by comparison with earlier generations of Cup yacht, the Twelve Metre was and is the largest inshore racing yacht of her day. Her choice ushered in an era that was as far away from the original yacht and concept of the America's Cup as it might be possible to get but which had yet been approached by a logical development.

America had raced to test one concept of yacht type against another. She had first sailed across an ocean to do it, and had then sailed against not one but an entire fleet of English yachts, around a local course.

When the races for her Cup had started, the Americans had not unreasonably insisted that similar conditions apply – but had given no significance to the already changing circumstances of the new contest. In the Squadron's August regatta of 1851, all yachts had raced against each other, but even in the first America's Cup match proper the seventeen defenders had raced against the lone challenger – with predictable result.

In the August regatta, *America* had been the only yacht built specially for the contest as well as crossing the ocean, but her opponents were likewise built to withstand the rigours of long life and long sea voyages. Even as early as 1887, the defending yachts were being specially and lightly built for the Cup races only. And while the *America* had had to race on a local, unknown course she had been given the benefit of the doubt over the one mistake she had made (leaving out the Nab Tower and thus saving her many miles of sailing), a mistake which made her victory virtually certain. No such benefits were afforded the challengers when they raced on the American's notorious 'inshore course'.

So over the years, the rules of the competition had modified, the effect of each modification being to remove the grosser inequalities of the competition. The courses had been altered and rendered less demanding of specialised local knowledge. The rules covering design had been altered to bring closer together the type of yacht each side brought to the contest. Amateur crews had replaced the professionals who had raced the earliest boats, which had made the original test not just one of each nation's type but of her working seafarers, too.

The early Twelve Metres at last saw the closest thing the America's Cup has ever been to a sporting, Corinthian contest.

It depends, of course, how you define Corinthian. In Britain, Corinthian means also patrician. It carries the overtone of doing well because one is naturally gifted, that a competition – be it in sailing, in running, in ski-ing, in anything – is designed to search out natural talent, that the worthiest winner is he who wins with least evidence of effort. That working at winning – the 'practice beforehand which ruins the fun' of Flanders and Swann – is somehow unsporting and frankly rather vulgar. Sadly for two British challenges, the Americans don't see it that way.

The Americans put enormous effort into defending the Cup. They built extra Twelve Metres; tested dozens of models for hundreds of hours (the *Sceptre* campaign managed a total of forty-one hours tank testing, in a tank with no wave-making facility); they trialled for months. They put in so much effort that the contests themselves were doleful mismatches. So one-sided were the *Sceptre* and *Sovereign* challenges that they caused not a little resentment in American yachting circles, resentment that the British did not appear to have put in an effort to match the trouble the Americans had gone to, an effort worthy of the traditions of the contest.

The British failures were almost entirely the direct result of mismanagement, of owning syndicates and individuals full of theories who imposed upon the yachts sailors lacking the necessary skills and then prevented them from acquiring them. The lessons, with hindsight, seem obvious yet forever the mistakes seem to be dangerously easy to repeat – but it is their magnitude which to the modern generation of Twelve Metre enthusiasts appears so unforgivable.

Yet this was a truly Corinthian period in the sportsmanship sense. The crews of the competing yachts sacrificed much and earned nothing, merely for the honour of taking part.

There was, too, a genuine camaradarie of sportsmanship amongst and between the crews. Once at the competition, they entertained each other, and dined together once racing had been concluded. On one occasion a crewman from one of the early Australian Twelves got married the day after America's Cup racing was over and the American skipper hosted the reception. Happily, that is one tradition that holds largely true today: when in Fremantle an Australian crew-member got married, guests at the wedding included sailors from virtually all the competing nations.

*

It was the Australian involvement, beginning in 1962, which heralded in the latest era in the America's Cup. First Sir Frank Packer, the newspaper magnate, challenged and quickly realised the benefits of the Cup to sales of his newspapers. He also, it has to be said, quickly realised the benefits that could be wrought in destabilising the opposition with a few well-planted or well-engineered scandals and outrages to keep the business rolling on a slow news day.

Then came Alan Bond. Bond is said to have ordered his first America's Cup Twelve Metre in a fit of pique at an American Twelve Metre man who was rude to him, but if this is so he was quick to exploit the promotional value of his Yanchep Sun City property development. More slowly, perhaps because subtlety is not a great Australian strong suit, he realised the benefits to himself and his own business profile in Western Australia.

France's Baron Bich, promoter of the Bic throwaway ballpoint pen, was another to see the America's Cup as a useful promotional vehicle, while Britain's Peter de Savary raised self-promotion through the America's Cup to the level of an art form.

Of Bond, at least, it can be said that while he realised and fully exploited the commercial value to his own enterprises of America's Cup participation, he had also been bitten by that craving that had driven Sir Thomas Lipton – that burning desire to attain the unattainable, to beat frustration of his efforts and finally beat the Americans. It was Alan Bond who finally won that 132-year-old race.

In doing so he brought the America's Cup full circle. In beating the Americans he removed what had become for all challengers the principal reason for entering the America's Cup circus at all. No one else could now become the first to take the Cup away from the New York Yacht Club defenders. There could now be only one sensible reason for bothering with the thing at all. Money.

CHAPTER FOUR

Defeat in victory

The *Lionheart* campaign was the last in the private rich-men's-plaything era of America's Cup racing, at least as far as the British were concerned. Challenging under the burgee of the Royal Southern YC the syndicate was headed by the man whose efforts, eight years previously with the humiliated *Sovereign*, had been so comprehensively outclassed by the American approach – but in 1980 Tony Boyden and several rich friends were back for another and this time final go.

There was a patina of commercial involvement – nothing so vulgar as commercialism – in that the campaign had the 'backing' of the Confederation of British Industry with a scheme whereby 1,500 British companies could become members of a corporate supporter's club upon payment of a fee which would now be regarded as ludicrously modest in sponsorship terms, even allowing for inflation. One Thousand Guineas had a nice, sporting ring to it and, perhaps more to the point, was considered the maximum an advertising director could write a cheque for without going back to the main board for full approval. To avoid the stigma of rich men at play (the CBI is very much the 'bosses' union') there was even a popular supporters' club. Yet while there was much trumpeting of this being a chance for British Industry to show the world the quality of its wares, the truth was that the funds were raised very much by a few rich individuals taking the hat round among their peers and getting them to cough up, albeit through their companies. Funding an America's Cup campaign was still something to be finalised in panelled rooms with whisky and soda, or over polished tables and port. In the event, British Industry was woefully reluctant to see the benefits which such an association might bring and the hat remained remarkably empty, despite the very modest amount being sought. Tony Boyden wound up footing most of the bill himself.

Tony Boyden himself was a member of the 'old school' Twelve Metre owner's association: privately wealthy, socially privileged and fiercely and proudly patriotic, though in that narrow sense that equates Britain with 'the old, traditional values'. It is a school which on all the evidence tends to put up a jolly good show and lose rather than adopt overseas' – much less American – methods and win. In an interview with profile writer Strahan Soames in *Yachts and Yachting* he icily declined to discuss money outside the strict parameters of giving a ball-park figure for the overall budget, and no less icily declined to discuss either his own financial involvement or indicate other than in the vaguest of terms where the money might be coming from. Strahan Soames, a dapper and most charming man, also of the 'old school', was hardly the world's most hard-nosed investigative reporter and being the subject of a Soames profile is rather like being hosed down with rose petals, but nonetheless Boyden was taking no chances. Discussing how the campaign was being paid for in real and serious terms was none of the public's business.

In the end, the campaign was both dogged and doomed by all the old, traditional problems. Honourable enough in their intentions, the owners treated the sailors as mere employees, there to put the owners' theories into practice and in the inevitable consequence when things did not go well, skipper John Oakeley was scapegoated and fired. He was replaced by a young man called Lawrie Smith.

Worst of all, however, was that the privately rich men turned out to be not rich enough. They baulked at the purchase of much-needed equipment, especially sails, and even placed, in the interests of cost-saving, a restriction on the number of times a week *Lionheart* could be taken out of the water.

Eventually, Boyden pulled the purse strings closed and the *Lionheart* campagn would have simply dried up, but for the arrival on the scene of a young, balding and vigorous millionaire called Peter de Savary.

A number of British yachting's eternal fringe figures – always around but never quite at the centre – later claimed to have been the one to hook Peter de Savary into Twelve Metre racing, but the most probable candidate is Kit Hobday, a mercurial public relations man with a taste for the high life, if not the most obvious means of visible support for it. Whoever it was, he did British Twelve Metre racing a most palpable service that was also something of a mixed blessing.

Peter de Savary bankrolled the final days of the *Lionheart* campaign, watched it crash out (quite literally – the British were finally put out of the Cup through colliding with the French) in a collapse brought about by poor funding, poorer management and last-ditch stop-gap remedies which failed to work, and decided that next time he could do better.

Cudmore at this time was still very much 'the Irish sailor Harold Cudmore' and in the public-school accented world of Twelve Metre syndicate membership it was quite unthinkable that 'we should have to recruit an Irishman' to sail 'our' Twelve. It was, after all, only three challenges ago that the natural choice of skipper should be the Queen's own sailing master; only two since the skipper had been a 'natural all-round sportsman' and the son of a Great English Explorer. Peter de Savary was about to change all of that.

His challenge for the America's Cup was lodged through the Royal Burnham Yacht Club, of which de Savary – originally from the Essex hinterland of that club – was an established if rarely seen member. The story of the lodging of that challenge makes a pretty good yarn of itself – among other jewels was the fact that, in typical de Savary style, the New York Yacht Club and the press were told the RB would be challenging before anyone got round to mentioning the fact to the committee of the RB itself and its new and incoming Commodore, and checking with them that the club would be happy to issue a challenge – but by the end of the year Peter de Savary and his Twelve Metre campaign were an up-and-running project with a full head of steam.

Immediately after Newport, de Savary had spurned *Lionheart's* designer Ian Howlett and turned instead to a young and newly successful designer called Edward Dubois. Howlett, de Savary had said – although without actually naming him, referring instead to the entire *Lionheart* campaign – at a dinner at the Royal Burnham was 'associated with failure, and I wish to be associated with success'. Dubois was certainly successful with a number of IOR racing successes to his credit and a string of prominent owners queueing to buy his designs.

Along with Ed Dubois, de Savary had engaged the services of Phillip Crebbin, a brilliant dinghy and keelboat sailor, twice his country's Olympic representative, who like Dubois was much admired by de Savary's advisor and sailing guru Kit Hobday. Phil Crebbin called Cudmore and asked him to come and meet this new man who wanted to race for the America's Cup.

By this time, the sailing world was rife with stories of Peter de Savary and what he would be doing, and everyone who was anyone in sailing and who could recognise a bandwagon when they saw it was keen to get on board. De Savary, having made most of his money outside Britain, was in the process of joining the City and as part of his move back to Britain had bought himself a gentlemen's club in St James', the St James's Club (well, no point in messing around with half-measures if you want a club in St James', is there?). *Lionheart* had been run by John Oakeley and a small handful of mates from the Hamble River, but for a few days de Savary held court in his new club, interviewing a galaxy of British sailing talent.

Most were members or habitués of the nearby Royal Ocean Racing Club, and most while on their way to see de Savary popped in to have a quick word with Janet Grosvenor, deputy secretary of the club and a mine of information about who is up to what and aboard which in the world of big boat sailing. Each in confidence hinted (some simply told) Janet whom they were going to see and why, but begged her to keep their secret safe until the announcement was official, and by the end of the afternoon she was hard put to keep a straight face as each new and exclusive arrival stuck his head round the rich dark-oak door of her office for a quick chat. 'I began to wonder' she later recalled 'whether he was putting together a Twelve Metre or a warship'.

De Savary had already bought Alan Bond's unsuccessful 1980 challenger *Australia* and among the many plans which would emerge – and be discarded – was one to purchase and equip a small cruise liner to act as floating, self-contained depot ship for the challenge, complete with on-board sail-loft, Twelve Metre dry-dock, engineering workshops, gymnasium and accommodation. There would be no more problems with inadequate back-up and not enough money to pay the boatyard for a pre-race scrub – Peter de Savary had arrived on the British America's Cup scene like something straight out of an Ian Fleming novel. For all that, there was that in some of his more crazy schemes which proved uncannily prophetic, and no one could be put in a mental home for suggesting that the logistic plan drawn up by the New York Yacht Club itself for its own campaign in Fremantle could have been copied from de Savary's Newport campaign of 1982/83.

It was in such an atmosphere of expansionist enthusiasm – just the sort of owner with whom he liked to work – that Cudmore met with de Savary, Phil Crebbin and Kit Hobday and discussed, as the communiques put it, matters of mutual interest. It looked as if the two might well see eye to eye on how wining campaigns are put together, and so in the next weeks Cudmore set to work with Phil Crebbin to draw up a working format.

The plan was announced at a news conference on 11 November, 1980 –

Remembrance Day – in the St James's Club to as large a gathering of the general sporting press and media as had ever attended a press conference about a yacht race. By the end of the afternoon, after a champagne and buffet lunch that spelled Opulence with a capital O, many may have known seriously little more about Twelve Metres and the America's Cup, but every paper in Fleet Street knew about Peter de Savary and the St James's Club.

The de Savary/Crebbin/Cudmore masterplan was to employ Ed Dubois as a design co-ordinator for the entire project and to retain Ian Howlett, *Lionheart*'s designer, to design a generic of the Freedom/Enterprise type of boat, the definitive Twelve Metre shape as it was then seen and the shape that had successfully defended for the Americans in 1980.

This boat would then be built and in 1981 go to America to race against *Australia* in her America's Cup rig and sails and with her Newport 1980 crew on board. In short, the 1980 America's Cup would be recreated, but with the British sailing a boat developed not from their own – unsuccessful – challenger but from the successful American defender. Thus would a major obstacle to winning the America's Cup – the inherent one-step-ahead advantage of the American defenders – be overcome. Instead of returning to Newport in three years' time with a boat capable of beating the boats that had lost three years previously and then discovering that the Americans had in the meantime moved ahead yet again, the British challengers would know straight away if they had such a boat, and could then develop from that to a boat to take to Newport for the challenge to come.

In parallel with this development, the design programme under its co-ordinator would gather together a more individual group of people to see if a development boat could be found to beat the now known quantity of the American-style boat.

It was a then more or less unheard of concept: Dubois, although himself a designer, would not actually draw the Twelve Metre but would instead co-ordinate the development of the entire project from design point of view, with other designers working not so much under as around him. This was the job eventually done to such devastingly good effect by non-designer but master strategist John Marshall in the '87 *Stars & Stripes* campaign, but in the jealous world of British design and its tradition of solo designers working alone at their ivory drawing boards it was to be a virtual non-starter.

It was also a plan uncommonly like the painstaking, step-by-step development campaigns which would be undertaken by the Australians who eventually won the 1983 America's Cup, designing the conventional *Challenge 12* and blooding and proving the developmental, radical *Australia II* against her. The irony was that all that would not become known until after the America's Cup had been lost and won, three years after Cudmore made much the same proposals to de Savary.

Finally, it was a plan that was not to be. During one of Cudmore's many absences on his racing programme, Peter de Savary either changed his mind or had it changed for him. He gave Ed Dubois the commission to design the Twelve Metre himself. At that time Dubois had no experience of Twelve Metres, had done no research and his only direct involvement in the America's Cup had been in watching the death-throes of the *Lionheart* campaign.

By the same yardstick, Cudmore had no direct America's Cup experience to point to either, only his proven ability at planning winning campaigns – and these were mostly in IOR boats. Dubois was an IOR designer on the crest of a wave of success, the IOR was a rating rule and so was the International Rule, to which the Twelves are designed. 'It's just another rating rule' was Dubois' counter to any – including this author in an interview for *Yachts and Yachting* – who queried his lack of experience when compared to the likes of Howlett. When the time came, Ed Dubois was able to supply, in *Victory '82*, a Twelve Metre firmly based on the American boats from information 'readily available' which was what, after all, the masterplan called for in the first place, but it wasn't the same thing. Was it?

Once the passage of time and events had released Cudmore from the confidentiality of the consulting room, he recalled with some feeling:

> Thus de Savary's first major intervention in the programme committed him to probable failure from the very beginning. At least a higher likelihood of failure – certainly it left him unlikely to win by innovation.

It may well be that de Savary had the move more or less forced upon him. Although in theory the masterplan sounded fine, Dubois at least found working as co-ordinator to the more experienced (at least in Twelve Metre terms) Ian Howlett an uncomfortable experience, while Howlett no doubt jealously guarded both what he regarded as his own professional stock-in-trade – his deep understanding of the Twelve Metre rule, developed from years of intense and almost exclusive study – and indeed his own professional dignity. This was not the first British yacht design collaboration venture to fail, nor would it be the last.

There was also the fact that 1981 was an Admiral's Cup year, and

Dubois had a tray full of Admiral's Cupper orders and a drawerful of Admiral's Cupper designs. Dubois had in fact first met de Savary in Newport not to discuss Twelve Metres at all but talk about Admiral's Cup designs, for a boat to be campaigned and skippered by Phil Crebbin. It was while this project was taking shape that de Savary had made his decision to have Dubois, not Howlett, draw his first Twelve Metre, presumably on the basis that the Admiral's Cup and the America's Cup campaigns would benefit mutually from keeping both design and management under the same roof.

Undoubtedly, *Victory '81* was perceived as much as anything as a means of permitting the big-talking but otherwise unknown newcomer to establish his bona fides with the sailing establishment in general but with Crebbin and Dubois in particular, before either would commit themselves wholly to the new America's Cup challenge. With John Oakeley's blood still drying on the boardwalk Crebbin was not about to become yet another sailor-victim of a megalomaniac owner, and Dubois with a fast-growing and flourishing general design business at his fingertips was only too well aware of the pitfalls and muggings that might await a fresh-faced young designer down the shadowy and specialised alleyway that was Twelve Metre designing.

As such *Victory '81* was initially spectacularly successful, becoming Britain's top ocean racer in the '81 season with a string of wins, a place in the vanguard of the Admiral's Cup team and becoming by the end of the summer Royal Ocean Racing Club Yacht of the Year. Given the vagaries and changes of direction which continued to characterise Peter de Savary's Twelve Metre decisions it is probably going too far to suggest that the distraction and consequent lost year of the Admiral's Cup campaign cost him the 1983 America's Cup, but it certainly put paid to any long-term Twelve Metre development work being seriously pursued. From now on 'shortage of time' would be a constant watchword in the British America's Cup efforts. Some lessons, it seems, are but slowly learned.

There was another consequence upon the America's Cup campaign of de Savary's dalliance with the Admiral's Cupper, the effect of which one can only but speculate upon. *Victory '81* was sold at the end of the '81 season to a new owner and taken to the US to be campaigned in the Southern Ocean Racing Conference, an early season circuit of almost as much importance as the Admiral's Cup itself. There, a serious error was found in her IOR rating. *Victory '81* was found to rate almost a foot and a half more than her British certificate indicated. The resulting scandal – for it was no less than that – had profound and far-reaching implications for both British and international offshore racing, but as far as the America's Cup campaign was concerned a committee of enquiry established by the RORC categorically cleared both de Savary and Dubois from allegations of malpractice.

All the same, a rework of her previous season's results on the new rating showed that *Victory '81*, while being no dog, was far from the spectacularly successful racer she had at first appeared. In the greater debate about rating procedures on both sides of the Atlantic, such a rework was noted but otherwise left unremarked – indeed, discussion of the subject was positively discouraged by the yachting establishment. *Victory '81*'s rating was far from the only one to be found to be in error around this time and official policy was and still is that results obtained with the erroneous rating must be allowed to stand unchallenged unless foul-play is suspected. Officially, her string of spectacular wins and her head-and-shoulders domination of the '81 season still stood. How much did such spurious success in his first season as an owner deceive Peter de Savary into thinking that he and his group had a Midas touch when it came to winning yacht race campaigns, that already and after only one season he himself had all the right answers?

There was nothing to be learned by sailing a Twelve Metre intended to win in September off Newport, in England in early May, so as soon as *Victory '81* could be got ready she was shipped to Newport to join *Australia*. Through that summer Cudmore and Phil Crebbin sailed one boat each, working closely together.

A major problem with *Victory '81* was that, because of the inexperience of all concerned, she had quite frankly not been put together very well and there were constant problems with rating and with the straightforward 'basics' of sailing her. Much more work than anyone had bargained for had to be done to bring her up to race specification and so there were constant delays in assessing her against *Australia*.

Dubois, too, was now having problems with de Savary – in the latter's view Dubois was not giving *Victory* enough of his time, while Dubois himself saw the situation differently. He had fulfilled his design contract, supplied the boat and now it was up to the sailors. To Dubois, designing de Savary's Twelve Metre was like any of the other design contracts his flourishing business was engaged upon (Dubois, by the way, always refers to himself and his business as that of a 'naval architect', not merely 'a yacht designer'). He had no wish to abandon this business while he immersed himself in the esoteria of the America's Cup. Ian Howlett, on the other hand, with no major design office to run was waiting in the wings whence, at the end of the short American season, de Savary summoned him, inviting him to come back into the programme on an advisory basis.

De Savary also dropped two more bombshells. He had decided he could not afford (and the programme could not spare the time) to build another boat and the whole separate development programme, some of which had included model work by a complete unknown called David Hollom, was dropped.

Much has subseqently been made of David Hollom's involvement with this radical group, but the reality is that at this stage there was more concern with merely setting up a management structure for the group than with investigating specific design avenues. Hollom's Project Acorn model *Royal Oak* was a thread, but no more. There is more to producing a radical Twelve Metre than building a model, as David Hollom undoubtedly knew and was subsequently to show, and without a proper design management team, de Savary's radical solution could never have been a reality. It was a lesson Cudmore would carry forward with conviction into the White Crusade.

In September '82, de Savary pulled another rabbit out of the hat by introducing *Lionheart* into the equation and inviting Lawrie Smith and British Olympic Gold Medallist Rodney Pattisson to sail her. The suggestion came direct from Ian Howlett who, having been called in by de Savary to give a second opinion on developments to date, had been not at all impressed with either *Victory '82* or with the way the programme was shaping up. De Savary then put to Cudmore and Phil Crebbin that he would like Lawrie and Rodney involved full-time in the programme 'to generate more competition' for the sailors already there – including themselves. If Cudmore's original masterplan had relied on a programme of rapid learning and careful, objective analysis in a stable environment it was more and more being eroded by de Savary's own apparently firmly held belief that he could only get an honest effort out of those to whom he entrusted his affairs by keeping them under constant pressure and the threat of unemployment.

Cudmore and Crebbin agreed to the new proposal on the understanding that only one or other pair would go forward, along with a final, nominated crew, into the Cup summer of '83.

The winter racing was carried out in Nassau, *Victory '82* having been grounded for major refit work. So at the expense of any development work on the Twelve Metre – even on sails and related equipment – *Lionheart* and *Australia* were shipped off for a winter in the Bahamas.

In late October, 1982, at another of his St James's Club press lunches, de Savary announced the new plan, indulged in fulsome praise of the

Dubois design and the team dispersed for an early winter break. Then, in an apparently extraordinarily speedy and isolated decision, de Savary without informing any of his sailors ordered a new Twelve Metre from Ian Howlett. Crebbin was on holiday at the time and Cudmore was in Hong Kong giving radio interviews saying what a great boat *Victory '82* was. He read the news that she was 'to be scrapped' and replaced by a new boat in the paper.

He was astounded: bare days before at the 'end of term' planning meeting, all the principal and long-standing members of the campaign – including Crebbin, himself, de Savary, Hobday – had concluded there was neither time nor point in now designing a new Twelve, given the still-undeveloped potential of *Victory '82*. After that meeting, de Savary had contacted Ian Howlett, asked him to fly urgently to meet him in New York, then flown him to Nassau to ask for his advice. Next day he ordered the new boat.

The racing in Nassau was complicated by the fact that *Australia* turned out to be a significantly quicker boat than *Lionheart* and that no one – not even the new sailing coach Peter Bateman – apparently kept accurate records of who beat whom and by how much. Cudmore kept his own records and as far as he was concerned the results in race terms were fairly conclusive, with himself and Phil Crebbin winning eighty per cent of their races when aboard *Australia* and something over fifty per cent when aboard the less competitive *Lionheart*. The only formal racing was a four-race mini-series in Bermuda in which Cudmore and Crebbin had been instructed to sail the limping *Lionheart* and Smith and Pattisson had been given *Australia*: it had been won by Smith and Pattisson but was enough for Peter de Savary to say that the winter's racing had proved inconclusive.

De Savary declined to honour his promise to nominate a final crew as the campaign prepared to return to Newport. Cudmore firmly believed that it would be suicidal to try to introduce a new boat into the programme while the crew was still undecided and therefore unsettled, particularly bearing in mind de Savary's savage selection techniques and belief in internal conflict as a useful motivator of Twelve Metre crews and personnel. There would simply be too many variables, too many grinding axes for anyone to make any sensible analytical assessments of either sailors or, indeed, of the new boat itself.

Thus, on a fundamental disagreement of strategy, Cudmore and de Savary parted company. It seems likely, too, that by this time Cudmore had lost any faith he might have had in the reliability of de Savary's judgement and decision-making process as an owner. He would not, and rightly so for de Savary was a complete novice at yacht racing in any boat, never mind Twelve Metres, have any faith in his judgement on sailing matters. That, from Cudmore's standpoint, would have been his own job – but de Savary seemed to change advisors as often as he changed his shirt and, more to the point, was determined to run the campaign his way, not Cudmore's.

'His best idea,' Cudmore complained at the time, 'is the one he heard last night,' while to de Savary he is reputed to have said, 'Your trouble, Peter, is that you take advice from far too many people.' 'And your trouble, Harold,' retorted de Savary, 'is that you don't take advice from me – and I can give you five million reasons why you should, one dollar each.' $US5m was the current budget and de Savary reckoned since it was his money, he might as well decide how it was spent.

De Savary had wanted to retain two crews throughout the summer, making a final choice as the end of the trialling and the Cup itself approached. Cudmore disagreed both fundamentally and from the point of view that here was de Savary yet again changing what at least one party to the deal had thought had been agreed between the two.

'If you lose me,' warned Cudmore, 'you'll have one crew anyway.' De Savary did not agree, and brought in Chris Law. If he told Chris Law that he would be given the opportunity to trial for the place at *Victory*'s wheel, it was not what he told the others, and within a short time – a matter of three weeks – Law was back home in England as the managing director of a roller skate business which de Savary had acquired. Smith, Crebbin and Pattisson had made it plain three people working for two places was bad enough – they were not going back to having four.

Another key victim of de Savary management was the man who had first brought Cudmore into the *Victory* programme and who had been its helmsman and technical director since inception: Phillip Crebbin. With days to go before the start of the final of the challengers' selection series, having patiently accommodated all the changes of plan, the unexpected – and often unexplained – arrivals, the alterations to strategy and twists of campaign tactics, having in short jumped through every hoop de Savary held up before him, Phil Crebbin had at last been told by de Savary 'right, you are going to race the boat from here on'.

The following morning de Savary announced to the press that Lawrie Smith would from now on steer the yacht. He had, apparently, yet again changed his mind (or had it changed for him) overnight – and had omitted to inform Crebbin of the change. In a branch of the sport not noted for its concern for personal sensitivities, it was still an astonishingly cruel thing to do.

It is little wonder then, that when the time came to people the new challenge several of the key players first and foremost made sure their own positions were secure.

Cudmore himself is unequivocal about the de Savary style of campaign management: it destabilises where it should motivate, detracts from progress instead of stimulating. Worst of all it is 'unstructured' (in the Cudmore racing lexicon, no more undesirable state exists). Crew members are more interested in their relative position than in the good of the programme, and when not sure of their place – not necessarily on the boat, but in the context of the campaign – they will not give of their best and certainly cannot be relied upon to devote all their energies to objective analysis of the essential development parts of the programme.

Looking back on the effects of 'creative tension', Cudmore now recalls that it brought *Victory '83* to the very brink of defeat, making it into the semi-finals (and against altogether different competition to that found three years later in Fremantle) by the slenderest of margins. It was only the arrival, as sailing coach, of a young American called Robert Hopkins which gave the yacht her final performance. He could see clearly the faults facing the programme and the inherent weakness of the boat, and in consultation with Crebbin – though allegedly opposed by Howlett – rebalanced the yacht by moving the rig forward. It was an intervention – in a programme more characterised by interventions than by continuity – which was to presage what was to come. In 1986 it would be the sailors who would at last dictate what sort of boat they needed, while in 1986 Robert Hopkins too was back in the business of coaching Twelve Metre programmes – for a Californian sailor by the name of Dennis Conner.

On Peter de Savary himself, Cudmore is no less unequivocal.

> His big failing is his unwillingness to be honest with the people he is dealing with. He will for a short-term comfort or to avoid confronting a problem make a promise which will subsequently not be kept and which comes home to roost in the longer term, when the truth comes out. Peter de Savary is not an organiser – he's a dealer, but no good at people management.
>
> But his principal inability is to make long-term plans and have the consistency of view to see them through. He much prefers short-term tampering, and very often can't solve a problem until he can get his hands on it. Twelve Metres require greater long-sightedness. He lacks the intellectual capacity for a lengthy and complex campaign.

It is unlikely that Cudmore would want to have a great deal to do with another Peter de Savary campaign, which is probably just as well. There is every indication that between the two men, feelings are mutual.

CHAPTER FIVE

Harold Cudmore – Who he?

Cork is the most European of Ireland's cities. To this area came the Phoenicians in the first era of Mediterranean expansion, and in subsequent centuries Vikings, Normans, Italian and French merchants and traders, to create and leave a legacy of broadened horizon and internationalism that is not typical of other parts of Ireland. In Cork, was founded in 1720, the world's first recorded yacht club – the Water Club of Cork – from which the Royal Cork Yacht Club claims direct descendancy, giving it claim to being the oldest yacht club in the world. The city itself lies in one corner of a vast and exceptionally beautiful natural harbour, the home and training ground for generations of Irish sailors.

It is from this dual heritage of merchant trading and sailing that Harold Cudmore springs. The eldest son of a reasonably well off middle-class business family, his summer holidays from school were spent more or less living aboard his father's thirty-four foot cruising yacht, either cruising when his father was aboard or pottering when he was not. In the Ireland of the late fifties, yachting (to be strictly accurate, 'sailing' – yachting was something they did in the south of England) was an unremarkable hobby for anyone who lived near the water, and in Ireland, shortage of water has never been a national problem.

Cudmore's earliest sailing exploits were in cruising rather than in racing – a reflection as much as anything of the nature and emphasis of Irish sailing at the time. At the age of fifteen, young Harold became the youngest person ever to be elected to membership of the Irish Cruising Club, a distinction he still holds and one of which he is enormously proud, not least because the ICC has no junior section and a strict system of qualification for membership. Part of the requirement is that a candidate's proposer must aver that he would be happy to allow the candidate to take his own yacht away in the role of skipper.

His racing talents began to show themselves first in a somewhat battered and leaky old International Cadet, acquired when the young Cudmore was twelve years old, and subsequently in the Jack Holt-designed Enterprise class, spearhead of the dinghy sailing boom which swept Britain and Ireland in the late fifties and early sixties. Hugely energetic and competitive, with a quick mind and a temperament not over-encumbered with patience, the teenage Cudmore was quickly one of the hot shots of the local and eventually national dinghy racing scene, winning the Irish Champion of Champions event in 1972.

Yet throughout, cruising was as important a part of Harold Cudmore's sailing as was racing, and in particular the retrieval and safe delivery of the yachts of family or friends from far-flung places back to Cork. As a result, Cudmore grew up with a wide and varied sailing experience, an experience of all kinds of boats and of all kinds of weather, which while by no means unique is nonetheless unusual among today's competition-bred younger racing sailors, the products of youth schemes, coaching sessions, and training seminars. It left him with an affinity with yachts and the sea which many top racing sailors lack. There are of course any number of sailors who enjoy both racing and cruising: what is so very unusual about Cudmore is that he combines this wide and deep feeling for the way of a yacht in the sea – in a word, seamanship – with a tactical racing talent of rare and extraordinarily high level.

From Enterprises Cudmore moved into the 505 high-performance dinghy, recently arrived in Ireland where until then the dinghy racing scene had been dominated by the unpretentious designs of the build-it-yourself era. Typically, Cudmore jumped in at the deep end, buying the boat and entering straight away the world championships, staged that year (1968) in Germany.

'I just bought the boat and a set of rigging instructions from the builder and a very fast experimental Banks mainsail which I assume they must have sold to me by mistake . . .' Then, as now, top sail-lofts tended not to waste their best products on also-rans.

At those championships, Cudmore found himself, to his unconcealed delight, boating all over some of the hottest names in the class and the next year went to Buenos Aires, to the world championship. It was only his second year in the class and he came second, and in the following year was fourth in the Europeans, held in Ireland (the 505 class is one of those which stages a European championship only when the world championship is outside Europe).

Yet his success even then was mercurial, erratic. On some days Cudmore would sail brilliantly, but on others, or at other events, his performance would be lack-lustre. Sometime around 1972 W M Nixon, then as now doyen of Irish yachting writers, wrote of Cudmore that if only he would stop fooling around and put his mind to it, he could become one of the world's greatest racing sailors.

For 1972 Cudmore bought himself a Flying Dutchman, the two-man Olympic dinghy, and without much difficulty qualified as Ireland's representative in that class at the Kiel Olympics. It was a year when Irish small-boat racing had suddenly leapt on to the international stage, with Cudmore's successes in the 505 giving notice of great things to come in the Dutchman, and with the Irish Olympic Dragon crew winning all before them at home and abroad and looking set fair to make Irish history with an Olympic yachting medal.

It was not to be. Illness among the Dragon sailors on the one hand and ill preparation among the Dutchman team on the other meant that Ireland's 1972 Olympic participation was noted more for the parties than the sailing, and the team came home empty handed and quite probably not a little thick of head. Yet the campaign demonstrated a side to the Cudmore character that was to become wider known in later years: a mischievious and sometimes self-destructive sense of fun – what the Irish call 'divilmint' – that says 'we must take this thing seriously – but there is no need to apply the same rule to ourselves.'

The sailors at Kiel were housed in a plush, multi-storey hostel, with the Irish on about the fifth floor and with only one lift to serve the needs of the sailors of many nations. Never ones to take physical training too seriously the Irish did not particularly relish pounding up and down the stairs, while those in the floors above had even less incentive to use shank's pony when a lift was available. The result was that everytime an Irish sailor wanted to use the lift, he found it had already been commandeered by those above. The remedy was simple and typically Cudmoresque – the control panel of the lift was hot-wired so that it always stopped at the Irish floor.

Then there was the time, years later, when the Congressional Cup was being raced on 17 March which, as everyone knows, is St Patrick's Day. His American hosts assured Cudmore that they took St Patrick's Day seriously, and Cudmore assured his hosts that, seriously and all as the Americans take everything, they could not take St Patrick's Day as seriously as the Irish did, and perhaps they might all like to come round to the house where he was staying on the appointed day and see for themselves.

For the party, no trouble was spared. The music was Irish, the cocktails were green and the small eats were imaginative variations on the potato theme. For Cudmore, the *piece de resistance* came when the hired help somewhat ostentatiously revealed that the small eats were running out.

'Don't worry,' said Cudmore, 'we have back-up supplies,' and seizing a small net on the end of a long stick strode purposefully toward the jaccuzzi. Before his guests amazed eyes, he fished out freshly cooked potatoes still wrapped in silver foil.

'You cooked the potatoes in the jaccuzzi?' asked one guest, scarcely daring to believe.

'Of course,' replied Cudmore with deadpan face. 'When it comes to cooking potatoes, y'know, we Irish don't frig around.' Thoughtfully he added, 'Let me know if you want a go in the jaccuzzi and I'll turn it down. It's a bit hot for sitting in just now.'

Only later did Cudmore reveal – and not to his guests – that of course the potatoes had been pre-cooked in a plain ordinary pot before being slipped unnoticed into the latter-day Bethesda. More to the point, the whole elaborate charade had been staged to allow him to win a bet that he could get this annual gathering of some of the greatest names in American yacht racing to eat boiled potato off the ends of cocktail sticks.

In the late sixties and very early seventies, the full-time yacht racing sailor was unknown in Britain. A very few yachts had full-time, professional crews but they were 'paid-hands', the last of the breed of professional sailors who had maintained and crewed the great yachts of the between-the-wars era of so-called amateur yacht racing, and who sailed – particularly in some of the 'better' Solent classes – as crew for 'gentlemen' and 'lady' amateur skippers. Cudmore, by now in his early twenties, had left school (undistinguished academically, in the best traditions of great leaders, but with the reputation of having read every book in the school library) and entered articles as an accountant.

That he gave up after two years, and went into the family business – a mundane but money-making calling involving the distribution of groceries to a national network of small stores. To the fast-thinking, impatient young man, it was a frustrating existence, the difficulties of which were reflected in a certain unevenness of keel both on and off the water. What he needed was a well-organised environment for his sailing talents, and these he found in a partnership with another, older, Cork businessman – Hugh Coveney.

To Coveney must go the distinction of being the first owner successfully to channel the Cudmore talent into winning consistency. Together they raced a modest sloop by the name of *Dalcassian* and in 1973 began campaigning in earnest in a new and for those days very *avant garde* design by French designers, Groupe Finot. She was *Allouette de Mer* and in her Coveney, Cudmore 'and a few of the lads' planned to 'do' Cowes Week. But there was a gale, they were late getting to Cowes and managed only one race before the Fastnet itself. It was a light wind, very slow race and six days in the engineless Half Tonner convinced Coveney that something a little bigger would not come amiss.

The following season he had a Ron Holland-designed One Tonner, *Golden Apple* – but more to the point, he and Cudmore put together what was to be the first of Cudmore's business-managed racing campaigns.

In *Golden Apple* they had some impressive results 'and some really great publicity' and in the following year the campaign team moved into high gear with *Golden Leprechaun,* the prototype of a Ron Holland design to be put into production as the Shamrock Half Tonner, one of the classic racing designs of the early seventies. There can be no doubt that the seeds of her subsequent fame and commercial success were sown with Cudmore's Cowes campaign of 1975: taking five firsts in six days in what was then still not only England's premier sailing regatta, but one of the most important in the world. The following year the trend continued, with his *Silver Shamrock* winning seven races on eight days of racing.

As four years before at the Olympics, Irish sailors were again jumping on to the apron of the international yachting stage – this time in IOR boats. In 1975 that consummate commentator on yachting trends, Jack Knights, was writing in *Yachts and Yachting*:

> The Irish were very prominent on the water in Cowes Week this year. The letters IR could be found on many sails . . . and a pair of Ron Holland-designed sisters took apart the large and competitive Half Ton Class 4.

And a year later he was writing:

> From Class 4, round about half ton size, came the undoubted star of the Week, the modified Holland-designed Shamrock-type 'Silver Shamrock', from Cork, skippered by red-headed Harold Cudmore. 'Silver Shamrock' won seven races in eight starts, usually by huge margins. Usually she was ahead of all, or nearly all of Class 3 which started ten minutes earlier. She appeared to outclass the other Shamrocks completely and did so six times with Cudmore steering and once, equally easily, with Doug Bishop steering.

Silver Shamrock was a turning point for Cudmore in more ways than one. Earlier that year – 1976 – he had begun work on the building of a new Flying Dutchman for the Kingston Olympics only to have his plans torpedoed by the hierarchy of the Irish Yachting Association who, perhaps remembering the erratic performances in the past, would not endorse his campaign. The excuse was that the campaign was too little, too late, but it is just as probable that the decision was made with the intent of slapping the Cudmore wrist and making him toe the official (and rather less flamboyant) line in the future. Thus thwarted, Cudmore decided on a full-fledged campaign for that year's Half Ton Cup in Trieste and *Silver Shamrock* was built with great speed.

Cudmore already knew exactly what he wanted in the boat, and went into every detail of her building and preparation with microscopic care. It was all very well being good, but it was even easier to look good if you had a fast boat in the first place. As Knights was to observe at Cowes, *Silver Shamrock* was quick more or less no matter who sailed her. (Doug Bishop, it should be clearly stated, was a top-class helmsman himself.)

In *Silver Shamrock* came the first example of Cudmore's almost unrivalled ability to put together the many elements which make a yacht win races: the attention to details of rating enhancement; the attention to weight distribution in her building; the details of her rig; her sails; the recruitment of her crew. In the next decade this was to become an especial Cudmore forte, culminating in the development of *White Crusader* into a yacht 'unrecognisable' (to quote a fair half-dozen of the Crusade's upper management) from her original state.

Silver Shamrock went on to win the 1976 Half Ton world championship, and subsequently went cruising with a certain amount of flamboyance to Venice, among other places. It was, to use a Cudmore catch phrase, 'a bit of fun'.

An indication of the Cudmore style may be gained from the remark of a journalist of this period, who commented that approaching Cudmore on the dock after a race it was impossible to guess from his demeanour whether he had won or lost. There was a truth in this – but only a partial truth. When a subsequent *Silver Shamrock* turned out to be so desperately slow as to earn that most damning of yachting soubriquets 'a real dog', Cudmore's good grace at losing (he never talks of 'not winning', only of either winning or losing – coming second is still losing) knew no bounds. 'It Takes A Lot Of Boats To Beat Silver Shamrock' ran the slogan on the front of the special T-shirts he had printed for the crew, with on the back the despairing rider 'And They're All Here'. As the regatta went from bad to worse, Cudmore eventually went up to the town hall and bought the yacht a dog licence which was ceremoniously taped to the mast as if it were an

Admiralty Writ. All enjoyed the joke, but there were those more percipient who saw through it to the motive beyond.

Cudmore was now firmly on the road of the full-time sailor: indeed was a pioneer of that road. Yacht racing was changing fast and there had grown up, relatively quickly, a cadre of young men both in Britain and America, and to a lesser extent in Europe, who devoted more or less all their time and thought to the problems and art of racing yachts and small boats. The Great Dane Paul Elvström, winner of four successive Olympic Golds, had shown the way by combining his addiction to yacht racing with earning a living by becoming a sailmaker, thus combining his sport and his business and in the process being able to work full time at each. Others had followed suit and in the seventies there not so much grew as burgeoned the species of amateur-professional, the sailor who worked in the industry during the week and 'played' at sailing at weekends.

It was a sham. The booming industry was supporting the sport by providing 'experts' to help aboard favoured customers' boats; the top sailmakers raced their own boats as part of their business promotion; the top yards set up 'works' teams to race a prototype or special one-off and each fortnight and month the advertisement pages of the yachting magazines trumpeted their winning exploits and demonstrated quite clearly just how seriously they took their weekend's 'relaxation'. Yet against such a background the sport and its rule-makers stuck firmly – and in a stance that would have required King Canute to have been an ostrich – to a pretence and to rules that yacht racing was exclusively amateur, that there could be no such thing as a professional yacht racer, that there should be no such thing as pecuniary reward for yacht racing.

Cudmore's involvement was of necessity ambivalent. He regarded it as one of his strengths that he never worked for a sailmaker or a builder or even a designer. The first *Silver Shamrock* had been a works' boat of sorts, and for a time thereafter Cudmore had repeatedly been involved with the designs of his friend Ron Holland, the New Zealander who had come to work and live in Cork, but his arrangements were made always with owners direct. His background and circumstances allowed him a limited financial freedom, and his chosen lifestyle with its determination to avoid the increasing immobility which the accumulation of material possessions brings did the rest.

He rarely kept the trophies he won. Those that the owners themselves did not proudly hold on to as their right (and why not?) he would give either to members of the crew or to the friends with whom he had stayed during the regatta in question. It was partly because he did not have anywhere to keep them himself.

He lived for the day, and for yacht racing.

The Cudmore racing pattern evolved around two areas, each distinct but each to be brought together for the America's Cup campaign of the White Crusade. The first was the continuingly successful big-boat management campaign, where Cudmore would act both as overall business manager and as racing skipper of the yacht; the second was the developing and highly individual world circuit of match racing tournaments. In these Cudmore would star, as it were, in his own production and in his own right.

He became the most international of sailors on the British scene simply because he had a voracious appetite for sailing and, far from demanding exhorbitant fees or complicated laundering arrangements for expenses, would accept virtually any invitation to sail on a yacht so long as he could fit it in. Of that time he used to say 'I have one great virtue. I turn up.'

His reputation grew as the number of successful campaigns increased. He masterminded the development of two Holland-designed sister ships *Big Apple* and *Marionette* of 1977: each yacht made their respective Admiral's Cup teams and *Big Apple*'s performance in the Cup itself prompted one commentator to remark that if the Irish could only get two more like her, they could well win the Admiral's Cup next time around.

Next time around they were back in force and in style and by the start of the Fastnet race, the final and all-important offshore classic which concludes the series, were points leaders ahead of the somewhat surprised talent of the rest of the world. Their enviable position was enhanced by a reputation for being at their best offshore. But this was 1979, the year of the traumatic Fastnet race which was devastated by storm. The high-flying Irish team came out of that Fastnet not at all well.

Cudmore came out of it on the end of a helicopter lifting strop. *Golden Apple*'s rudder had broken off and, although the crew had not summoned assistance, a rescue helicopter on the way to another casualty had chanced upon them and its crew urged them to leave the yacht. Cudmore himself, who in the earlier days of delivery trips had sometimes had to get yachts out of worse messes than this, was bitterly reluctant to leave, but common sense and the other members of the crew prevailed. 'Gone to lunch, back later' read the note he left on the chart table.

A One Ton world championship win with a grand slam – five wins in the five-race series – a Two Ton Cup and two maxi World Cups were among other wins, along with a host of lesser prizes to attest to the success of his management expertise. Yet the most spectacular success of all came during the White Crusade itself with the performance of Graham Walker's Admiral's Cup campaign in 1985.

It began conventionally enough but with better omens than most. There was no shortage of money, nor of time. The design was the best possible, construction was painstakingly detailed and as advanced as it was possible to be: state-of-the-art, as the heavily overworked American phrase has it. The crew had within it all the elements of success. Initial trials showed the yacht to be possessed of mouth-watering potential.

Her first serious test against the other Admiral's Cup team hopefuls came in the first official selection trial race, held over a course that took the fleet overnight down the English Channel to Portland and back around the Isle of Wight. She sank.

True enough. She sank through a basic failure of seamanship: close-tacking with her companions near the shore at night, she lost track of her exact position by a sufficient number of metres – between ten and 100 – to strike a charted but otherwise unmarked wreck. No doubt about it, poor seamanship – and with Cudmore, that so-called great seaman-racer, in command. Cudmore himself accepted full blame but fortunately Graham Walker was not to be deterred and backed another yacht with its owner Lloyd Bankson, a standard production boat, to replace his beloved but short-lived *Indulgence.*

Till then, the boat in question had been an also-ran, to put it at its most generous, but under Cudmore's direction there was effected a transformation that more than justified her new name of *Phoenix*. Nothing major was done to her, but the cumulative effect of the complete re-think was as radical as if a new rig, deck, hull and keel had been put under her masthead wind indicator. Every deck fitting came off and was either discarded or re-located; excess weight was ruthlessly removed; sheeting positions were altered; sails re-cut; ballast more carefully assessed and positioned. From being barely able to make it into single figures in the results, she made it into the British Admiral's Cup team and thence to the position of top individual yacht in that forty-five-boat, fifteen-nation series. It was a spectacular demonstration of what is meant by the term campaign management.

Back in 1976, Cudmore had been one of the first sailors outside the US to make the link between constant match race practice and winning the America's Cup, although there is little doubt that then it was no less the high profile, adrenalin-surging nature of the one-to-one combat that fired his imagination. His growing international profile and his self-admitted virtue of 'turning up' began to earn him invitations to compete on the growing international circuit, and once he began to win, the invitations came thick and fast.

Two characteristics above all marked his performances, both the direct result of his fiercely competitive – aggressive, if you prefer – style: his vociferousness on board and his punishing use of the rules.

There are two schools of thought regarding the use of the rules in match racing, even today, and in the mid-seventies as the sport developed into an independent discipline they were even more marked. One regards the complex yacht racing rules, rules which essentially seek to define in any possible circumstance and in every conceivable juxtaposition which of any two yachts shall have right of way over the other, as a code of conduct for keeping the yachts apart, for preventing collisions principally by not allowing the two yachts to come close enough for a collision to occur.

The other regards the very complexity of the rules as a most useful tool for wrong-footing the opponent, for at worst keeping him off balance and breaking his sailing pattern and for at best manoeuvring him into a position where he commits a prohibited move – a foul – over which a protest may be lodged and for which the protest jury will subsequently declare him to be disqualified. It is to the latter school of thought that Cudmore wholeheartedly subscribes. It was not, in the early days, an attitude which won him universal popularity either with fellow competitors (particularly, British competitors who were at the time notably lacking in international match race experience) or with some race organisers. It was one, however, which won him a lot of races.

In 1981, this author had the dubious pleasure of squaring up to a Cudmore in full cry in the Lymington Cup of that year – ironically enough while racing with Edward Warden Owen, Cudmore's subsequent companion in the White Crusade. The following extract from *Yachts and Yachting* describes the occasion.

> Seconds after gunfire we saw him creaming towards us, a bow wave under the forefoot of his mushroom-coloured OOD like a destroyer after a contact. In he came from windward, reaching fast on starboard with a scything, curving wake that clearly meant business. Warden-Owen on port bore away to keep clear; Cudmore, already calling 'Starboard!', bore away more to force Warden-Owen to gybe and make Cudmore a present of his transom.
>
> 'Hold your course,' called Warden-Owen.
>
> 'Starboard!' called Cudmore, and pulled the helm towards him. It is this technique of Cudmore's which so upsets his competitors. They cite Rule 35 ('the right-of-way yacht shall not so alter course as to prevent the other yacht from keeping clear;

or so as to obstruct her while she is keeping clear') and say that in altering course while holding the right-of-way Cudmore is preventing them from keeping clear.

'There was no collision,' says Cudmore. 'You were able to keep clear – how can you say I prevented you from doing something when in fact you were able to do it?' The rule, Cudmore insists, does not say he has to sail in a straight line from the moment he goes on to starboard tack and as long as he does not force a collision by his course alterations he is not preventing or obstructing the other yacht. It depends how you define 'obstruct'.

Cudmore's technique is to keep the pressure on: pushing, harrassing and calling until his opponent is so rattled and shell-shocked that he bungles into a mistake – and there will be Cudmore, hopping up on the cockpit sidebench, waving his arms, shouting, dancing back down again, pressing home his advantage.

He comes at us from astern and to leeward. 'Up! Up! Come on – you must keep clear or I'll protest – come on, keep up.'

'I'm clear,' calls Warden-Owen, looking back (and thus the wrong way: advantage Cudmore). 'You must allow for my stern swing – you must give me room.'

'No! No! You're windward boat. I know the rules. You must keep clear – Come On – GET UP! GET UP!!'

Owen luffs again, now above close-hauled. His stern swings towards Cudmore's bow. Cudmore, standing now on the sidebench, yanks the tiller towards him extravagantly, swinging his yacht's bow away with an exaggerated sweep (you never know, the jury might be watching), the wash curling up under the forefoot.

'That' it,' he yells. 'That's our protest – I'm protesting. Protest – protest – I had to alter my course to avoid a collision – I would have hit you – you've forced me to alter course.'

He leaps down off the sidebench, still calling, and actually turns a complete circle in the cockpit as he hops on to the opposite bench to get at his protest flag, yanking at the securing tape. 'That's it,' he calls again. 'That's it.'

Now Cudmore keeps further away. He reckons he has a potential protest win up his sleeve should disaster strike on the water, and there is no need to risk a more dubious incident which a jury might not see his way.

'Oh. Bother him,' says Edward Warden-Owen, or words to that effect.

In fact, Owen had Cudmore stitched up with a minute and a quarter to go, outluffing him at the port end of the line and forcing the Irishman to peel away on to starboard outside the end of the line while Owen fell back on to port. All he had to do now was sail up the line, turn and come back on starboard while Cudmore, coming back, would be on port and Owen could start as he pleased. Unhappily, he mis-timed it, getting back to the port end of the line too early, too close to the line and having to do a last-minute gybe-around while Cudmore coolly dipped his stern, re-seized the advantage by tacking on to starboard and sailed off into the distance.

'Oh bother,' said Owen again.

*

Thus Cudmore, over more than a decade, established his reputation, a reputation second to none in Britain and few in the world for methodical, business-like and above all successful management of yacht racing projects, and for rare ability in that esoteric branch of the sport which pits just one boat against one boat. They are the two elements which together face their most demanding test in the America's Cup.

He also established another reputation – and one he might prefer to be without. The reputation of having one of the most frenetic skippering styles in the world.

His peripatetic, leap-aboard way of life had taken him to the Antipodes, to skipper a yacht racing under the Australian flag, which had in her crew as bowman a sailor who was not of the level of expertise that Cudmore would have preferred. About six foot four inches in height, weighing some sixteen stone and with hands reminiscent of the grabs on a Rotterdam dredger he made up in enthusiasm and strength anything he lacked in finesse and skill and fortunately he was very enthusiastic and very strong.

After one particularly shambolic mark-rounding, Cudmore – a fully paid-up member of the Adrenalin School of Crew Management – could take no more.

'Jack – Jack! Here Jack, steer the bloody boat, Jack.' Jack, the navigator, working quietly below, came rushing on deck to find Cudmore already on his way forward.

Reaching up to grab the unfortunate crewman by the collar, Cudmore began to berate him roundly, pulling his face down to within an inch of his own, by now close to purple, rage-infused face.

'You,' he screamed, 'have got to be quite the most fuckin' useless fuckin' idiot I have ever seen on any boat anywhere in all my fuckin' life.'

'And I hope,' he added, as the full size and physical power of the giant he was manhandling dawned upon him, 'that you'll look on this as constructive criticism'.

CHAPTER SIX

Genesis of a Challenge

What Philip Tolhurst wanted to talk to Harold Cudmore about was the sailing and development programme of an America's Cup campaign that could most charitably be described as embryonic. Cup fever had for a time run high in the wake of the *Victory* campaign which, despite the comings and goings of the hired help, was widely and with good reason perceived as certainly the most worthy that Britain had put forward, at least since the days of Sopwith.

Post-83 Cuptalk was dominated by the miraculous benefits bestowed upon *Australia II* by those vaunted wings, and so far there had been no one in the Australian camp who had even hinted that the wonder design might not have been all she had been cracked up to be. In such a light, the received wisdom was that had there been no Australian breakthrough, *Victory '83* could well have won (here we go again, remarked some British commentators) – and indeed there was no denying that she had beaten all the other challengers except for the eventual Cup winner.

Set against such buoyant perception were the shudders still rippling through establishment breasts at some of the more flamboyant aspects of a de Savary-style campaign. Peter de Savary himself had indicated that he would not again go it alone but would combine forces and funds, but there seemed a general feeling that putting sponsorship money into a Twelve Metre campaign in which de Savary or someone like him was involved would be a somewhat pointless exercise, publicity-wise. The PdS – whoever he turned out to be – would burn up the money and hog the limelight.

There was, too, considerable debate about whether it would even be worth going to an America's Cup in Australia. Now that the Cup had been wrested from the Americans, what was the point of the competition? 'Where is the money to be made in Western Australia?' asked this writer in a speculative piece in *Yachts and Yachting* in February, 1984, which dismissed the likelihood of de Savary becoming involved again and for good measure added 'come to think of it, where is Western Australia?'

There was, at least in the minds of some – devious minds, perhaps, but experienced nonetheless – the notion that de Savary was playing a very clever game, making all the right noises about going again so as to avoid panicking anyone else into challenging but then not proceeding with his much gossipped-about plans having successfully blocked, until after the deadline, the plans of anyone else. The point of such a manoeuvre would have been that it would have left Peter de Savary as the unchallenged British Twelve Metre patron with a clear field of operation when – as most informed observers felt was the likely course of events – the Cup eventually went back to America. The only real disagreement was how long it would take the Americans to win it back.

Finally, with quite literally minutes to go to the 4 pm London-time deadline (midnight Perth time) the Royal Thames Yacht Club of Knightsbridge had telexed through to the Royal Perth YC a challenge. The club held in its hand a blank cheque from Admiral Sir Ian Easton, KCB, DSC to cover the cost of the entry fee – and strict instructions not to cash it.

Easton had stumbled across his challenge. He had been approached by a young and unknown amateur designer called Warwick Collins with some radical ideas on keel design and a convincing scenario for a technically-oriented British challenge. Collins had failed to persuade anyone with the necessary clout either in a yacht club or in industry to back his scenario and came to Easton – the two had collaborated on a military defence project – for last minute help. Would Easton affect an introduction to British Aerospace through his friendship with another retired Admiral, Sir Raymond Lygo, then chief executive of BAe? Easton, wondering just what he might be letting himself in for, affected the introduction.

Lygo made it plain that as chief executive of Britain's major aerospace concern he could not possibly sanction any sort of BAe involvement simply on the basis of the Royal Navy's old boy network, but if Collins could convince BAe's boffins and marketing people he was on to something, BAe might well be interested. Collins convinced them he was, indeed, on to something and together Collins and Easton set about trying to find a yacht club to put forward the still skeletal challenge.

Eventually it was the Royal Thames which agreed to act on their behalf, but not for them. The Thames, by curious coincidence, had been the nominated club of the first ever America's Cup challenger, and had challenged again only once – in 1964 with *Sovereign*. Now it found itself with two potential challengers, Easton/Collins and a nebulous group fronted by de Savary's former guru Kit Hobday, and it was taking a firm line with each: they must convince the club that their ideas had the substance, in other words the money, to see them through to fruition or the club would not lend its name to their enterprise.

Collins had persuaded BAe to sponsor initial testing work and as part of that sponsorship to invest the required entry fee of $A10,000 – about £4,000 at then current exchange rates. The accounting procedures of big companies being what they are, BAe could produce at such short notice only a letter of credit, which would surely – the company being not without standing in the financial community – be sufficient, but Tolhurst, representing the Royal Thames, insisted upon a cheque. With a snort of irritation at such pettyfogging, Easton pulled out his own personal chequebook, signed a cheque and thrust it at Tolhurst – and the Easton challenge for the America' Cup was born. Armed with the cheque, Tolhurst hurried round to the club's telex and threw the Thames' hat into the ring. They would decide later just whom the hat belonged to

Easton and Collins, along with Hobday, attended a main committee meeting of the club a fortnight later where first Hobday and then Easton, now thoroughly briefed by Collins on the technical aspects of the plan, put forward their relative proposals. Tolhurst, a member of the club's sailing committee who had been closely involved with the Royal Burnham's challenge and was thus listened to with some attention by the club when speaking on Twelve Metre matters, was asked for his opinion, and within an hour the Royal Thames decided to endorse the Easton challenge.

Easton himself had no intention of remaining even titular head of the campaign for longer than was absolutely necessary, and immediately began a search for someone – preferably from the Royal Thames – who would take over as chairman; someone who could command the respect of the yachting establishment, whose sincerity of belief in the challenge matched his own and who could attract the necessary funds from industry and commerce. But as the days turned into weeks, none such could be found. Meanwhile, and in the manner of an admiral with a background in strategic planning, he put together a command structure for the campaign, based on and extending Collins' own technical structure, and began to search for names to fill in the blanks. Cudmore's terms for becoming involved were simple and to the point: he would either have complete charge of the sailing programme and be the unchallengeable skipper of the yacht, or he wasn't interested. The last thing he wanted was another de Savary episode.

Easton had by this time already established his design team with Phil Crebbin as the putative technical director, something else which Cudmore found very attractive.

Easton recalls his first meeting with Cudmore vividly:

> He came on very strongly – as Harold does – and frankly I was a little put off, although I can understand precisely why he felt the way he did. He knew a lot about sailing, a lot about Twelves, and de Savary had given him a very rough ride and ballsed the thing up really, so now Harold had two main concerns.
>
> The first was he didn't want to have the thing bitched up by people who didn't know anything about Twelve Metres, but who came in from the outside. Let them go away and raise the money, was his stance, but let the sailors get on and run an America's Cup campaign. This was completely understandable.
>
> Also, he didn't want to be in a situation where he went half way down the road and then at the last minute the prize was snatched from him and handed to somebody else. He came on very strongly on this line: it must be left to the sailors.

Other aspects of the de Savary campaign, however, were more palatable, in particular the overall strategy of having two design groups working to explore as many avenues as possible.

Easton himself was primarily interested in running a campaign based on the philosophy proposed by Collins, of using the country's enormous technical resources and talent to develop a radical, breakthrough boat and with it win the America's Cup, just as the Australians had apparently done. The plan was not so much to design a new type of Twelve Metre, but to design a new type of sailing yacht, and fit the concept into the Twelve Metre rule. Cudmore, on the other hand, has a deep mistrust of what he calls 're-inventing the wheel' and was fearful of putting all the campaign's eggs into one development basket. As June and July rolled into Cowes Week he started talking to Ian Howlett, the man with most Twelve Metre design experience in Britain, and by the end of the summer had persuaded Easton, against the latter's better judgement, that at the very least the radical campaign should have a conventional Howlett design up its sleeve, just in case.

Cudmore's philosophy then was to use the Howlett boat as a benchmark from which to gauge and develop the potential of the radical boat and then build a third boat, based on the lessons of the first two, with which to go forward to the America's Cup itself. 'It was a wonderful plan,' he recalls, 'considering we had no money'.

Money was already proving to be a problem. Angry and then bitter at what he saw as the usurpation by Easton of his own position as progenitor of the challenge, Collins had withdrawn, stating in firm tones that if the campaign were run Easton's way, it would fail. Having as he saw it been responsible for introducing British Aerospace to the campaign, he felt it his responsibility to convey the same news to them and – whether for that reason or another – BAe did not proceed with either sponsorship or indeed technical support for the challenge, other than making available some computer time. Kit Hobday had also by this time been to Sir Raymond Lygo to assure him that Easton's challenge would fail. The first potential sponsor thus disappeared before the show was even properly on the road.

It is both an irony and a fact that throughout the life of any British Twelve Metre America's Cup campaign there always seem to be as many people in yachting circles determined to see it fail, and to do anything they can to assist such a process, as there are who wish to see it succeed. Throughout the life of this campaign, again and again, the phenomenon was to occur, with the added curiosity that the great majority of those who were allegedly scuppering attempts by the campaign to close sponsorship deals and raise funds appeared to be senior members of the Royal Thames Yacht Club itself.

The nature of commercial activity in London being what it is, great use is made by senior executives of social contacts. On more than one occasion it was to happen that a major company would be approached by the campaign, express interest and a presentation would be prepared and pitched. The company would become even more interested. Specific figures and terms would be discussed and the basics of the deal would be cut. Then a senior executive or board member would recall that he knew so-and-so, who was a member of the Thames and he would give him a call, just for a second opinion. Inevitably, the prospect would go cold. Although solid documentary evidence would never be produced the pattern and personalities became so evident that the challenge was able to establish a dossier of the names of those whom it believed were, for motives best left unexplored, quietly putting the finger on their efforts.

All this time, the radical design team under Hollom, Wallis and Pearcey was proceeding with work at the National Maritime Institute, towing a selection of 1/10th scale Twelve Metre models up and down the towing tank at Teddington, and being paid precious little to do it. Pearcey through his contacts had been able to persuade NMI, as it then was, to look on the work as a promotional venture, recouping the costs either when the challenge itself became firmly funded or through other Twelve Metre work they might attract. The fame that had been earned by the Netherlands Ship Model Basin, where *Australia II*'s keel had been tested, had alerted other professional testing organisations that Twelve Metres could be big and lucrative propositions both commercially and in terms of publicity and status. Fast-growing popular yachting mythology now has it that Hollom, Pearcey and Wallis used the very same tank in which Barnes Wallis had tested the Dam Busters' famous bouncing bomb, but the myth is the result of artistic – or to be strictly accurate cinematic – licence. The tank was the one actor Michael Redgrave bounced his ping-pong balls up and down for the film of that famous raid – Barnes Wallis in fact used the smaller tank next door, housed in a building too small to accommodate a camera crew when the film came to be made.

In a desperate search for more development money, Easton went back to Peter de Savary who had early indicated a willingness to put in some funds, although not to bankroll the entire campaign, but the two could not agree on terms. In particular, de Savary made it plain he wanted both Cudmore and Phil Crebbin, whom Easton had by now appointed Technical Director, completely out of the organisation. Easton demurred, but as other avenues of exploration still refused to yield up their lode he went back to de Savary to pin down the financial aspects of handing over chairmanship of the challenge to him. It quickly became plain that Easton had misunderstood de Savary's proposals and the lone admiral, determined not to give up, started looking around yet again.

It was now September of 1984, and the message was starting to come through loud and clear that, far from being just another yachting event, the Fremantle America's Cup was likely to be very big indeed. The first proper world championship of the Twelve Metre class ever held took place in Sardinia. Until 1983, the New York Club had effectively blocked world development of the Twelve Metre as a class with its unofficial but widely known dictum that any US Twelve Metre group which sailed against 'foreign' Twelves would be serving merely to assist the foreigners in trying to reach US Twelve Metre standards and, for such unpatriotic activity, would be very unlikely to be considered by the club as a potential candidate in any future defense campaign. Since the majority of the world's Twelves were American, their and their sailors' absence had meant that previous attempts to institute world-wide Twelve Metre racing outside the America's Cup were doomed to failure.

Now, in Sardinia, there were Twelve Metres and sailors from Italy, France, Canada, the US, Australia and New Zealand. Despite the fact that there was no official British entry, the championship was won by *Victory '83* under Italian ownership with, among others, Derek Clark her British America's Cup tactician in her crew. Also in Sardinia along with the competitors was the class's political wing – the International Twelve Metre Association and its founding secretary, who just happened to be Philip Tolhurst. Ian Easton was also there, without a Twelve Metre and therefore without a vote in the Association's proceedings.

Also present at that championship, watching progress and talking behind the scenes to any who might become available for a British campaign, was Harold Cudmore.

Philip Tolhurst, as befits a lawyer, revels in the convoluted and often prickly world of Twelve Metre politics. At this time both the class and its primary reason for existence, the America's Cup, were in a state of fluidity bordering upon the vaporous. The New York Yacht Club, which until the loss of the America's Cup ten months previously had been obstructively hostile to the formation of ITMA, was now pleased to be a model member, and the other American syndicates, freed of the consequential burden of NYCC disapprobation of their actions, could now come out of the closet and be openly enthusiastic.

The Royal Perth Yacht Club was already indicating that it saw its possession of the America's Cup as a windfall which could be turned to considerable financial advantage. The International Yacht Racing Union was on the one hand endeavouring to claim, as copyright holder of the design rule, ownership of all television rights associated with any event in which the class participated and on the other, as world custodian of the Corinthian ideal of yacht racing, to prevent any commercialisation of the event with its infamous and unworkable Rule 26, forbidding any form of advertisement – including a name which might even remotely be suggestive of a commercial product or sponsor – to appear on the yacht, her hull, crew, sails or equipment.

With all these imponderables the new class association had to come to terms and quickly – among the most pressing being working for the removal of Rule 26. Without its removal, there was little incentive for any company to sponsor a Twelve Metre campaign, for the simple reason that the yacht racing rules would more or less forbid all but the most subtle and indirect exploitation of the sponsorship in promotional terms: hardly the most tempting reward for an investment of £2m, which was the price of the basic package Tolhurst himself was trying to sell to British sponsors who might wish to be associated with the British campaign. As secretary of the International Twelve Metre Association, Philip

Tolhurst had a number of motives for wishing to see Rule 26 dead and buried.

Yet while the world was beginning to announce its interest and its tentative plans – suitably veiled and filleted of all significant intelligence, of course – for the next America's Cup there was from the British naught but stony silence. 'All will be revealed in January,' Easton told a small group of invited British journalists.

Back in England Cudmore contacted Easton, who confirmed to him that Phil Crebbin had been appointed technical director and – although not in so many words – that de Savary had come and gone and as a consequence he, Cudmore, was now back in favour.

The problem still remained of finding a leading yachting figure as chairman. One of the earliest choices had been Graham Walker, a relative newcomer to British international yachting but, even after only a few seasons, a man with a reputation for mounting highly successful campaigns. Walker, a businessman with a background in wine and spirits retailing, wholesaling and company acquisition had, at a little over forty years of age, merged his successful drinks business with the Argyll group, realised a more than comfortable level of private wealth and gone to live in Jersey to take up the role of a businessman somewhat now removed from the retail counter and the marketing front line.

He had almost taken over the chairmanship of the syndicate once, but a serious motor accident had all-but crippled his son Max, and Walker had pulled out of day-to-day involvement in virtually everything but restoring his son to health. The basement of his home in Jersey had been turned into a full-fledged physiotherapeutic gymnasium, and Max's slow and painful recovery had occupied his father fully through the summer. With his son on the mend, Walker's mind began to turn to the forthcoming 1985 Admiral's Cup and in November Cudmore flew to Jersey to catch up with Walker and discuss Admiral's Cup plans.

The net effect of the visit was that Walker's dormant interest in the Twelve Metre programme was re-awakened. By December, he was again fully briefed on the, somewhat parlous, state of affairs in general and of the finances in particular and, like Easton had been when first approached by Warwick Collins, he was appalled at the thought that Britain might not be represented in Perth at what was clearly going to be the beginning of a new era in the history of yacht racing's most singular and vaunted prize.

On 9 December, he agreed that in the light of the continued failure of Easton and Tolhurst to close a deal with any of the many firms they were approaching, he would personally put in what was regarded by all as merely the seed money necessary to keep the development work moving and thus keep alive a base on which to build the campaign.

A linchpin of Walker's involvement was that Cudmore should be confirmed as skipper with Phil Crebbin continuing to mastermind the design and development programme and on 2 January 1985, a press conference was held in the Royal Thames Yacht Club to confirm that the club would be going ahead with its challenge and outlining its management structure and nature. The challenge would be mounted by a company to be known as America's Cup Limited. Graham Walker was to be chairman, Admiral Sir Ian Easton was to be a director of the company and assume a presidential role in the campaign; Andrew Spedding, Phil Crebbin, David Arnold and Philip Tolhurst were respectively operational director, technical director, financial director and company secretary and Harold Cudmore was to be sailing director of the company and skipper of the yacht. The campaign would be under the hands-on control of the four executive directors – Arnold, Crebbin, Cudmore and Spedding, each responsible individually and collectively to Graham Walker. It was to be a sailors' challenge, after all.

Apart from a man from the *Sun* who wanted to know whether the Australians would have any in-built local advantage because of the tides (Cage Roads off Fremantle where the Cup was to be held is in fact virtually free of tidal influence, with a rise and fall of only a few inches and with negligible tidal streams) most press questions revolved around the question of Cudmore's security of tenure as skipper. David Arnold answered the question about the tides – he was at that time the only member of the programme to have recently visited Perth and Fremantle, never mind sailed there – and Cudmore himself answered the personnel questions. He was sailing director, he said, with complete and sole rights of hire and fire when it came to the crew of the boat. No final decision had yet been taken about who would be the skipper – that would be taken by him when the time came. Did that answer the question?

Also present at that press conference were the Hollom/Wallis/Pearcey design team – introduced to the general although not the specialist press for the first time – and sail designer Angus Melrose, then enjoying a reputation as the second finest Twelve Metre sail designer in the world (the finest being Tom Schnackenberg who designed *Australia II*'s sails). Of Ian Howlett there was neither sight nor mention.

At this time, the complete public stance of the campaign was on the development through technology of a radical new Twelve Metre. With the breakthrough of *Australia II*'s winged keel rendering all other Twelve Metres obsolete overnight, and with the complete change of sailing conditions between Newport and Fremantle requiring a totally different type of Twelve Metre from that developed for all previous America's Cups, the field was seen as being wide open with everyone having to start again more or less from scratch.

Very quickly after that press conference the campaign at Cudmore's insistence finally was able to make an arrangement with Ian Howlett. He had been at first unavailable because of commitments to de Savary, then to the Italians who had purchased *Victory '83*. Now and with certain reservations he joined what would become the White Crusade.

Howlett's reservations particularly and understandably concerned the principal design group, only one of whom (Stephen Wallis) had any experience of designing or building full-size Twelve Metres. Asked to join the design group on equal terms he flatly refused, feeling and saying that it would not be a marriage of equals. In effect, he would have to teach them all he knew and they could teach him nothing.

He was not, he said, against the idea of a design group in principal, but it would have to be a group of intellectual equals. Accepting that such a group as himself, Melrose, Crebbin and Cudmore would satisfy his criteria, he was eventually given a brief to produce an evolutionary Twelve Metre, along with the option of modelling and tank testing a radical design.

Still the money failed to roll in, and still Graham Walker privately paid the design and development bills. Two major companies to come close to signing substantial sponsorship deals were Tate & Lyle and Trafalgar House. In the latter case detailed proposals were drawn up including the colour schemes and the graphics for the chosen yacht, to be called *Trafalgar* – to which honourable name it was hoped Rule 26 with a proper regard for British naval tradition would turn a blind eye. Neither proposal came to anything: independent enquiries to Royal Thames members warned both companies off investing in the challenge.

In the summer of 1985, relations between the challenge and the Royal Thames grew steadily worse, culminating at the end of the year with a concerted effort by a number of senior members to kill the challenge off completely.

Officially, the reason was that with its funding still uncertain the challenge could not guarantee success and it would be better to stop now, rather than risk ignominious failure later which would undoubtedly reflect badly upon the club. The club had given and extended two deadlines by which the challenge was to declare its financial security – now was the time to pull the plug. In particular, there was concern that the club's financial status with its lack of limitation of liability could be seriously damaged – perhaps ruined – by a challenge that incurred considerable debts which it might somehow be unable to meet, despite the firm assurances to the contrary offered by Graham Walker.

Unofficially and privately, the members of the challenging syndicate complained bitterly that if certain prominent members of the club would rally round, as might reasonably be expected of them, and lend their support to the challenge – even if they would at least desist from their known clandestine efforts to sabotage its fund-raising activities – the financial situation could rapidly be resolved. In a bitter and painful episode, David Arnold was summoned from his cabin in the club having retired, following dinner, at midnight and by 4 am had been forced to offer his resignation as Rear-Commodore.

In a sense, the club had a point. In the increasingly commercial environment of an America's Cup campaign there might indeed arise a conflict of interest between the role of an officer of the challenging company (Arnold was financial controller) and a flag officer of the club. It was the manner, rather than the substance, of the dispute which caused a bitterness and rift which was never entirely healed.

At last some solid sponsorship appeared, in the form of a deal with British Airways. With the competition on the opposite side of the world, the airline offered a substantial amount of sponsorship in kind in the form of free and reduced air travel and air cargo fares between England and Perth. At travel agent's rates, the deal was worth about £250,000: it wasn't much out of £5 million, but it at least meant the team could get to the venue.

It was also hoped that the announcement of the British Airways sponsorship might tip the balance with other blue chip names tentatively poised to come aboard, but it was not to be. A succession of professional so-called fund-raisers and sponsorship brokers passed briefly across the stage, ranging from West Nally and IMP to Michael Stacpole, who shortly after joining and leaving the challenge's publicity effort achieved a fleeting notoriety for his efforts in non-publicity on behalf of his long-standing friend Jeffrey Archer.

Ian Easton particularly recalls with despair those days.

All these people would come in, full of promises about what they could achieve and who they could bring in through their own special contacts. They usually wanted fifteen per cent of any money they raised, which seemed quite a lot to me if you're talking about three million pounds, but on top of that they had to have 'expenses' for their design people or their studio or whatever. Some of them said they would come in on a 'no foal, no fee' basis but none of them ever did. We just couldn't afford them and so we'd get someone else. Then they would want money as well.

The trouble was, you kept thinking 'well, maybe this £7,000 will be the sprat that will catch the mackerel' and thinking that you might land the big one. But it was very depressing, because of course all this time we really had no money, and Graham was paying to keep the design work going while the designers themselves were working for very little, hoping that it would all come good in the end.

Hardly surprisingly, Ian Easton does not have a very high opinion of the London public relations executive as a breed.

Construction of the Twelve Metres began in May 1985 after delays caused by lack of funds, the internal row with the Royal Thames and finally the company originally awarded the contract, Whistocks on Constable's River Deben, going into receivership. Cudmore and Crebbin had persuaded Easton, somewhat against his better judgement, that the Howlett design rather than the Hollom should begin construction first: the Hollom/Wallis/Pearcey team had asked for a few more days to continue work in the tank and on the computer and with any further delay it would be quite impossible to get the boat to the world championship in Fremantle the following February.

Attendance at this important championship – the first racing series for Twelve Metres to be held on the new America's Cup waters – was seen by both Crebbin and Cudmore as crucial to putting together a viable campaign, and both argued strongly – Cudmore in particular – that the obvious boat to take to the worlds was the benchmark boat, not the team's secret weapon. For one thing, the benchmark's conventional design would be the better tool with which to gauge where the opposition had got to should they turn up with either conventional or radical designs. For another, should the team's own radical design turn out to be a breakthrough, the advantage would be thrown away by showing their hand too soon and giving the opposition advance warning along with time to either copy the idea or rethink their own.

So, in one of those occurrences which are at the time perceived to be of little consequence but which later assume a profound significance, the decision was taken to move the Howlett boat – the benchmark, back-up boat – on to the production schedule ahead of the boat around which the entire challenge had until that moment been centred. From now on, the hoped-for breakthrough, radical design would become in every sense the campaign's number two boat, to be known officially only as *C2*.

By late 1985 a solution of sorts to the financial problem had been found with the creation of British America's Cup Challenges plc, a sports-promotion company funded under the British government Business Expansion Scheme. This scheme permitted investment in high risk companies – and was there anything with higher risk than challenging for the America's Cup? – to be set in advantageous terms against tax and BACC was yet another Tolhurst-inspired package to find funds where none seemed to exist.

The prospectus of the new company invited investment on the grounds that the America's Cup was an event out of the participation in which money might be made. The company took the view that Twelve Metre ownership and America's Cup participation were no one-off affair, but rather a continuing activity from which money could be made through the avenues of sponsorship, brand and product endorsement, the promotion of Twelve Metre events around the world and, in general, intelligent and proper sports management. The issued capital of the company was £3 million and, apart from minor shareholders such as Ian Easton with his £1,000-worth and less than £100,000 from other Royal Thames members, it had one major shareholder. His name was Graham Walker.

Tolhurst also performed one more signal service for the challenge. He secured for the naming ceremony of the first of the two new yachts the wife of the then Commodore, now Admiral, of the Royal Thames Yacht Club, His Royal Highness Charles, Prince of Wales. Not only did the presence of the Princess of Wales ensure for the challenge the highest possible public profile, it perhaps more importantly put a seal of royal approval and interest on the challenge which would encourage Graham Walker to persevere in his by now more-or-less solitary efforts, and which eventually – although not without one final spasm – put paid to any more shilly-shallying on the part of the challenging club. In a club like the Royal Thames, if HRH is for it, who dare be agin it?

Crusader was named, shrouded in muslin to hide her keel and underbody, in an elegant and low-key ceremony in mid-December that laid emphasis on the fact that in this campaign, money was being spent on essentials rather than razzamatazz. Strictly speaking, the veiling was not so much to hide the keel as to hide the fact that the keel was not there. Delays in her construction start followed by a further delay when Howlett discovered a flaw in his calculations meant the boat was four weeks behind her desperately tight schedule.

As the final shipping date to get the boat to Fremantle in time for the world championship had come and gone, there had been a brief-lived scheme to airfreight the yacht and keel ('now that's what I would call a dramatic entrance' remarked Cudmore as he gleefully pondered the prospect) but BA's support, though highly valuable, did not run quite that far. The plan to go to the worlds was abandoned.

In the event, the failure to attend the Fremantle worlds and its consequent loss of vital hands-on experience of racing Twelves in the demanding Fremantle conditions would later be identified by virtually all the sailors as the most significant single contributing factor to the problems which beset *White Crusader*'s final racing programme.

In a desperate stop-gap measure Chris Griffiths, an offshore race-boat owner who was keen to help the campaign in practical terms, chartered the woefully uncompetitive *Challenge France* for the world championship and she was sailed by a (very) mixed crew of French and British sailors under Cudmore's command. The sails, as *Yachts and Yachting* recorded at the time, looked like the bags all the other yachts' sails had come in and the leaky old yacht had had to be pumped around the course, even abandoning one race when in a sinking condition. It was experience, of a sort, but hardly to be compared to the practice that the Kiwis, the French and the Americans were by now putting in.

In one last bid to attract large-scale funding and to galvanise public support, *Crusader* had gone on display at the January 1986 London Boat Show and was then shipped to Australia.

Four weeks later, without so much as a splash of champagne, the anonymously white hull of the boat that would become *C2* was floated away from Cougar Marine on the Hamble River where she had been built alongside *Crusader* and loaded aboard ship. Spedding and his advance party had left in November to begin to put the compound and workshops in place. Chris Law – after months of private negotiation with Cudmore concerning the conditions of his precise role – officially joined the campaign as one of two helmsmen-elect and immediately left to set up the sailing programme and Cudmore himself finally boarded the plane on 22 March. The White Crusade was at last underway.

CHAPTER SEVEN

Role of the Yacht Club

Since its inception on 8 July 1857 – six years after the schooner had won the trophy itself in the Squadron's August regatta – the America's Cup has officially been a contest between yacht clubs, rather than either individuals or nationally selected teams. Yet from that day to this the role of the yacht clubs has been neither clearly defined nor even agreed upon. It has always been a subject of controversy.

Furthermore, the role of the yacht club in the contest has always been viewed differently on the opposite sides of the Atlantic across which so much of America's Cup tradition and precedent has been fashioned. No doubt the reason for that is that for the first 132 years of its existence there was only one US club – the New York Yacht Club – centrally involved in the Cup, while the twenty-six challenges that it took to depose the NYYC were spread among a dozen different clubs from three countries with another three countries and an uncounted number of clubs peripherally swept up in the challenging process.

The dye of confusion was cast by George L Schuyler, spokesman for the *America*'s original owners, when he presented the Cup to the New York Yacht Club and laid out in a covering letter the sentiments and conditions which formed the basis of what is still today known as the Deed Of Gift: the foundation stone on which all the rules of conduct for the America's Cup are based. As a document the letter was at once as well-intentioned and as self-contradictory a little note as one might wish to see; as a foundation stone for anything it was of singularly unsatisfactory shape.

The original Deed offered the Cup for challenge from 'any organized yacht club, through one or more of its members' for the purpose of 'making it perpetually a challenge cup for friendly competition between foreign countries'. In other words it was to be a contest between nations, via yacht clubs, fought out by individuals. While the defenders were soon able to bring these three wildly differing interests more or less comfortably together, the challengers would never be able to do so with anything like effectiveness – in a way, would never even try – although it took until 1987 before the strains imposed by Schuyler's original muddled but well-meant thinking would finally tear open the fragile wrappings of the illusion they enfolded.

It was the three-way cross that caused the problem. It meant, in effect, that the country could claim all the glory, the club enjoy all the pomp and ceremony and the individual would do all the work. Yet unique among international sporting trophies (so much of what the America's Cup is about is, truly, worthy of that overworked word, which is what doubtless lends it its unholy fascination) there is no national structure from which a challenging team is selected. A nation's America's Cup squad is not like its football team, its hockey team or even its Olympic sailing team. A nation's America's Cup team is self-appointed, answerable only unto itself.

Nor, although the Deed of Gift stipulates that 'the contest' shall be one between clubs, can an America's Cup squad be regarded in any way as a 'club' side, as with a side from a rugby football club, a cricket club or – in the sport of sailing – a team-racing side of the sort that competes for its yacht or sailing club in the National Team Racing Championship or an international team sailing event such as the British–American Cup. Only twice has a British America's Cup challenger been anything like representative of a club. The first time was when the Royal Corinthian Yacht Club hastily assembled a crew to sail *Endeavour*. On that occasion Sir Thomas Sopwith refused to compensate his professional crew properly for the winter earnings they would lose if they went with the yacht to America instead of going back to their winter trade as fishermen. The second occasion was when a dozen members of the Royal Yacht Squadron grouped together to produce the *Sceptre* challenge.

In every other case the record shows that the progenitor of the challenge is an individual. Usually – and this was very much the case with the White Crusade – the first thing the individual decides to do is challenge for the America's Cup, and the second is shop around for a yacht club to take him and his challenge on board. And most usually, as Admiral Sir Ian Easton, Alan Bond, Tony Boyden, Sir Thomas Lipton and James Ashbury, to name but five, have all discovered, the answer from the club of their choice is 'No'.

Yet once a club agrees to put forward a challenge, its powers over the challenge's destiny become enormous while its responsibility for it remains nominal – and in the event of the challenge's success, the individual can find himself robbed of the fruits of his victory at the very moment of triumph. It is one of the most curious ironies – indeed mysteries – of the whole America's Cup phenomenon that the last people to realise the full significance of Schuyler's stipulations were the individuals themselves. How could such otherwise astute brains as those of Lipton, Packer, Bond and even Conner fail to see the consequence of the success they so single-mindedly strove to achieve?

There is a story, probably not apocryphal, that after his 1983 victory Alan Bond was in Australia watching with some friends the video of his moment of triumph. He had spent millions of dollars trying to win the America's Cup and had done so at his third attempt. His money had built and paid for *Australia II*; it was he who had found the designer and stuck with him through the years of learning and of trying this, trying that; it was he who had found and persuaded and cajoled the crew to give up so much; it was he who allowed one of his company's senior executives to spend so much of the company's time and money playing boats instead of digging oil wells or running supermarket chains or all the other things other big businessmen insist their executives do; it was he, Alan Bond, who had by anyone's assessment won the America's Cup. Now, he watched himself attend the prize-giving he had so long waited for and dreamed of.

'And that's when we lost the fuckin' thing,' he exploded as he watched Robert Stone, Commodore of the New York Yacht Club, hand the America's Cup not to him, Alan Bond, whom everyone – absolutely everyone – knew had won the 'thing', but to some virtually unknown individual in the crowd, his face recognisable to only a handful of those who had followed the 1983 Cup with the closest of interests and the keenest of eyes. In newspaper offices and on yachting magazine desks there wasn't even a stock mugshot of this man among files that bulged with pictures of Bond: Bond at press conferences, Bond in the New York Yacht Club being granted a peek at the Holy Grail. Bond out watching the races aboard *Black Swan*; Bond at balls and at parties and at dinners. Quite a few newspapers could not even spell the man's name: Peter Dalziell, Commodore of the Royal Perth Yacht Club.

The Cup which Bond had tried so hard to win and finally lifted was not his at all, for in 1857 Schuyler had written as a final paragraph to his covering letter, 'It is to be distinctly understood that the Cup is to be the property of the club, and not of the members thereof, or owners of the vessels winning it'. If Bond had any doubts about the matter, they were soon removed when it became plain that to defend the Cup he would have to stand in line with anyone else who applied and that as for playing any part in organising that defence (or making money out of it): forget it. That was the yacht club's job. It was, quite literally, 'thank you, Alan'.

Someone who did realise – before it was too late to do anything about it – the full significance of the final paragraph of Schuyler's original letter was Philip Tolhurst, the Dragon-sailing lawyer who first became hooked on the Twelve Metre scene during the de Savary days and who became company secretary for Graham Walker's British America's Cup Challenges plc. Tolhurst had the advantage over Bond and the others in that he was an officer who had changed uniforms between wars.

In the 1983 challenge, Tolhurst was a member of the Royal Burnham Yacht Club's America's Cup committee and its legal eagle under the direction of its chairman Frank Kemble. To Kemble must go the distinction of being perhaps the shrewdest America's Cup committee chairman any British club of modern times has had the good fortune to appoint, and under his guidance the Royal Burnham brought a clarity of vision to running their challenge which was a model for other clubs to follow. Among the Burnham's coups was the well-timed revelation concerning IYRU rulings on wings on keels which finally shut the whingeing of the New York Yacht Club as they twisted and turned in the search for an excuse not to have to face up to *Australia II*.

Even more important, the Royal Burnham America's Cup committee gave considerable thought to what would happen should they (not, note, Peter de Savary) win: 'we are the challengers, Peter de Savary is our candidate' remarked Kemble with a twinkle in his eye to a question this writer put to him on the subject in 1982, the year before the racing would take place. It was plain from his other answers that the Royal Burnham, if not their candidate, were fully well aware of the significance of Schuyler's stipulation. One gained the impression, however unfounded it might have been, that no one felt it particularly incumbent upon them to make sure the candidate was no less aware. Had *Victory '83* and not *Australia II* made history, it would have been David Geaves, the Burnham's Commodore, and not Peter Dalziell to whom Robert Stone would have handed the America's Cup. It is only speculation on this writer's part, of course, but it could well have been that Peter de Savary would have found himself in just the position that took Alan Bond by so much surprise.

In April 1984 Kemble's man Philip Tolhurst was a member of the Royal Thames Sailing Committee as well as secretary of the International Twelve Metre Association and was thus the obvious person for the Thames to turn to for detailed advice about all these Twelve Metre candidates hammering on the door. As the challenge developed, Tolhurst's interest and skills made him a no-less natural choice as the man to handle the challenge's legal affairs. Thus, game-keeper turned poacher, he would have known all about the potential ambush to which so many otherwise astute challenge leaders had apparently given so little thought.

As the challenge took shape, Tolhurst and the challenge's executive director David Arnold were able to forge an agreement with the club that would fully protect the challengers' investment and make sure that what happened to Bond could never happen to them. It was an agreement that was forged with no little amount of pain, and it was but a part of a relationship that was frequently far from easy, for either side.

We have but conjecture to tell us what in 1868 was in the mind of the upwardly mobile James Ashbury, Manchester manufacturer of railway locomotives and would-be parliamentary candidate for the English East Coast town of Harwich, when he entered the first ever challenge for the America's Cup. Historians ascribe to him much the same motives as later writers ascribed to Alan Bond and Peter de Savary, probably with the same over-simplistic level of accuracy. Whatever the motives, Ashbury's first challenge was not so much rejected as not even entertained, the New York Yacht Club pointing out that he could not challenge as an individual but must do so through a yacht club.

Ashbury's first proper challenge was in fact through our very own Royal Thames, and for his second he suggested, when the New York Yacht Club began to play hard-ball over the rules, that if they cared to read their rules with care he could demand to sail the series of twelve races for which he was asking under the burgee of a different club for each race (he was a very clubbable man, James Ashbury and belonged to each of the twelve clubs he nominated) and take the America's Cup home after the first race he won in the name of the club under whose flag he happened to have been sailing on that day.

That Ashbury's suggestion was not seriously entertained on the American side of the Atlantic shows how already the pattern of differently interpreting the role of the yacht club was emerging, although in fairness to Ashbury it is probable that he did not expect the New York Yacht Club to accede to his idea. The Americans were being obdurate in not allowing him the opportunity of sailing tune-up races, having just completed a trans-Atlantic voyage in cruising trim, as required by the New York Yacht Club rules of the time.

Yet it was already becoming plain that, to the defenders, yacht club participation was the *raison d'être* of the competition; to the challenger it was a matter of mere convenience. The club's involvement was necessary merely to overcome a letter of the law. The level of the clubs' involvement and even enthusiasm may be judged by the fact that the Royal Thames took until 1963 to challenge again while the Royal Harwich evidently found the whole experience so enthralling they did not again express an interest until 1987. The club, in other words, was merely the posting box, the channel, for the challenge, never its motivating force and indeed could become almost an albatross around the challenger's neck – not least because that was frequently how the club viewed the relationship between the challenger and its own neck.

Such a pattern marked, to a greater or lesser extent, the club role in all subsequent British and probably all other challenges. In some cases, as with the Royal Thames endorsement of Ashbury's *Cambria* challenge or the Squadron involvement with the gallant Lieutenant Henn, the club role barely went beyond acknowledging that the challenger was a bona fide member of the club. What he was up to, over there in America, was really up to him.

In other cases, as with the Royal Yacht Squadron challenge with *Sceptre*, the pendulum was at the other end of its swing. That challenge was probably the closest there has ever been to the sort of contest Schuyler must have been envisaging, with a syndicate of twelve members having shares in the yacht and running the challenge as a collective club enterprise, with no motive apparent other than national pride and the desire to maintain a sporting tradition. Even so, support within the Squadron for either the challenge or even the idea was far from unanimous. One member, when approached to lend his support, had suggested that Hugh Goodson the syndicate chairman should see a psychiatrist (probably quite a good idea, really, for *anyone* who expresses an interest in becoming involved with the America's Cup) and at that year's annual general meeting of the Royal Yachting Association (British boating's national co-ordinating body) it was argued with some force that the money being raised might better be spent on helping Britain's Olympic efforts.

The balance has tended to lie somewhere between, with the added complication that the Deed gives the club as a separate entity the opportunity to exercise ultimate authority over the conduct of the challenging campaign, while recognising that the campaign will be the effort of at most a few individuals. At best, the Deed is a guarantee of Corinthian and sportsmanlike contest, at worst it can become a Meddlers' Charter.

The Royal Thames lodged Britain's only challenge for the 1987 America's Cup by default but from unassailable motives. By the time the challenging deadline had arrived there was no clear-cut declaration on the part of any syndicate or owner to undertake a challenge, but there was much rushing around and rustling of the bushes, particularly by Kit Hobday who may or may not have been acting in concert with Peter de Savary. Clearly, if the time were not to run out and leave the British irredeemably out of the '87 Circus, some sort of holding operation was called for, simply to keep the options open.

The Royal Burnham which, as a relatively junior club in the unwritten but clearly discernible hierarchy of the British yachting establishment, had handled the 1983 challenge in such an exemplary manner, had for its own reasons decided that it could not challenge again without knowing exactly what it was letting itself in for. The Thames, as one of the most senior yacht clubs (certainly the oldest) on the British mainland, stepped in and picked up the torch.

The club always made plain to its prospective challengers (Easton and Hobday, in the first instance) that their first task would have to be to convince the club that they would be able to put up a challenge which would not only take place but which would perform with credit, if not succeed. In this, the club took a position that was both proper and legitimate; what would later become a bitter complaint was that the club in general seemed to require one hell of a lot of convincing – not once but over and over again – while some senior members in particular clearly did not see it as any part of their or the club's role to lend the challenge their support.

The greatest problem the challenge that became the White Horse Challenge experienced with its club was equivocation, a lack of wholly committed and uncompromised support, both tangible and moral. It was a problem that undoubtedly arose in major part from differences of perspective. It also involved, inevitably, that slow-burning fuse that lies within the central core of any enterprise that involves a great deal of spare-time, amateur activity from a disparate group of people: personality.

John Foot, the Vice-Commodore of the club who initially gave his imprimatur to allow the challenge to be lodged in the first place, would within eighteen months apparently do his utmost to have the challenge withdrawn. It was a turnabout which Graham Walker, the quiet-spoken enthusiast whom the challenge would eventually find to pay its bills, could scarcely comprehend, much less condone. Walker himself, by his own admission unbelievably naïve, could neither understand nor come to terms with the attitude of many other members of the club – each individually more wealthy than he – who simply would not put their hands in their pockets and pull out their cheque books for sums they were better placed to afford than was he to see both Britain's and the club's good name placed with honour in the contest.

Cudmore would see the club's role as purely supportive of the challenge efforts but without – because of lack of acceptable qualification – the right to wield authority or even influence over the sailing programme. John Maddocks and Stephen James, trustees of the club and the latter its solicitor, would view the naked commercialism of the modern America's Cup as something anathemical to a private club. The potential consequential liabilities of becoming involved were something the club would have to be greatly protected against, at the challenge's expense and by putting the greatest possible distance between the club and the challenge. Easton would view their attitude as unnecessarily hostile and their apparatus as being unnecessarily costly to the challenge in terms of both time and money. David Arnold would come to view both their actions and their tactics as cruelly hurtful, insensitive to a degree and questionably motivated. Virtually everyone in the management of the hard-pressed challenge, so desperately strapped for cash, would find it impossible to forgive or even respect Stephen James when a five-figure invoice arrived for his services while apparently acting as a member of his club's general committee.

And further from the epicentre of events, lines would be drawn and attitudes struck in reflection of what was taking place. Those in the club who had ideas on how to conduct a challenge which did not coincide with the way in which this challenge appeared to be developing felt themselves under no obligation to keep their reservations to themselves. Those down the line and nearer the sharp end of the challenge, picking up what they could of events but hearing by definition only one side of the story, rallied instinctively behind those they felt had been slighted or not properly supported, away from those whose feet stayed dry and whose jackets remained buttoned.

From such brave beginnings, relations between the club and the challenge slid steadily downhill in 1985 and probably reached their nadir as 1985 moved into 1986. The split became public when two senior members of the Royal Thames were heard in another club discussing the challenge and its chances of success in a manner that was far from flattering. So damaging were the things they were saying that Philip Tolhurst, as company secretary and lawyer to the challenge, found himself writing to the Royal Thames pointing out the potential legal consequences of such behaviour. He was, of course, himself a member of the club, and had indeed been on both the sailing committee and the America's Cup committee until forced to resign from the former to prevent alleged conflict of interest.

The reaction from the club was swift and firm – if Tolhurst could name the members concerned and prove the allegations (the latter would not have been difficult – the occasion had been very public) the Royal Thames would act with severity. Tolhurst, sensing an opportunity to cool things down on both sides, wrote back to say that the challenge had no wish to provoke a situation where senior members might be forced to resign or even find themselves the defendants of a law suit for libel – a course of events that could only make matters worse. Thereafter any breach between challenge and club was kept severely under wraps.

Shortly after, Arnold himself was required to resign as the club's Rear Commodore, but the ultimate crisis was reached as late in the campaign as December of '85 and January '86, a bare ten months before racing was due to start. The first yacht had already been built and named *Crusader* by Her Royal Highness the Princess of Wales, and had already had to miss the vital World Championship in Fremantle as a direct result of lack of funding. The cause of this was in no small measure due to lack of support from the club, when the most serious attempt to close the campaign down was mounted by the club, apparently led by John Foot, John Maddocks and Stephen James.

Their declared motivation was that the challenge, through its admitted lack of funding, was going to be ill-prepared and its performance in Fremantle would not be likely to bring the club credit, while the financial risks associated with continuing without guarantees of unqualified financial security were potentially too damaging to the club, which might be left to pick up the pieces. It was an argument which, no matter what its merits, placed little or no weight on the no less obvious consequence of pulling the plug at so late a stage: the total destruction of British Twelve Metre credibility for the foreseeable future.

In the end, the differences between the Royal Thames and its challenge were resolved amicably and to the general satisfaction of all concerned, the crux of the solution being an agreement divorcing the club from both the commercial activities associated with promoting a modern challenge and from the liabilities which such involvement might entail. It also placed control of the commercial operations firmly in the hands of the challenging company, which was potentially a vital guarantee should the challenge have succeeded. It is a model of its kind, certainly better than the one that Alan Bond discovered to his cost he did not have, and evidently much better than the one Dennis Conner had with the San Diego Yacht Club. From BACC's point of view, the agreement was vital: should they have won what Michael Fay described as the 'America's Cup Industry' it would have been theirs to profit from. Whether the Royal Thames would then have been as happy with the arrangements is another matter, notwithstanding the infamous though unattributed quotation from a senior member:

'Of course, the last thing we want to do is win the bloody thing. Imagine having to organise a defence!'

Largely removed from the face-to-face dealings at the Royal Thames and concentrating on the sailing campaign, Cudmore could assess not only the difficulties his own challenge was having but the similar problems being experienced by his opposite numbers in Fremantle.

America II had quite a problem with their yacht club, the New York Yacht Club, particularly in terms of authority over the programme. There was substantial Texan money involved and the New York Yacht Club was inclined to interfere with the running of the programme to such an extent that the Texas backers threatened to withdraw their funds – ask for the money back – and they eventually were able to reconstitute the New York Yacht Club America's Cup committee to their liking. The NYYC Commodore actually resigned over the matter from their America's Cup committee.

The Italian example is interesting because all their challenges were yacht club based, because of the different way their yacht clubs are organised. Clubs like the Yacht Club Costa Smeralda are already pure commercial organisations, founded from the beginning for commercial purposes, so do not run across the problem of the America's Cup being grafted on to an old-established club structure with a wide range of member's interests which have nothing to do with the America's Cup.

Elsewhere, there is a general feeling that the clubs have become largely irrelevant. The clubs are no longer generators of the funding or of the direction of the campaign, if indeed they ever were – which I doubt. For the future, there will undoubtedly be much greater use of yacht clubs of convenience: but there is the usefulness of the established, traditional yacht club being an institution, so there is an up side.

For example with the right sort of yacht club use can be made of an infrastructure of race management expertise, to everyone's benefit. Then again there is the value of having the use of the club base building – especially a prestigious clubhouse like that of the Royal Thames.

Yet it is terribly important not to forget that the yacht club side of it is part of the heritage, and it must always be borne in mind when tampering (modifying, changing – call it what you will) with the America's Cup that its long history and its historical associations are a very great part of its special mystique. It genuinely must not be allowed to become 'just another yachting event', however glittering, or it loses its unique identity.

Apart from anything else, it then descends into head-on competition on equal terms with other claims on sponsors' money. At the moment the America's Cup has something very special and unique to offer sponsors. Its stock-in-trade, principal asset, must be very carefully preserved throughout any changes to the immediate format.

There is a great feeling in the class that traditions must not be cast away. Even with regard to the yachts, and changes to them. We are dealing with a 1906 rule that has in its way stood the test of time. The Twelve Metre is still a fantastic boat. There are a lot of rules that came along since 1906, were hailed as great improvements and much smarter rules. They don't look so smart now.

CHAPTER EIGHT

Out of their heads

Nineteen eighty-three and the revolutionary design of *Australia II* was the dare-devil, glamourous stroke that the America's Cup needed to pull it from the esoteric reportage of the specialist press and hurl it on to the front pages of newspapers around the world. Easily grasped, if not understood, the idea of the wings on the keel of the Little White Pointer turning established practice on its head and giving the Americans, of all people, a short sharp lesson in technology was straight Roy of the Rovers stuff. It had all the necessary ingredients for popular appeal, including the attractive mental picture of Ben Lexcen, *Australia II*'s affable and lovable designer, conjuring the wings out of thin air before having his revolutionary weapon tested in utmost secrecy behind the closed doors of a Dutch test tank. Not since Archimedes ran naked down the street yelling 'Eureka' can a technical breakthrough have seemed so unprecedented or so captured public imagination.

In practice, and sadly from a media point of view, Twelve Metre yacht design is rather more complex a process than merely sketching wings for a keel on the back of a fag packet, although it is at the same time one of the most exciting aspects of the America's Cup that it is a competition in which design innovation, and the prospect of it, play an important part. 'Exciting', however, is a relative term.

What lends the America's Cup its special fascination and the greater part of its particular character as a sporting contest is that the two contenders never meet until the first race of the America's Cup itself. There is traditionally not even a common reference point by which the potential of the two contestants may be judged: they reach the America's Cup arena by different routes, emerging from different backgrounds to sail against each other for the first time only on Opening Day. In this respect, the America's Cup is first and foremost a designers' contest.

It seems likely that there is no other one-to-one test in the calendar of sport that puts such a complete barrier between the contenders until the day of the contest itself. Even heavyweight boxers meeting for the first time to decide a world crown will normally have fought at least one or two common opponents on the way to the title fight. Racing cars practice together over the same track. Horse racing has a form book inches thick, athletes have Previous Personal Bests, football teams have league tables.

America's Cup yachts do not even sail on the same courses during their separate work-up periods.

In passing, it might be worth remarking that this phenomenon is not only what lends the America's Cup its peculiar fascination, it is also what often makes the event itself so boring to all but the true cognoscenti. For what most usually happens is that after the months of speculation, the rising tension of defender and more recently challenger racing, the inevitable sideline intrigues, gamesmanship and allegations of illegality the two yachts come to the line and within the first fifteen minutes of the first windward leg it becomes markedly apparent that one of the two is quicker than the other. The racing becomes a formality, a mere confirmation of the hopes and claims of one camp, a sad dashing of the aspirations of the other.

This, indeed, is the normal pattern: it has happened more or less comprehensively in every post-War challenge since 1958 and it happened again in 1987. Only in 1983 with all its drama was the America's Cup itself an exciting sporting contest. The failure of the general sporting press – and thus of the general sports-following public – and of the television producers and commentators in Australia in particular to appreciate the significance of the unique structure of the America's Cup then led to considerable disappointment and disillusionment with the entire event. A public which had been hyped by its media to expect 'the greatest sporting contest of the century', as one television network billed it, was cruelly disappointed and potentially embittered by finding itself watching a three-hour two-boat procession.

America's Cup Twelve Metre design is a process that starts from its end and works backwards to its beginning. In this respect it differs from most other forms of yacht design, which typically begin with the designer having a good idea or a client asking for a yacht which is to fulfil a wide range of frequently conflicting requirements.

The America's Cup yacht has to fulfil only one requirement, and beat only one other boat. That is its sole reason for existence. One of the things that made the 1987 contest so fascinating as it unfolded and so interesting in retrospect was the fact that the eventual convincing winner had such a difficult job making it through the qualifying rounds. Dennis Conner knew exactly what he needed in *Stars & Stripes* to win the America's Cup off Fremantle in February – and the boat he needed to do that was substantially different from the boat he needed to beat all the other Twelve Metres in Fremantle during the very different weather patterns of the months of October, November and early December.

In going so decisively for his design concept for *Stars & Stripes* he left himself precious little room for manoeuvre against his opponents who had chosen different, more versatile design routes – routes which in the end were shown to be paying for their versatility with ultimate speed. It was a consummate display of crystal ball gazing on Conner's part, but it had a good deal more to do with painstaking science than with witchcraft.

There are two ways to design a Twelve Metre to win the America's Cup, and for 1987 the British tried both. The first way is to have a bright idea – preferably a burningly brilliant rethink of the very basics of what makes a yacht sail quickly – design it, test it, discover it works and build it in total secrecy, launching it upon an unsuspecting and probably sceptical world at the last possible moment so that, when the cynics have had to eat their words, there is no time left for the opposition to produce a copy.

It was much the route chosen by Bond, Lexcen and Warren Jones for *Australia II* and it was very much the route chosen by Tom Blackaller, Gary Mull and the backers of *USA*. It is, of course, a route so charged with romance and potential drama that it cannot fail to be a winner with the press every time. It is also a route hugely attractive to first-time backers of America's Cup challenges, and it was the route favoured by Ian Easton and the original conceivers of the British challenge.

It is a route not generally favoured by the top sailors. Mediocre sailors – that is to say most sailors and yacht owners – have a private dream of finding themselves in charge of some supercharged design that only has to be pointed in the right direction and it will outstrip all opposition. It is the dream that keeps alive all design-led racing classes, such as the offshore handicap classes and the Metre classes themselves, and it is the dream that keeps in business most of the world's yacht designers.

The top sailors, being blessed in equal measure with more experience and hence less gullability, favour the developmental rather than the inspirational route. Partly they know that it needs only a very tiny edge of performance for one boat to look a great deal quicker than another, and partly they believe of themselves that to win all they need is at least an equal boat. The edge they can provide themselves. While ordinary sailors have dreams about getting themselves a super-fast boat, top sailors have nightmares about finding themselves riding a slow one. Top sailors are often distrustful of designers.

The developmental route designs its Twelve Metre by logic. Having analysed every conceivable element that will be involved in the competition, from the predicted weather pattern and sea conditions on the course to what the likely opposition will likely do, the design is drawn to fit the exact specification which, perforce, will have emerged: a sort of technological Join The Dots. This was the Cudmore-inspired Howlett route which eventually produced *White Crusader*.

When the two boats arrived in Australia to be tested together, Cudmore had good cause to bless his insistence on covering the inspirational dream with a developmental back-up.

The first day they were able to go sailing together with the two boats must have made everyone in the syndicate sit up and think very hard. Until then, everything had been conjecture. The whole ethos of the campaign had been structured around having a revolutionary boat, now they were going to see for themselves how close they were to being on track.

Cudmore, Crebbin and their crews had already been testing the Howlett design – the two were by now simply known as *C1* (the Howlett boat) and *C2* (Hollom/Wallis/Pearcey) – and were cautiously pleased with her. There had already been some informal racing against *South Australia* and this had been more than encouraging: now, already possessed of a yardstick for the Howlett design, it was time to put the two designs together and measure the new boat.

We put the boats in the water together and took them sailing and the first day we went out *C2* was disastrously slow, like half a knot off pace. I mean a *real* horror story.

The public were there and the press and quite a few VIPs so we quickly devised a system of hiding it and they actually couldn't tell. We would trial the two boats together, and when they began to get far apart or if *C2* couldn't keep up we would call *C1* and tell her to go to the CB net. It sounded as if we were merely telling them to switch radio channels on to a private frequency, which is completely normal and a fairly routine occurrence. What it was in fact was a simple coded message to tell them to 'sand-bag', to slow down without making it obvious, just so as not to show the other boat up. It really was that bad.

So that first day out *C2* was a disaster, about half a knot off pace. That evening we very quickly sank her in the water and got her back into some semblance of pace but I would not allow the boat to be rated, because she simply would not have come out as a Twelve Metre.

Then we went on quite a long development programme with *C2* which included a new keel and the additional winglets. She got close to *C1* then, but that was before we began fully to develop *C1*. Thereafter *C2* was never really in contention as our race boat, although after every day's sailing the question would always be asked of those who had been sailing aboard her: 'if you had to go out and race the America's Cup tomorrow, which boat would you take, *C1* or *C2*?' Always the answer was '*C1*'.

In some ways, it was hardly surprising that the Hollom design should initially be slower than the Howlett. *C1* had 'come out of the box' in beautiful shape and needed only refined tuning to show that she had the potential to be a quick Twelve Metre. But then *C1* was the product of Britain's most experienced Twelve Metre designer, the only man other than Ed Dubois to have had a Twelve Metre actually built and the only one with any practical experience of sailing real Twelve Metres. It would have been the most damning indictment of Ian Howlett's abilities had the yacht not sailed well from her first moments afloat. There was, by definition and by commission, to be nothing unusual about her: she was to be as conventionally state-of-the-art as it was possible to make her.

That was not at all the case with the boat now called *C2*. Indeed, the amazing aspect of the whole British campaign was that their original number one designer had never before designed, let alone built, a yacht that was big enough for anyone to sit in. Not only that, but, again by definition and commission, *C2* was to be as unlike any other Twelve Metre in the world, as radically different, as it was possible to make her. It was hardly surprising that she had a few rough edges.

Nor was it less surprising that disappointment in *C2* should be so wholesale, so total and so immediate. For two years, the campaign had survived to a great extent on a myth of its own making, that the long test programme, so cloaked in secrecy, would produce a wonderboat that would waltz away with the America's Cup quite literally on wings of high technology, for was not one of her boffins the very man who was responsible for the wings of the Harrier jump jet, that singular and remarkable success story of British design and ingenuity? Even if the myth-makers themselves had initially been sanguine about the veracity of the story, two years of feeding it to press and potential sponsors alike must surely have rubbed off just a little. With time now so desperately short it must have been a devastating blow to discover that *C2* could not simply wipe the floor with *C1*.

In fact, the truth is that *C2* was no dog, more that she was a boat very close to the bottom of her development curve whereas *C1* was a boat that went into the water quite a way up her own. There simply proved not the time to expend on the extra development that *C2* required, especially since there was no guarantee that at the end of what little time could be spared the campaign would have a winning yacht, or even a yacht with all her bugs removed. After the America's Cup was over, she would be brought back to her builders in Hamble to have done to her those modifications that could not be done in Fremantle, and the real worth of her potential more fully explored.

Meanwhile, as time began to run out, there was much work to be done on the Howlett design, and this involved as much two-boat sailing as possible.

Both boats line up about three boat lengths apart with the bow of the windward boat in line with the stern of the leeward boat, so that it is far enough forward not to cause an upwash effect but not so far forward that it doesn't roll the leeward boat. Then you start drag racing along and you both start tuning and sailing and steering and you gradually work out who is gaining and who is losing. Once you get more than an extra two boat lengths apart you then re-position, you constantly keep re-positioning and you just spend the day working away and judging which boat is quicker and why.

With the modern technology and its instrumentation and telemetry, we had a system with both boats where one would talk to the other electronically and on the screen we could see the other boat's numbers. Thus, if one boat was suddenly gaining you could look to see if he had had a windshift even though he would be only three boat lengths away. It was surprising how often that would happen, but these would come through waves and would average out. After a period of time both computers would give you how you were doing against the other boat.

In a slightly different wind direction the computers judge how well each boat has done and give you the answer in metres. So fine is the judgement that you can sail along for half an hour and gain twenty metres for one boat and that's a *BIG* gain.

So you could compute all this in and say 'That's it'.

Again on a good day, with a good breeze well established, we might go out to the race area and go into a start sequence. We used a system called the Rabbit start. You drop a buoy in the water, one boat comes round the buoy on starboard tack while the other boat would line up on her. The boat on starboard tack sails long and the port boat dips him and then the starboard boat must tack within about six boat lengths, then you have a race on your hands.

Then we would do one of two things, either a two mile windward leg or the full America's Cup leg of 3.25 miles. We normally wouldn't bother reaching because reaching is just so boring, and that was something which caught us out in a big way when we started racing. We learned all our lessons on reaching pretty quick in the series!

Then you race the return leg, run down and round the leeward mark. If the boats were well positioned close together we would keep going another round, if not we would reposition and start again. After the second or the third time at the windward mark we would drop the headsails, on the run down we'd have lunch and start again at the leeward mark. It's a long, hard graft.

By the time the racing timetable, moving inexorably closer, had arrived, *White Crusader* had been improved beyond all recognition of the boat that had been so good when she came out of the box. The only snag was, so had most of the others and, in contrast to what happened in the *Victory* campaign, the development sailing had all had to be done at the expense of hard, hard crewing practice.

In a different context, this in itself need have presented little problem. Dennis Conner, in particular, was another who was concentrating hard on development rather than crew practice and in the initial round-robin racing to come his sail handling and crewing were going to look very rough indeed on several occasions. The difference was that Conner had with him a hard core of people who were on their third and even fourth America's Cup. *White Crusader* had no such reserves of deep experience.

David Hollom and his design ideas were a cornerstone of the campaign from the word go, and in a sense were inherited by the management team established by Ian Easton when the campaign finally got under way. What David had was convincing, very correct, but then it was as if he had gone to the tank and totally redesigned the boat. Comparing David's original concept with the boat that was built as *C2*, it is tempting to say 'if we had built that – the original idea – we might have been right'.

'That' in fact was a boat with the centre of buoyancy well aft, wedge-shape almost, although the wedge was disguised by the long pin-tail. In the tank the shape had to be modified, and the general concensus was that the final boat did not behave as the model predicted: that old problem of scale effect again. The full-size boat didn't accelerate out of tacks.

It may be this is correctable, but in Fremantle there simply wasn't time to do it. The boat herself is not that slow, not that bad a boat, but whether her potential is worth pursuing is something that will probably be known only when she is fully developed.

In reality, *C2* was never considered to be the boat. She got close to *C1* before *C1* was given her new keel configuration and in flat water actually won races, but mostly she was sailed out of rating, so we could level the boats.

If one wanted to sum it up, one might say that her designers went down this complex, extended tank programme, convinced themselves of a radical change of design from the original concept and incorporated that into the final boat. In other words they used the tank to design which is a very difficult thing to do. The tank is best if it is used only for testing.

Ian, taking his brief of an evolutionary boat, produced a boat not tremendously different to the final version of *Australia III*. However, he did not go back to basics and evolve a design from scratch for Gage Roads and this was to have unfortunate consequences later as we began to perceive that despite having the design talent in fact he had not got the profile correct. So we eventually ended up with a compromise boat rather than being just conservative. The Kiwis, on the other hand, had built a very careful middle-of-the-road boat but it wasn't compromised.

But in a boat that wasn't the shortest, wasn't the narrowest, wasn't the fattest, wasn't anything – it was in the middle – what do you do? What the Kiwis said was 'we need high stability so we throw all the lead down there', and went all out for that design feature. But we didn't. So we ended up with a compromise.

As we went further down the track we began to appreciate where we should be and we were in the process of getting there, but we never quite got there in the time we had left available. It was Conner's boat that would have always been the problem.

We know what he has done but we could never have put *White Crusader* there: Conner actually used a different boat to the rest of us. Whereas, if you take *White Crusader* and the *Kookaburras* you wouldn't be able to tell the difference easily.

The things we still had to do included yet more stability in another redesigning of the keel, a spacer between the hull and the ballast of the keel, further refining of the keel's shape so that it went through the water well. With these modifications, *White Crusader* would have had a profile more similar to that of the *Kiwis*. The difference was that they had got there immediately, which coupled with their very good crewing, was what propelled them in such style through the round robins.

Conner went a different route. He had a different shaped boat, different numbers, different approach and he seems to have proven perhaps that having gone back to first principles he had made a complete one-step advance. His *'85*, the other boat he liked and brought to Fremantle, was more similar to the other top boats among the challengers, although a bigger boat.

Ian Howlett has enormous experience and thus a great many of the capabilities required to win the America's Cup. His performance this time was superior to his previous showings because this time he operated well within a peer group. Now the question is can we get together a new group and make the step up to winning the Cup. Probably yes is the answer.

But we will need more inspirational input. Ian himself is best seen as a possibly brilliant technician rather than an original-thinking designer, and one who is now responding to the sailors. What Conner had was a situation where the sailors would say 'well, what we need here . . .' and the designers would produce it. The problem now is that the whole competition is moving to a new venue, and we must all go back to the empty piece of paper again, start designing a new boat for a new set of conditions. We must, in the jargon, hit the numbers again. The sailors can do that, and a designer like Ian can put the numbers in place.

The down side is that such a route will not produce an inspired breakthrough.

This then brings in the question of using other designers. The tragedy with Ian Howlett is that he does not work easily with other people. A great strength in Fremantle was that he was comfortable in his group: Phil Crebbin or myself would say 'we need such-and-such', Ian would go away and think and come back and say 'here's how'.

So what are we left with for a conclusion about the boat herself? There has been a certain amount of comment about the level of contentment, cohesiveness – call it what you will – on the boat. Let me tell you something about happiness on boats, because from the attitude and deportment of the sailors on board it is in fact possible to tell quite a lot about the boat herself.

When things are going well, everyone on the boat is happy. It is when things are not going well, when the boat does not have an edge and everyone on board knows it does not have an edge, then that is when you start to get unhappiness on board. And then you get unhappiness off the boat as well.

It's easy to criticise from off the boat. If the boat performs well against an opponent, she's a great boat. If the race goes badly, the sailors are screwing-up.

In our own case one can rightly criticise the sailors in the race against *America II* in the Louis Vuitton final round robin, where we did have the same speed or perhaps even an edge. We should have beaten her. That's the one boat we should have beaten.

French Kiss was quicker than us twice in the heavy conditions in which we met her. Certainly she was straight-forward quicker the first time, the second time she was a bit quicker. That led us to a more aggressive manoeuvre than we should have had at the end of the second leg in conditions which were not far from the limit. Well, I called that – because I did not perceive that we would beat her if she got round the mark ahead of us.

There is a photograph of that incident which shows *White Crusader* submarined back to the mast on that manoeuvre. We were blamed – I was blamed – for sailing the boat into *French Kiss*'s quarter wave, but there was no other boat photographed all summer doing that, into an opponent's quarter wave or anywhere else.

Granted, I should have known that about the boat, we knew all about the lack of freeboard forward. But my judgement was that if we didn't get around that mark first, we would get beaten.

Jumping up and down about the semi-final is all very well, but it is not addressing the question that when the boat was delivered to Perth she was slow compared to the boat that would have been needed to beat *Stars & Stripes* in the America's Cup itself. *White Crusader* in her original configuration was probably eight minutes off the pace for a full America's Cup course. Together we brought her up to about four minutes off; I think it rather more constructive to look at that in the context of the next time, and what might be achieved.

There is no doubt, and I know of no one who really disagrees with this, that the hull of *White Crusader* was not as good as the top two boats, which were *Stars & Stripes* the eventual winner and the New Zealand boat. In the end she was as good as *Kookaburra*, but slower than *Stars & Stripes, New Zealand* and *USA*. She was, I would agree, good enough to get into the semi-final.

In the end, though, I never argue with designers – I have been bad-mouthed by the best of them – because they have to sell boats. I only race them.

CHAPTER NINE

Eleven knights to ride a White Horse

Eleven men crew a Twelve Metre. It does not sound a great number, but finding just those eleven men is crucial to the success of any Twelve Metre campaign. There are any number of ways to go about the search.

One is to advertise widely and interview those who reply. It is a technique widely used and respected in sporting and adventure programmes from mountaineering to living on desert islands; from jungle trekking to scientific expedition. 'Wanted: resourceful people, strong on loyalty but short on imagination . . .' It is a technique common enough in sailing circles. That eccentric and charismatic long-distance sailor H W Tilman found many of his young crews in such a manner, while for his first round-the-world yacht race Chay Blyth added the bizarre rider that the initial interview would be held in a crofter's hut miles from anywhere in the wilds of the Scottish Highlands. It was supposed that a successful arrival, on time, at the designated tryst would indicate resourcefulness and initiative on the part of the would-be crew member, but as a method of selecting good sailing men it probably said more about its inventor than about his victims. For his own crusade, Cudmore needed sailors, not fell-walkers.

A top skipper already has around him the nucleus of a crew which he calls upon as each regatta or campaign demands, and in the climate of the semi-professional racing circuit that has developed in international yacht racing over the past decade Cudmore's communication chain is second to none. Like mercenaries anywhere, the top crew men have their own contacts, network building upon network, so that a call to one will result in a call to others no less ready to rally to the flag. This was one method which would be tried.

The other would be to do what any well-run, growing organisation does when it needs good people fast: go headhunting. As Cudmore puts it, 'you seek out a list of the best people in the game and approach them'. Simple as that.

The advertisement approach was considered and rejected early on. The implications of placing advertisements are that the recruiting organisation has the time to interview at least a sensible number of applicants, has an opportunity to test them and can give them some sort of mutually exploratory trial in an immune area. For the White Crusade there simply was not the time, nor indeed the resource. If you want to trial a crew for a Twelve Metre it helps to have a Twelve Metre to trial on. Thanks to the lack of success of those who had spent the end of 1984 and the beginning of 1985 trying and failing to find funds for the campaign – not to mention the success of those who had been trying to and succeeding in queering the pitch – Twelve Metres were things the campaign was woefully short of at the time the crew was originally being assembled.

But, through that efficient and masonic grapevine that exists in the world of top big boat sailing as at the top of any sport, the word was put out that those with the required experience should make contact.

Not all the contacts were from those in whom Cudmore was particularly interested. There were in addition any number of applications from people who had simply read in yachting magazines or even in the newspaper about the campaign, and who were keen to catch America's Cup fever. In most instances, a letter asking for details of experience which might be appropriate – full-time sailing; expertise in boat building; a record of success in world championship events; any of the necessary first steps to this level of sailing – was enough to, tactfully, inform the hopeful applicant that it was unlikely his services would be required.

In addition, Cudmore went on a thorough search to find the best crews in the country, so that the challenge would not be restricted to a group of apprentices and friends. Every area of endeavour where the participants could be seen to have the right sort of experience to something approaching the required level of excellence was systematically explored. Those with existing Twelve Metre experience were obviously the most valuable, but the challenge went also to the Royal Ocean Racing Club to explore the ocean racing fleet and to the RYA for Olympic, dinghy and small keelboat class champions and crews, it even went to the – highly successful – Youth Squad, seeking advice from the coaches who, together, make the British RYA's race training and coaching schemes among the best in the world.

In the end, the group who finally arrived and stayed in Fremantle were predominantly full-time, professional sailors on the world circuit and not necessarily based in Britain. Previous British challenges have relied heavily on the Services to provide many of their crews. No other country does or did, and the reputation of the RYA's coaching schemes notwithstanding it has to be something of an indictment of the level and depth of international sailing talent in Britain that in his search for even a base nucleus of sailors who could together crew two Twelve Metres Cudmore and the challenge should sweep the cupboard so completely bare. Not long after arriving in Australia, setting up camp and taking the Twelves racing in the twenty-five-knot winds and eight-foot seas off Western Australia Cudmore remarked to *Yachting World* that he did not believe there were many sailors left in Britain who would have been capable of joining them.

Once the Twelves were in the water and racing, the enormity of the task facing the crews in preparing for the battle to come was borne in upon all of them. Chumley Prime's famous Quote Of The Day roll of honour, which by the end of the campaign would stretch from one end of the sixty-foot Portacabin rigging shop to the other in the link-fenced compound which was the base headquarters, records for posterity the day the crew were joined by Paul Stanbridge, a head-hunted latecomer from the hard-bitten world of maxi-yacht racing. Stanbridge had just completed the 27,000-mile Whitbread Round the World Race as bowman on the maxi *Atlantic Privateer* (maxis are the biggest IOR racing yachts in the world, eighty feet or thereabouts in overall length, crewed by between eighteen and twenty-five strong men and as tough a training ground as any wool clipper or Grand Banks schooner) and was preparing for his trial sail aboard *Crusader*.

'We find this hard,' an unimpressed Cudmore briefed him, 'and we're good sailors. You're going to find it bloody difficult . . .'

Also from the world of the maxi sailors came Louis Rich, who had been sailing aboard *Kialoa* and *Matador* and Mel Coleman who graduated to the maxi *Matador* from the mere sixty-footer *Jubilation*. It is men like these who are the mercenaries (the term is used as a tribute to their professional skills rather than as any sort of pejorative) of the sailing world, always to be found where the boats are biggest and the racing is hardest.

An obvious source of crew should have been the *Victory* campaign, and in the initial planning of the challenge it had been intended that the Perth campaign would grow naturally from the momentum generated by the de Savary campaign. In the event, this momentum turned out to be more ephemeral than tangible, although for some time its myth was maintained as a useful public-relations prop when there was little else of substance with which to reassure the doubting. There was nothing in the way of hardware that was in the end remotely useful, and even in development terms the box, when it was finally opened, proved to be more or less empty.

Over $US1m, for example, had been spent by the *Victory* campaign on sail development yet when the time came to carry on this work for the White Crusade not a single photograph from the many thousands taken and developed as part of that programme could be found. And this despite having Angus Melrose, the man most singly responsible for *Victory*'s sail programme, as *White Crusader*'s principal sail-designer.

Such lack of continuity spread into the recruitment of the crew, due largely – yet again – to the lack of funds. While four syndicates in Australia, nine (the number eventually reduced to six, then five) in America and the Kiwis in New Zealand were pushing ahead with their plans, building boats and going sailing, British talent was leaching away. Cudmore was unable to hold them on only the likelihood of their being able to race for the Cup aboard a British Twelve Metre.

Some went to other syndicates; others went sailing elsewhere; some simply became too committed to other things to be able, when the time came, to give up their all to join the Crusade.

Not unnaturally, there were no plans to have aboard from *Victory* either Rodney Pattisson or Lawrie Smith, but one person Cudmore particularly regretted losing was Andy Burnell, one of the two genoa trimmers aboard *Victory* and a regular member of Cudmore's match racing and IOR crews. Another was Derek Clark, Phil Crebbin's sometime wireman in the Olympic 470 and tactician aboard *Victory '83*. Clark, a highly-strung, hyper-active and aggressive competitor, had of all Peter de Savary's 'boys' been probably the most determined to be on the Twelve and had become a brilliant computer analyst of Twelve Metre sailing. After Newport he had stayed with *Victory* when she went into Italian ownership and won the 1984 Twelve Metre World Cup held in Sardinia. There he had been sounded out by Iain Murray who was putting together Kevin Parry's Australian Task-force syndicate.

'I don't want to become a mercenary,' Clark said at the time, 'but I do want to race in the America's Cup,' and, in the absence of a firm offer from the Royal Thames syndicate – even, at that stage, a firm assurance that they would definitely be in Fremantle – he had thrown in his lot with the Australians. He moved to Perth in January, 1985, just in time to establish the necessary two-year residence qualification for membership of a nation's America's Cup team, and became tactician aboard *Kookaburra*.

David Powys was another, an Australian-born multi-national sailor who as well as being aboard *Victory* was a regular Cudmore aide. He hung on in England for as long as he dared, hoping that the Crusaders would be able to commit themselves to fleshing-out their programme with sailors.Then he could wait no longer and risk losing the chance of sailing aboard a Twelve Metre – any Twelve Metre – in what even by 1985 was already shaping-up to be the yacht race of the century and he left for his native Australia. He, too, sailed aboard *Kookaburra*.

Some *Victory* crew were still available. Almost the first to be recruited was Andrew 'Spud' Spedding, the *Victory* shore boss and operations manager. So crucial was his role seen to be that not only was he the first to join Cudmore and Crebbin but he, like they, became a director of the company eventually formed to operate both the yachts and the campaign.

Victory's mainsheet hand, Chris Mason was with the Crusade as was Mark Preston who had been reserve grinder in Newport. From other Twelve Metres came Craig Nutter and Chris Church, both from the brave but pointless *Courageous* attempt to span the gulf between the Newport and the post-Newport eras of Twelve Metre sailing. Craig Nutter sailed with *White Crusader* in most of the races, Chris sailed in some.

Also with a Twelve Metre background was Michel Maeder, a French-Swiss sailor who is both something of a phenomenon and something of a Cudmore protégé. Just under six foot but powerfully built and with a luxuriant mane of black hair and a moustache that any Mexican bandit would be proud of, Meader had sailed in two French Twelve Metre campaigns in Newport, as well as in any number of Admiral's Cuppers and maxi yachts. He has raced with Cudmore for many years, graduating from deckhand to valued match race tactician and sail trimmer. Now, he has left his mentor's side to race against him on the world match race circuit and to have his own maxi yacht command, but when the call went out to get himself to Fremantle, he went like a shot. He sailed in *White Crusader* as genoa-trimmer.

From the world of Olympic sailing came Chris Law, Jerry Richards, and Mike McIntyre. McIntyre was Britain's Olympic Finn representative in the Los Angeles Olympics and he had sailed in the '85 British Admiral's Cup team selection trials. Jerry Richards is the long-standing crewman of Chris Law in his Olympic Soling campaigns but in 1985 had forsaken Law's unlikely-looking Admiral's Cup campaign to join Cudmore in his, along

1 Phil Crebbin (left), the Challenge's Technical Director. He and Cudmore had co-operated well on board *Victory* but Crebbin's de Savary experience left him reluctant to race aboard the new Twelves.

2 Cudmore eventually chose Chris Law to steer *White Crusader*. Law is a brilliant helmsman in his own right although less successful than Cudmore as a skipper. He is a strong, confident personality – the partnership was not without tensions.

3 Graham Walker, the quiet, determined owner, reluctant to be in the limelight. He stepped in to fund the Challenge's early stages expecting others to help, but was eventually left by the Royal Thames to go it virtually alone.

4 Admiral Sir Ian Easton, the retired officer who simply refused to accept that there should be no British challenge for the 1987 America's Cup.

5 David Arnold, financial controller for the Challenge, who was forced to resign from the position of Royal Thames Rear Commodore over alleged conflict of interest.

6 Andrew 'Spud' Spedding, Operations Director and the White Crusade's shore boss. His Fremantle compound remarked one US journalist, was 'the only one that actually looked like a boat yard'.

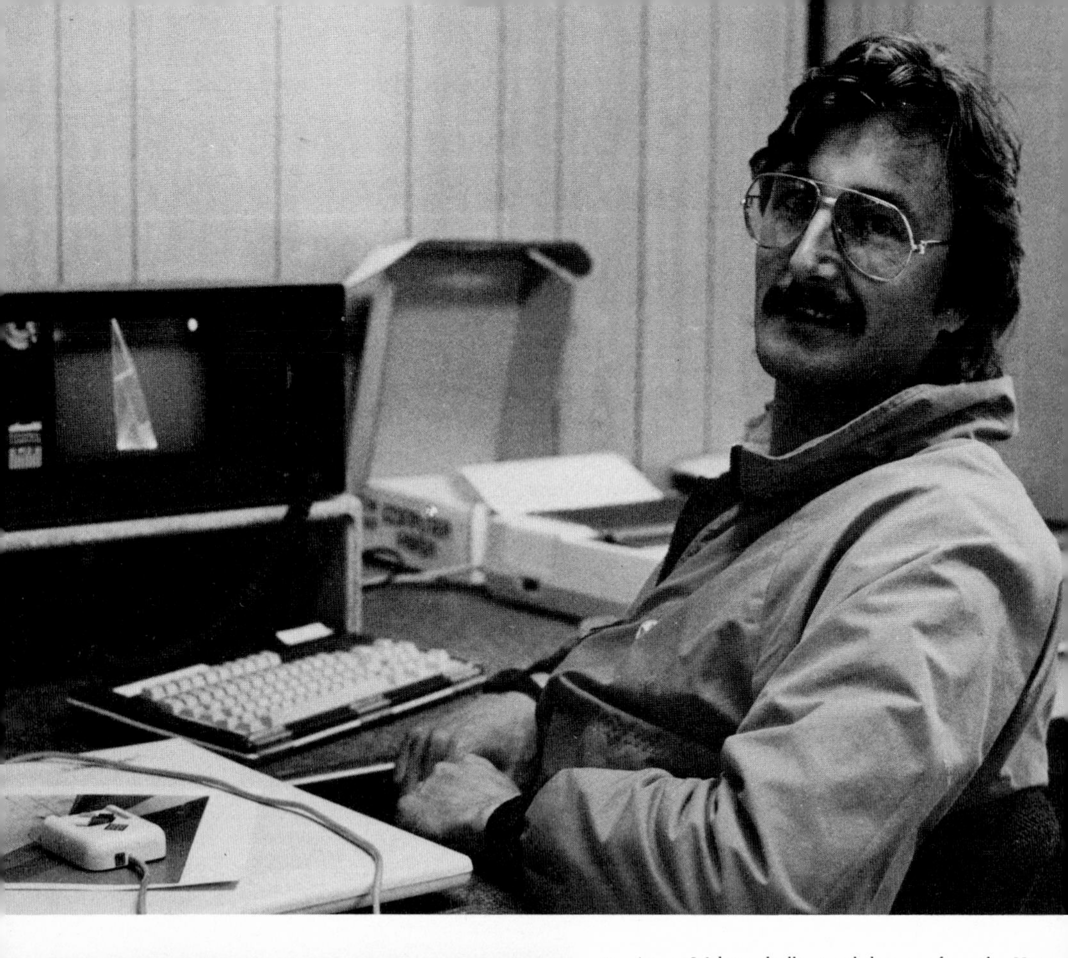

7 Angus Melrose, brilliant sail designer from the *Victory* programme who joined the White Crusade to mastermind the sailmaking programme. Downwind problems with the boat were attributed to his spinnakers and when Ken Rose and then Eddie Warden Owen were brought into the sail programme, Melrose was less than completely happy.

8 *White Crusader's* designer Ian Howlett, brought into the design programme at Cudmore's insistence, and originally briefed to design a 'conventional' boat as a bench-mark to test the new radical design around which the original programme was based.

9 D/C 2 – the boat that never was. Time ran out on developing the radical ideas, such as the very big, pointed stern which her design incorporated, and she was never seriously considered as the choice for race boat.

10 Study in concentration: racing a Twelve. Eddie Warden Owen steers C2 while the crew keep their weight to windward. Only the genoa trimmer in his cramped 'foxhole' cockpit sits to leeward. Twin steering wheels allow the helmsman to steer from where he can have the best view of the sails and the oncoming seas.

11 Many hours were spent testing the two boats against each other, always following progress with the fast semi-rigid inflatable 'Bouncer' which ferried spare sails, and with the computer-equipped tender. Fremantle conditions were markedly more windy than those at Newport.

12 Aboard the Twelve. Mike McIntyre, Olympic sailor and part of the on-board management group, operates the coffee-grinder winch for the mainsheet. The outer of the concentric steering wheels operates the rudder; the inner one, usually locked-off in position, works the trim tab.

13 In the early part of the Summer of '86 *White Crusader* often raced against *South Australia*, one of the potential Australia defenders. Always, she showed a comfortable and comforting edge of speed.

14 The two Twelves roar along together 'their white wakes sizzling past the cockpit and the steady roar of the quarter wave drumming in the helmsman's ear. Aboard each there is only silence as the two crews concentrate on the last tenth-of-a-knot of speed and the tacticians watch for the results of their crews' endeavours.'

15 *White Crusader*, designed for just one purpose – racing other Twelve Metres.

PHOTOGRAPHY BY KOS

with sailmaker, small boat champion and potential helmsman for the Twelve Metre, Eddie Warden Owen.

One young man joined from the ranks of the RYA Youth Squad. Down in Fremantle, when the British dock compound had just been erected and all was a chaos of aluminium sheets, packing cases, rubble and concrete dust, in walked a young man with Twelve Metre fever in his eyes. His name was Mark Chisnell and he was completing a do-it-yourself world tour after coming down from university. He was an international-level world youth sailor, a member of Britain's current Olympic dinghy training squad and held a masters' degree in computer sciences – and he wanted a job with Britain's America's Cup campaign.

'Can you use a brush?' asked Chris Law, who was more or less the first person Chisnell met.

'Yes.' said Chisnell.

'Then start sweeping up this mess.'

And the master of computing sciences set to work. In the weeks to come, as moustached and muscled mercenaries from the maxi boats and the veterans of earlier America's Cups strutted their stuff and talked of past campaigns, while the key hoofers planned and plotted and occasionally emerged to oversee, he beavered away, shifting rubble, sweeping what seemed like tons of cement dust, painting the Portacabins. Anything, until the great Twelves should eventually arrive, be de-coccooned, rigged and finally spread their Kevlar/Mylar wings. He might, he had been promised, get a sail.

Eventually, as the development programme began and someone remembered they had heard him talk apparently knowledgeably about computers, he took over the operation of the challenge's data gathering and performance analysing computer systems and became an indispensable member of the campaign. He even got to sail aboard the Twelve. And all because he could use a brush and was not afraid of hard work.

In the back of *White Crusader* Cudmore planned to have himself and another helmsman/tactician. Unusually – indeed alone – among those with the ambition to skipper an America's Cup racer he had no great desire to steer the yacht himself, except when the pressures of the immediate situation demanded it. All who have seen Cudmore sail, sailed with him or against him rate him as an outstandingly good helmsman and, like everyone else, when he set out to establish his reputation he steered the yachts he raced. But over the years of campaigning larger and larger yachts he 'grew out' (to use his own phrase) of steering, preferring to concentrate on the management of the yacht, deciding strategy and dictating tactics: just as a warship captain 'fights his ship' without actually grabbing the wheel.

Cudmore prefers instead to recruit a good, preferably brilliant, helmsman who then concentrates simply on steering without the distraction of having to worry about where to go, or what the opponents are doing. The difficulty with such an arrangement is that most helmsmen who are that good are – at least in their own opinion – also good enough to have overall command. It is in straightforward human terms difficult for a helmsman who is good enough to have reached the top on his own abilities and racing judgements to make himself not just a part of but an extension of another skipper's thought processes, even if he is sufficiently far above normal human failings to be able to view his role as more than simply making another skipper look good. Cudmore's own part in the partnership is no less difficult, for he must establish such a bond with his helmsman that he maximises his use of the other's talents while directing him in his own thinking: the two must think, not just as one but as Cudmore. If it goes wrong, the entire system crashes – sometimes literally – in a tangle of garbled communications, incomprehension and jagged edges of personality. If it works, it is wonderful; but with hindsight, Cudmore's belief in such a system turned out to be the final obstacle which eventually brought the Crusade to the end of its road.

First and natural choice for the shared responsibility at the back of the boat was the man who had proved ideal in the *Victory* campaign and who was already technical director of this one, Phillip Crebbin. Crebbin, however, had been so traumatised by his shabby treatment by Peter de Savary that he could not be persuaded to commit himself to rejoining the afterguard of another Twelve Metre. Additionally, he felt his role as technical director – responsible for the co-ordination of the development programmes for both Twelve Metres and all their equipment – was quite enough of a plateful without going sailing as well, so Cudmore looked elsewhere.

Almost as soon as he had finished talking to Philip Tolhurst at that initial meeting at the Lymington Cup, he approached Chris Law to see if Law might be interested in joining him. Law indicated that he might well be, but that there were many gates to pass and ditches to cross before the enchanted castle could be reached.

Until then, Law and Cudmore had always raced against, never with, each other. Their most regular meeting place was yearly, at this very Lymington Cup, and it always seemed their matches were drawn with a particularly keen edge. Individual honours between them were uneven but close, with Cudmore still ahead. Law had been runner-up in the competition almost as many times as Cudmore had won it, but always the final honour seemed to fall to Cudmore.

In fact, Cudmore had been in the process of recruiting Law to the *Victory* campaign when his own breach with de Savary had interfered, but it was obvious that for the two to get together there would have to be some adjusting of personal egos.

Another possibility was Olympic Flying Dutchman sailor Jo Richards. He and Cudmore had successfully sailed together in the helmsman/skipper combination on a number of boats, most notably *Justine III*. In her they had won the One Ton Cup, world championship of the One Ton IOR level rating class with an unprecedented five firsts in the five-race series – but Richards had recently married and his wife had just given birth to their son. A new wife and a new son are no fit baggage to be taken on any crusade.

Fourth contender for the hot spot was Eddie Warden Owen. A champion in any number of dinghy and small boat classes, he had steered Graham Walker's all-conquering Admiral's Cupper *Phoenix* to stardom under Cudmore's command and the partnership had worked well for both of them. Owen had been far from a mere lackey to Cudmore's whiplash tongue and could give as good as he got, yet knew when to bow to the latter's greater experience or insight. The two respected each other greatly.

These, then, were the key men whom Cudmore assembled around him as the White Crusade got down to business on the far side of the world from Knightsbridge – and almost the first thing they confessed was that they were short in one crucial department. They might have been good at sailing, but they were no good at lifting heavy weights.

The seas off Fremantle are the biggest in which Twelve Metres have ever tried to race, and the winds the strongest. Although there is no limitation on the sophistication of the electronic instrumentation that the yacht may carry, no restriction on the money, the science and the technology that may be expended in her design, no prohibition on the number or cost of the sails she may have in her wardrobe there is one area of operation where only blood, sweat and tears may be poured out. Those sails must be raised and lowered, sheeted and trimmed by hand.

The power of a Twelve Metre's sails is harnessed and controlled by massive capstan winches which, although permitted sophisticated gearing systems, may not be mechanically activated. Instead the power comes from enormous handles, mounted on pedestals in the middle of the boat and universally known for some arcane reason as 'coffee grinders'. In a three-hour race, the Twelve Metre may have to tack a hundred times, the tacks as little as a minute apart, and on every tack the genoa must be let go and re-sheeted on the other side not just with brute strength but with precision timing and co-ordination.

In physical terms it is the equivalent of having two men lift, say, half-a-dozen bags of cement and place them neatly one on top of the other without splitting, damaging or crushing any of the bags – and have them do it within the space of twenty seconds.

Even in Newport, such a regime demanded huge physical effort: in Fremantle virtually every syndicate made or confirmed an important discovery. The sport of sailing simply did not breed men strong enough to race a Twelve Metre flat-out for three hours in the Fremantle conditions.

Chris Law had organised a search to find the men to out-power the competition. Following the racing in the world championships the previous January Tom Clarke, then sports editor of the *Daily Mail* and since moved to the sports chair of *The Times* was the man who came to the syndicate's aid with a competition run by the paper to find 'The Strongest Man In Britain'. On the appointed day and after due publicity in the paper the final applicants assembled before a mock-up of a pair of coffee grinders and began to do their grunting stuff. Instead of hauling in sails they actually hauled aloft drums of cement, but the work loads and work pattern had been devised to resemble as closely as possible those endured in short tacking a Twelve Metre, and the simulation was carried to such a degree of accurate detail that they even had Harold Cudmore to offer verbal encouragement, just like the real thing. It was, no one would dispute, extremely hard work.

The *Daily Mail*'s Winch Winder competition provided *White Crusader* with two of her five grinders, although one potential grinder travelled all the way to Australia only to discover that he did not like sailing.

Clive Roberts at least had a boating background of sorts. He was an Olympic oarsman and thus would only have to accustom himself to boating in waves and looking the right way, but Paul Rushent and Sean Campbell, also oarsmen, had no sailing experience at all. Paul, universally known as 'Jabba', became a household name when, as final selection drew near, he was featured in a television programme manfully taking a 'private' dressing down from Cudmore: just him, Cudmore and four million television viewers.

The experience marked him profoundly. Not only did the dressing-down have the desired effect and Jabba's efforts and commitment to the Crusade increase to the level where he became a regular member of the final crew –

no mean feat for a man who had never sailed before in his life – but they brought him a fame that was as widespread as it was unexpected and unlooked for.

One day the *White Crusader* team met – with a certain amount of mutual awe – the England test cricket side who happened to be playing a series in Perth. As the two sets of international sportsmen mingled, Jabba was spotted by Ian Botham: 'Ah – you must be Jabba,' proclaimed the doyen of English cricket. 'Yes,' said Jabba, with a twinkle, 'and you are . . .?'

CHAPTER TEN

On the Campaign Trail

There is good reason why the long-drawn-out slog from drawing board to finishing line is called a Twelve Metre *campaign*. The parallels with a military operation are obvious, and close.

First, there is the planning, the gathering of resources. Then there is the departure for foreign shores, the establishing of the beach-head and the setting up of camp. Then there is the fighting itself, with its preparation beforehand, its short, sharp battles, its debriefings and its preparations for the next round.

Logistically, a Twelve Metre is an expensive machine to keep in fighting order. Once you have solved the problem of getting to the battle zone, you must have somewhere to keep it, to work on it, safe from prying eyes. Its weapons load of sails requires constant attention, arming and re-arming, as well as continual replenishment and refinement. Its attendants must have somewhere to work on it, its fighting crew need shore support, and everyone must have somewhere to live and something to eat.

The military analogy cannot be taken too far. Twelve Metre sailors are seldom ambushed in their beds and so far the only bomb attack on a Twelve Metre has turned out to be a hoax.

To solve the financial burden of operating the Twelve Metre group so far from home, the Thames' challenge adopted an innovative approach to the problem of housing both the Twelve Metres and their sailors. Spedding and Arnold are what in modern management jargon are called lateral thinkers, which is to say they both have a great deal of common sense and are not afraid to use it. Instead of trying to find rented accommodation for their sailors, which is what most other syndicates were doing, with the obvious effect on prices, they went out and bought it.

Crusader Castle, as it became called, was a former private nursing home on the edge of Fremantle, far enough away from the centre of town to ensure quiet and privacy, yet close enough to be convenient to the dock and compound. With everyone from the Royal Perth Yacht Club to the Government of Western Australia telling the people of Perth in general and of Fremantle in particular that the arrival of the America's Cup and its participants would be the biggest economic boost in the State since the Gold Rush, even long- and medium-term rents around Fremantle took such a leap as to make the purchase a very shrewd move. Little could be done to make the Twelve Metres themselves anything other than fast-depreciating assets, but at least the campaign would not be pouring money down the drain in just housing its foot-soldiers.

Spud Spedding is one of those to whom outward appearance means but little. A lightly-built, slightly shambling figure with an owlish face and bushy, mutton-chop whiskers (in gardening terms they would be described as 'well-established') he looks more like a yeoman livestock farmer than operational head of a £4m logistics programme. In fact, for much of the time he *is* a yeoman livestock farmer ('I run a boulder farm on Dartmoor' is a favourite introductory line) but for *Victory* and again for *White Crusader* he was the genius who kept the yachts afloat and racing, working with a diminished minimum of shore helpers.

Other syndicates had larger, more elaborate and above all tidier compounds than the British. Indeed, it is difficult to think of any front-line syndicate which had a compound less pretentious or more apparently unruly. But appearances can be deceptive. While one noted British reporter was wont to comment with scorn on the British effort in general and on their dock and compound in particular, it was an American journalist who paid Spedding one of his most valued compliments of the whole campaign: 'This,' he remarked on leaving Spedding's office, 'is the only dock in Fremantle that actually *looks* like a boatyard.' Spedding was delighted.

In this boatyard and its nearby shed, almost nightly modifications to one or other of the Twelve Metres would be carried out as the development sailing progressed. Unimpressive it may have looked to those who judge efficiency by the yard of storage rack or the number of notices prohibiting entry to all but authorised personnel – but the British were the only challenging syndicate to have the foresight to acquire for themselves a shed large enough to act as full-size Twelve Metre sail-loft and high enough to take a Twelve Metre and her enormous travelling lift. Not even the vaunted Kiwis nor the high-spending Conner could work on their boats under cover. With Arnold's hard head for business again working overtime, the Crusaders occasionally rented out both shed space and computer time in the sail-loft to other syndicates when they didn't need them themselves. It helped pay the rent.

There is a notion that yachting is somehow a leisurely pastime. The very word conjures up thoughts and images of champagne and wicker chairs, cucumber sandwiches and summer afternoons. While there may yet be the lingering legacy of such Edwardian days among those who come to spectate at an America's Cup, there is no such connection for those whose life it is to race the Twelves. A Twelve Metre race is a tough proposition. Cudmore himself describes it thus:

In Newport one usually used 2s and 3s [Code sizes for the genoas – the lower the code size, the larger the sail and the lighter the wind]. Out here in the summertime you might start with 3 and go to 4. In Newport you would never use a 6 through the whole season; you never put one on; out here you use it quite regularly.

We took people out of rowing, inernational rowers, and they came in fit, powerful men. Still we built them up noticeably over a period of time. They were so much more powerful when they had finished with us than when they had started and they judged that this sport was immeasurably tougher than their own. Sailing a Twelve is not just a couple of minutes of a race but a sustained requirement for physical effort that is immeasurably tougher than rowing in the long haul.

In tacking a boat where you have four grinders, the boats will tack in say forty-second cycles, close tacking. It takes about six months for fit men to get to a stage where they can sustain this indefinitely – and for an America's Cup that is what they must be capable of.

The pre-start manoeuvres are particularly tough on the person on the mainsail – the genoa trimming is not so bad – but if you are doing a slow wind up into the wind it really can be awfully tough, much tougher than tacking after the start.

After the start a worked-up grinding team will have the technique up so well they only apply themselves fully for something like three or four seconds, maybe a little bit longer. The sail can be sheeted almost home with the winches in top gear.

So you have this ten-minute work-up – the pre-start – although a lot of the boats eased up on their pre-start manoeuvres. They were just taking too much out of the crew. After the start then you can find yourself tacking every forty seconds to a minute sometimes in trying to break a cover and this can be really tough – yet very often we'd go on like this for ten or fifteen minutes, accelerating and coming back at the other boat, which is punishingly sustained effort.

Once at the top mark, one of the guys would pull up the pole [spinnaker pole], jump the spinnaker halyard – that's not the tough bit, it's an eight-second explosion of energy – but then taking down the bastard of a genoa, dragging and pulling it in, then folding that genoa and bagging it and putting it away, that's tough.

Then doing a series of gybes and getting down to the bottom end. Genoa up again is not a big deal but that spinnaker coming down is hard physical graft. Then you go straight into a tacking duel immediately afterwards . . . and you're only starting leg three of an eight-leg race.

The physical requirement of these boats is right up there with some of the really tough sports. From all accounts it wouldn't be up to professional boxing, where you do fifteen rounds, but because of the broken pattern of exertion, the lack of rhythm, it is demanding. Certainly the comparison is with a lot of the serious sports, such as football where you are running all the time, but with football you are so fit that you are running within your capability and then you have quick spurts.

In football you are not fighting anything. So much of sailing a Twelve Metre is simply fighting it.

An interesting sidelight on the sailors' approach to fitness in particular and dedication in general occurred when the *White Crusader* squad were hosts to another visiting English international sporting team, normally the subject of considerably more public attention, adulation and acclaim.

The first surprise was the discovery that the visitors appeared as honoured to meet the sailors as the sailors were to meet the visitors. The second was the manifest lack of physical condition of the majority of key hoofers in the cricket side.

And most alarming was the things they did to their bodies. By this time, most of the *White Crusaders* were in a peak of physical condition, on careful though not strictly imposed diets and too keenly aware of the ill-effects on reflexes and stamina of residual alcohol to take much more than a beer or two, if any at all. With genuine surprise they watched their visiting fellow international athletes hit the booze with a vengeance, to such an extent that at least one of their number – no minor player either – was at last taken home suspended between two of his not-much-soberer colleagues.

'They're just a bunch of lushes!' remarked one amused and bemused sailor, as much in awe as in horror.

In fairness to the visitors, it has to be recorded that the next day and in true Roy of the Rovers style one of the principal revellers knocked off boundaries like he was in a coconut-shy and went on to take a match-winning number of wickets. There are some people who sail best with a hangover, too.

*

The problem of fitness is one which will receive an increasing amount of attention as Twelve Metre sailing becomes more demanding. The British, like all syndicates, took fitness very seriously and discovered afterwards that next time around they will have to take it even more seriously still.

That whole physical side is terribly important. Even before we went to Australia we went to Southampton University and the sailing Olympic advisers John McFadyen and Gerry Berrel in the physical education department there. We got them to go down to the Twelve Metre when she was still in Hamble and discuss with some of the crew who had been in *Victory* about what the requirements were. Then they drew up training sequences which reflected the differing work patterns and requirements of different positions on the boat.

Then I asked Mike McIntyre and Clive Roberts to help – both are Olympic sportsmen and already thoroughly at home in a gymnasium, though Mike was the one to be our link-man. We didn't have a specialist trainer so someone like Mike who was trained for Olympics and being the type of guy he is, serious, conscientious, he would undertake the role thoroughly.

He got to Fremantle and with the knowledge a lot of the guys had from the rowing and from sport generally (we weren't training nineteen-year-olds we were training twenty-five-year-olds so they had been around the sport for six or seven years), with that knowledge and background, and Mike to carry forward that knowledge we were able to put it into a sensible programme.

Of course, we made some mistakes. Some of the weight lifting was done perhaps to an excess, there were quite a few injuries. In fact to analyse the injuries over a period of time is quite interesting – we had a lot of people with muscular injuries. Quite a few suffered that injury where the tendons get so big they rub on the sheath of the muscles and that is a real problem to solve.

Clive Roberts had an operation, two or three others used Cortisone, that's a pretty savage sort of drug to be involved with in sailing . . .'

Michel Maeder and Gerry Richards, the two trimmers, were to run into this trouble that might more usually be associated with iron-pumpers and similar grunt-stunt sports. Not least because of the need to keep the squad as few as possible but also because the simple crew learning time was so short, they had been sailing in a sustained way right the way through the build-up, both while *White Crusader* and *C2* were being trialled the one against the other and after the programme had perforce become a one-boat campaign.

Just as racing came up Michel Maeder had to take four weeks on the dock and Gerry Richards went down between round robins one and two. Fortunately, both men caught the problem just in time, but it demonstrated that in the most physically demanding positions in the crew – grinding and sail trimming – men were on their bodily limits.

That is what many people who still think of yachting as some sort of rich man's pastime don't realise. We are getting to a stage of physical fitness where we need a level of sports medicine. In Perth and Fremantle the local standards are pretty high so we were able to use local skills but next time I think we will have to be more professional about something like that.

Later on in the series we brought in Tina [wife of squad member Martin Amy] who is a physiotherapist. She came in to do injuries and had a steady stream of people constantly being worked on. The physical demands of the game in Perth were such, and the physical demands on people were such – simply because of the tough conditions – that we should really have addressed this as a whole new problem area and brought in specialist people. Whereas this time, like our whole programme, the funding limits made us very very careful what we spent our money on.

Further to dispel the notion that yachting is a genteel pastime, the daily routine of the campaign began at 0615 each morning, with a PT session at 0630. The nature of the session would vary but always last an hour. Two days a week the entire squad would perform that latest vogue in rendering hard labour palatable – aerobics – and two days a week there would be a run of a mile or two, ending up in a park and going straight into light exercises and loosening up. Then would follow a session of competitive grid sprints and tougher routines followed by a brisk run back to the house by a shorter route.

On other days the squad would just road-train for the whole period, running out for half an hour and then running as fast as possible back to the house. 'Some people could get their exercise over in fifty minutes', recalls Cudmore, 'others would need a taxi'. Ever mindful of the need for group welfare, he insisted that each member of the group take $5 in case they got lost 'earlier on'.

The campaign also took out group subscriptions to both a local swimming pool and to a very fine gymnasium called Laurie Potters, where on wet mornings – contrary to popular myth it rains coldly and frequently during the West Australian winter – the squad would work-out.

Carrying the entrepreneurial spirit further, the campaign did a deal with Lombardo's, a freshly-built (more correctly rebuilt to unrecognisable standard) restaurant overlooking Fishing Boat Harbour and a symptom of the wave of expansionist re-vitalisation being enjoyed as Fremantle itself prepared for the Cup. Each morning most of the squad went there for breakfast. It was a deal which cut both ways: it solved the morning cooking problem at Crusader Castle and it carried Lombardo's through the long winter, but how much profit the restaurant made is debatable. On one occasion Cudmore watched one of his grinders fill his plate with a dozen eggs, and for some of the healthier appetites, burning through up to 12,000 calories a day, seven or eight would have been considered average.

After clearing Lombardo's out of eggs and bacon, the crew would get down to the dock for about 0830 and begin the chore of humping the basic sails from the loft. Each night after racing, in a routine that saved literally tens of thousands of dollars in wear and tear and depreciation, every sail used that day was taken out of its bag, washed and hung up in the huge, hangar-size sail-loft. Next day, genoas would have to be packed and spinnakers bagged and the basic group brought to the dock. It was a big job for two boats involving ten people for half-an-hour.

The first job then of the afterguard was to decide the sails – the Twelve Metre's weapon load – for the day against the forecast, and these sails would be loaded on board the two Twelves while the one boat of the pair that had spent the night on the hoist to allow minor work – replacement winches, for example – to be done by the overnight crew would be put back in the water.

At 0915 began each day's crew briefing, the daily system of keeping everybody 'up to speed' and an opportunity if the crew wanted to raise something. It kept everyone in touch with everyone else, briefed about everything from what the PR people were doing to the thousand and one other things it takes to run a Twelve Metre program.

Not least of the functions of the daily briefing was the maintenance of morale. Good commanders from Hannibal to Noel Coward have known the value of a happy ship, and in the closed world of the compound, the Castle and the daily grind of chore heaped upon chore, boredom and a subsequent falling off of motivation were a constant danger. Happily for the good of the Crusade – not to mention the sanity of the Crusaders – there were those in the compound with a firm grip on reality, not the least being the sanguine and unimpressible Spedding and his alter ego, facto factotum and general right-hand man Chumley Prime.

Soon after arriving and setting up camp, these two had instituted a special award whose earthy title might be most genteely translated as This Week's Silly Person Award. Every Monday, or indeed on any day when an especially silly thing had been done, the new Fuckwit Of The Week would be required to step bravely forward and receive his – or occasionally her – proudly delivered citation.

No one was immune, including Cudmore who was an early winner when he was responsible for *White Crusader*'s first collision, with *South Australia* during practice.

Other notable Fuckwits included the crewman who put his shoes on the oven to dry but failed to remove them before they caught fire, and the Royal Thames dignitary who emerged from a hard day below decks on the committee boat with his fly-zip undone. Geoff Meeks, the noted South African sailor whom Cudmore briefly imported as a tune-up helmsman and Jules Mantle, the awesomely capable Girl Friday who ran the day-to-day logistics of the compound, were declared worthy joint-winners when they laid the windward and leeward marks of an impromptu match race course either side of a mudbank in the Swan River, and Chumley Prime himself was once required to step forward and be recognised. He had spent many hours and $165 fitting his car with a roobar – the great metal shunting frame Australians put on the front of their cars to protect the vehicle in case of collision with a wandering kangaroo – had then gone off into the bush and emerged three days later with the front of the vehicle unmarked but the side expensively stove in. A cruising Emu had gone into it at twenty mph.

Even the much-loved Eileen Caulcut, a founding race officer of the Royal Lymington Cup, Vice-Commodore of the Royal Lymington and an internationally recognised expert at match race organisation was not immune. Out in Fremantle at the syndicate's request to help with the practice racing, and acting also as a representative of the Royal Thames, she had been given notice that she had been honoured with an award – a sort of sailing Oscar – back in Britain for her years of significant contribution to British international match racing. Due for some leave from the compound, she planned her flying round-the-world trip with care: a visit to some friends in Los Angeles and then back to Perth via London, leaving her a bare twenty-four hours back home to check over the house, see her sister and pick up the award. She arrived at Heathrow late on Monday night, made it to the Savoy in London to collect her award on the Tuesday, and flew out again early on Wednesday morning. Unfortunately the award ceremony was on Thursday. She was declared a worthy winner.

Another daily routine was checking the notice board – uncompromisingly designated as the only official method of circulating information. There were just too many people rushing around doing too many things for any more personalised system to be operable and, once again, no one was excused the need to check the board. If you didn't know what was going on, that was your problem. More often than not, it was Cudmore himself who would be caught out, failing to notice some domestic detail posted during the day.

The sailing team would be on the water between 0930 and 1000. The twin diesels of *The James Capel,* the campaign tender would roar into life, the long white hulls of the two Twelve Metres be eased from their berths stern first, turned and taken in tow and with the fast, semi-rigid support boat *Bodyline* and the appropriately named high-speed telemetry platform *Bouncer* (Spedding is a considerable and dedicated cricket buff) in attendance, the *White Crusader* would turn its head to the open sea.

CHAPTER ELEVEN

We Are Sailing

America's Cup sailing is first of all the putting together of a total programme. It is much, much more than merely taking a Twelve Metre to sea and winning a few races, although the delight of the contest is that in the end; that's what it all boils down to. But there is much, more much to it than that initially.

Initially there are such things as the cash and the authority to operate the programme. It is at this first hurdle that so many British programmes have fallen down; too often the initial people are incorrectly equipped in terms of capability and talents and they pre-empt the management decision role. But as you can see from Dennis Conner, who has been the most successful Twelve Metre sailor of the last decade, he has above all solved that problem, although he himself would admit to enormous problems when he was operating through the New York Yacht Club, which eventually led to their losing the Cup.

There is no doubt about the bitterness that Conner felt toward the New York Yacht Club and this time, with his own challenge through the San Diego Yacht Club, run in his own way, he was able to show himself in his true merit. And that was a complete dominance of the America's Cup, reminiscent of the days before the challengers had got properly together.

So that's the first step. The second is taken once that initial management structure has been set up, and that is to pull together a design programme to understand exactly what you are trying to achieve. Again one of the great lessons of this Cup and of the last Cup is that America's Cup is a boat speed competition. The fastest boat tends to win: the sailors only make a marginal difference. That's a lesson that has been learned – or should have been learned – by everyone who was at Fremantle. America's Cup is above all a boat speed test, so design aspects are crucial.

There is perhaps a parallel in motor racing, that however good the driver if the car isn't fast and immune from breakdown it doesn't matter. Good drivers can switch to top teams and suddenly become world champions, or world champion drivers get caught in bad cars and suddenly disappear. It is the same with America's Cup.

Design of the yacht is integral to the success of the whole campaign and while the designer will put together the potential boat there is still in most boats available to the crew the ability to turn that boat into a champion. If *Stars & Stripes* had had a less talented set of sailors involved in her development she would not have won the America's Cup, for the sailors have a crucial part to play in developing the boat speed.

Yet, ironically, once everything has been prepared the importance of their role diminishes.

If, for example, Dennis had taken ill the day before the America's Cup and, say, Tom Whidden or even Chris Dixon or for that matter the British crew had sailed her, *Stars & Stripes* would still have won, probably by the same margin.

First of all the design must be right. Then when the first boat is delivered the programme goes into testing and judging that against the initial design philosophy. Identifying the aspects which are crucial – for example, sails. Ideally it is not necessary to make too many mechanical changes to the boat but the process is one of putting together these very complex decisions about areas which are not in themselves complex, so there are a lot of small fairly innocuous problems which have to be put together into a complex whole so that, provided all your percentages point the right way, you end up with a big percentage over your competition and a winning boat.

Thus there is a link between crewing ability, sails, rig design and then the ability to sail the boat. So far Dennis Conner has proved to be the best in the world by quite a long way at putting together that whole mix.

This is the great attraction of the America's Cup and it is one of the reasons why the sort of tycoon-type tends to enjoy getting involved, because he can see the complexity of the problem and the importance of correct decision-making. The danger is that you can only have very skilled people making the decisions.

The most dramatic example of both the benefits and the problems of having tycoons run the campaign is the 1986/87 New Zealand campaign. That programme was very well run from off the boat, yet ultimately it was a lot weaker than the programmes whose people were all knowledgeable. For example Michael Fay's opposite number Malin Burnham is himself a top Twelve Metre sailor, Star boat world champion – and he runs a bank. In other words he is Michael Fay plus the sailing ability.

So Dennis Conner is not alone in his campaign. John Marshall went from being president of North Sails to being Dennis's design co-ordinator while enjoying his own very successful racing career, including sailing in previous America's Cups. This is the sort of level Dennis Conner is operating at, with the ability to pull all these talents together and hold them. That's what gives that group the margin and this is one of the lessons that Britain has to learn to win the America's Cup.

Until more than just one or two individuals in the campaign group have that competence level and they've learned how to work together I do not think Britain can win the America's Cup. Certainly no individual designer, no matter how capable, will be as good as a properly organised small design team working with an extended technical group.

It's the same with the management of the programmes. This time our management group was not very experienced. Only two of the four executive directors [Phillip Crebbin and Andrew Spedding] had done a full America's Cup, I had only done a small early part of one. We had two drivers for the boats, both very talented but both with only a few weeks of America's Cup experience. At least we have now acquired a knowledge level. If another British group is formed without previous experience, they will just have the same learning curve to climb.

Once the programme is well down the track and sailing the boats there are large areas of boredom. It is not interesting sailing. Testing Twelve Metres is a very boring, painstaking chore and you need a very special sort of mentality such as that of Dennis Conner to sustain that sort of effort through the continuous boredom. A lot of top sailors are rather boring people.

It is something that whoever is sailing the boats for Britain next time will have to face: there will be years of continuing application to work without much glamour.

Then, and only then, when you have proven that you have fast boats and a full, competent and complete organisation, you finally get out to race.

What Cudmore calls 'the extended organisation' of the Twelve Metre camp is like a small armada. As the morning mists begin to clear and the day gets ready for the developing sea breeze, the tug takes the Twelve Metre in tow, the warp groaning and stretching, tightening round the centreline towing post and leading tautly out through the port quarter fairlead as the Twelve Metre's 60,000lb deadweight comes on to it, then sagging into its long, shallow curve as the big yacht gathers way. The trial horse tags along on a long tether from the tug's starboard quarter or, in a more affluent campaign, dutifully follows her own tug out to sea.

The telemetry chase boat and the fast high-speed sea boats take up station, and the VIP boat with its visiting syndicate members, sponsor's guests, invited television crew or whoever is on board for the day, follows out to join the waiting spectator fleet.

The course is merely a designated patch of open water, patrolled and kept – hopefully – clear of other traffic to allow the Twelve Metres uninterrupted space for their private battle. It is not so much a race track as an enormous

The Full America's Cup Course

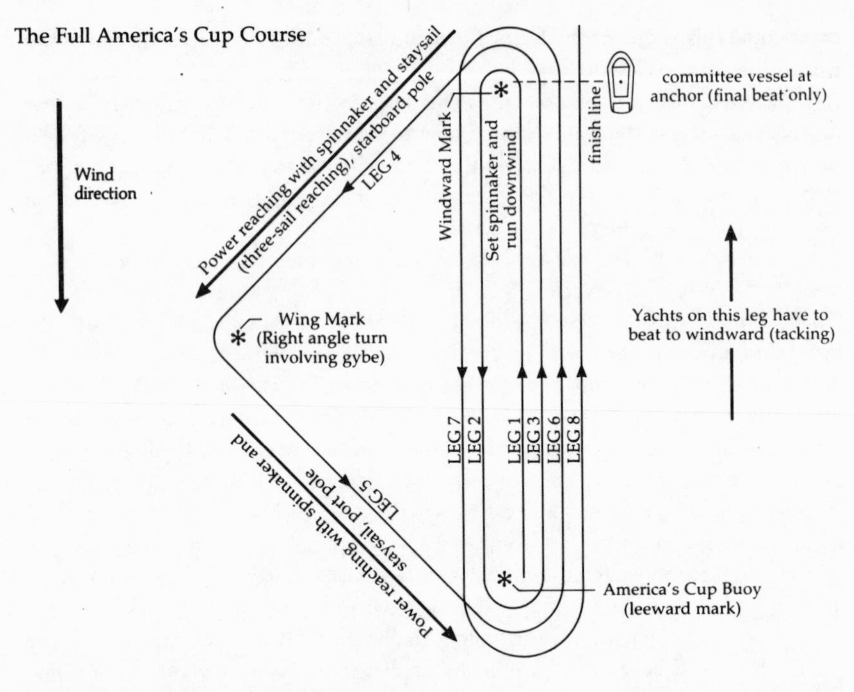

Usually Called	Leg No	Point of Sailing
Opening Beat	Leg 1	Beat to windward (upwind)
First Run	Leg 2	Run with the wind (downwind)
Second Beat	Leg 3	Beat
First Reach	Leg 4	Reach across the wind
Second Reach	Leg 5	Reach across the wind
Third Beat	Leg 6	Beat to windward
Final Run	Leg 7	Run downwind
Final Beat	Leg 8	Beat to windward

Note: If wind shifts a new windward mark may be laid, pivoting the course around the America's Cup buoy (leeward mark), thus:

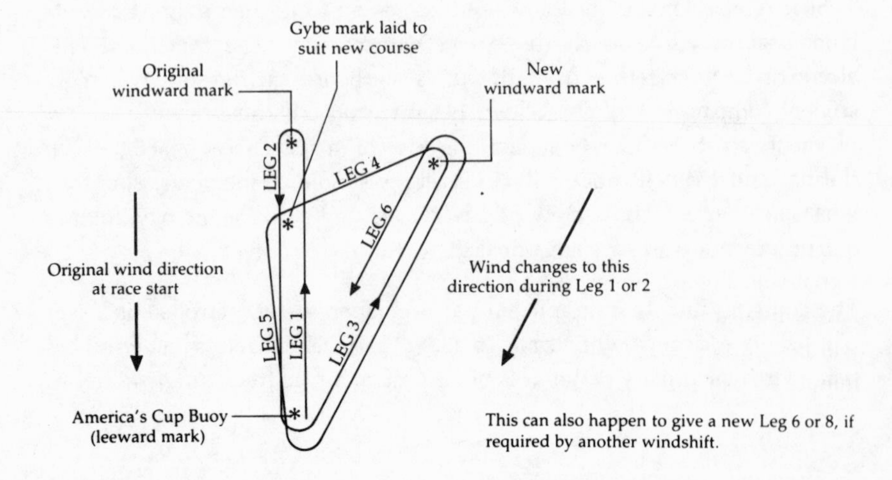

prize-fight ring. There are no marked-out lanes, no bends and banked curves, no hurdles, jumps or ditches. Its only physical, visible boundaries are three or four marker buoys and the race committee's own vessel, used to mark one end of the starting and finishing lines.

The positions of the buoys vary from day to day, depending upon the direction of the wind. Only one remains constant: the America's Cup Buoy itself, laid permanently to mark the pivotal centre of the course.

The starting line is laid hard by the America's Cup buoy, close to it and as near as possible at right angles to the wind's direction. It is marked at one end by the mast of the anchored committee vessel and at the other by a small, round orange marker buoy anchored about 400 yards away. There are no tapes, no white lines painted on the sea's surface, no red and green lights to mark the precise line for the competitors or tell them when they may start.

Instead, each skipper must judge for himself the distance of his boat from the imaginary line, knowing that he may not cross it until the starting signal is made, knowing too that in an ideal start he will cross it a bare split-second after that signal, and with his yacht already travelling at full speed. Since it can take up to two minutes to wind a stopped Twelve Metre up to her full speed mastering the time-and-distance judgement of the rolling start and the final run-in for the line is one of the crucial basic skills in the racing skipper's armoury.

In all, four signals are given to signal the start of the race. The first, the timing signal, is given at fifteen minutes to go, and the next, the warning signal, at ten minutes before the start. The fifteen-minute signal, a single cannon shot, is merely to warn the competitors that the racing sequence is being set in motion. It is the warning signal – the ten-minute gun as it is popularly known – which signals the start of the duel itself.

Strictly speaking, all starting and all race signals are made from the committee vessel by code flags, the guns themselves being merely to draw attention to the flag. It is just another of those arcane hang-overs from the days of Nelsonian naval signalling that go to make up the complex tradition of yacht racing, but it is a fine point and on board the Twelve Metre it is the navigator's job to know which signals to expect when, and to know what each flag or flag combination that may be used is intended to mean.

The preparatory signal is given exactly five minutes before the starting signal, and precise timing is crucial. Exactly five minutes later, the starting flag will fall from the signal yard of the committee boat and the race itself will be on. Between these two, one more signal is given, at precisely one minute to the start: no gun is used, but the one minute flag is hoisted to warn competitors that the final countdown is proceeding.

During the race, the yachts have to round seven marks in order, and then sail to the finish line. Hallowed by long tradition off Newport, the America's Cup course was altered slightly in Australia to make allowance for the differing geography of the racing area but the essential elements of the battle remain the same: a test of the sailing ability of yacht and crew directly into the wind, directly away from the wind, and back and forth across the wind's direction: in the sailor's language a beat, a run and two reaches.

The first mark of the course is laid directly upwind from the starting line, and at a distance of 3.25 nautical miles. The America's Cup buoy itself is the second mark of the course, that same 3.25 miles dead downwind of mark one. The third mark is again 3.25 miles dead upwind of the America's Cup buoy: so if the wind has not shifted during the opening part of the race the Twelve Metres will use the same mark as for their opening windward leg. If the wind has shifted, mark three will be a new buoy, specially laid while the race is actually in progress, and its direction from the America's Cup buoy, in degrees magnetic, will be signalled by code flags from the committee vessel to the Twelve Metres as they approach the America's Cup buoy.

Mark four is laid out to the left of the direct line between the America's Cup buoy and the windward mark, so that the three together lie on the points of a right-angle triangle, with the right-angle at Mark Four. Thus are formed the two reaching legs of the course, each lying at 135 degrees to the direction of the mean wind blowing over the course.

Once back at the America's Cup buoy, the Twelve Metres again turn to windward, racing up the next beat to Mark Six. Again, the race committee has the option of laying a new mark to cope with a windshift over the course area or of using the previous windward mark and, again, if a new windward leg has been set its direction will be indicated to the Twelve Metres by code flags from the committee vessel.

Back then to the America's Cup buoy for the last time, running dead downwind from the windward mark, before turning for the finish line and home, 3.25 miles away into the wind's eye. The finish line itself will be formed, in similar configuration to the start line, between the committee vessel and a marker buoy lying off its left-hand side so that the line is as near as possible at right-angles to the wind direction.

That, then, is the America's Cup race course: 24 miles of racing around a handful of nondescript markers on an otherwise featureless tract of sea. Each race takes – assuming the wind holds – just over three hours, and in the event of the wind failing a time-limit of six hours prevents competitors and spectators alike from having to sit out there all night.

With ten minutes to go to the start time, the warning signal is given and the yachts come under the yacht racing rules. Under the additional special regulations for the America's Cup – known as the Sailing Instructions – the two Twelve Metres are obliged to sail into the racing area by crossing the start line from the 'wrong' side, each yacht being assigned to a different end of the line to ensure that the pre-start manoeuvres, where the two helmsmen feint and parry, trying to place their yachts in the most advantageous position for the start itself, begin from as even a situation as possible.

You have to decide in the ten minute manoeuvring before the start what you want to do in the race itself, and this dictates wholly the sort of start you want to make and thus to some extent the tactics you employ during the manoevuring. If you want to go to the left-hand side of the course on the first beat – maybe you feel there is going to be a shift in the wind direction that will favour that side – then you need to start to the left of the other boat – if the line is equal.

On the other hand if there is a strong bias towards starting at the right-hand end of the line, but you want to go left after the start, then you have to decide that you'll take the advantage of the bias but you must start with enough of a gap between you and the boat (to leeward) so that you can go along with him, and not be forced to tack away.

Bias is caused either by the line not being laid at right angles to the wind direction, or by the wind shifting in direction after the line is laid. As the wind shifts the angle at which the yachts can cross the line alters, becoming more acute on one tack but more obtuse on the other – and it is advantageous both to cross the line on the favoured tack and at the end of the line which corresponds to that tack.

On an unbiased line, two yachts starting at opposite ends of the line on opposite tacks, each headed toward the other and sailing at the same speed, will meet half-way between the ends of the line and a distance directly upwind of it.

On a biased line, the yacht starting at the favoured end on the favoured tack will have the shorter distance to sail before crossing her opponent's line, and will cross ahead. In simple terms, if the wind shifts to the right after the line is properly laid, the right-hand end becomes favoured, and vice-versa.

The sailing yacht cannot sail directly into the wind's eye, only at an oblique angle to the direction from which the wind is blowing – and making that angle as small as possible is the great goal of designer, sailmaker and sailor alike. The ability of the yacht to sail as close as she can to the wind's direction is called her pointing ability, and the closer to the wind's direction she can sail, the higher she is said to be able to point.

There comes an angle when extra pointing ability – measured at this level of refinement in single degrees – can be had only at the expense of speed, and a fine judgement must be made as to the point where the extra distance gained to windward by pointing high is more than lost by the drop in speed, measured in tenths or even hundredths of a knot. The sailor chooses to sail 'low and fast' or 'high and slow'.

Low and fast and high and slow, provided the relative losses and gains cancel out, are legitimate options and races can be won by either boat if the distance each yacht covers directly toward the upwind mark (the Velocity Made Good, or Vmg) in any given time is roughly equal. High and fast is what everyone wants to be relative to the opponent: low and slow is bad news all round.

In a race between two yachts of the same design, each sailor would know that his yacht had much the same pointing ability and speed potential as his opponent, but in a race between yachts of even slightly differing design, such as the Twelve Metres, the yachts themselves will probably have differing characteristics – performance profiles, in the jargon – and these differences will crucially affect the way each skipper will elect to try and sail his race.

So through the start is linked the tactic of the race, bearing in mind the manoeuvrability of your boat, any difference in your performance profile from your competitor. For example if your boat sails lower and faster you may decide that you can't start to windward of the other boat – you must have the leeward berth.

If he knows that about you, he will fight for the leeward berth also, so as to start to leeward of you and thus be able to embarrass you immediately after the start by climbing up under your bow, giving you reflected air – the upwash of air from his own sails, which will interfere with the flow of air across your own sails, slowing you down and making you point even lower – and thus he can force you to tack away. If he can do that, you have immediately lost the initiative, lost ground on him and are already in trouble. Not too good.

If he wins the leeward berth from you, you may be forced to start either at the other end of the line or on the opposite tack from him, sailing away from him instead of in the same direction.

So you begin to permutate the endless possibilities: the oscillating breeze, the shifting breeze, the probability that your weather information is accurate, your judgement as you go up the track. So as you go through the sequence of manoeuvers at the start, manoeuvring against the other boat, being aware of the rules, using your crewing, your ability to stop and start the boat, position it, you are also thinking the tactic you want and what best fits it.

The intricate pre-start manoeuvres are a battle in their own right, and have a twofold purpose. The principal object is to come away from the line with an initial advantage over the opponent, and in this position and potential are more important than mere speed or even who crosses the line first. It is perfectly possible for a yacht to cross the line some seconds after her opponent but still have 'won' the start by virtue of being better placed to take advantage of anything from line bias to a major windshift – a point repeatedly made by their specialist advisors, such as John Bertrand and Cudmore himself, to the horse-racing-trained commentators inflicted upon the America's Cup in Fremantle by Australian television producers. It was a point missed just about as often as it had to be made.

A secondary object of the pre-start manoeuvring is to disadvantage the opponent, or even so confuse and discomfit him that he is forced into a rule-infringing error. Because of the high calibre of America's Cup sailors this aspect of the pre-start is less important in America's Cup than in lesser match racing events, but nonetheless it is one of which advantage can sometimes be taken, especially if a skipper knows that his opponent is potentially faster, so that merely starting equal is not going to be sufficient. If this is the case it is time to get what Cudmore euphemistically calls 'aggressive'.

The simplest ploy is to herd the opponent away from the line, keeping your own boat between him and the starting line until you are both so far away from it that neither can get back before the starting signal has long gone. If successful, the starting signal becomes irrelevant and the line itself merely a gate through which the two of you, already now racing upwind for the first mark, must pass.

The herding can be done in a number of ways, most of which require the herder to clamp his yacht on his opponent's tail. Then, every time the opponent tries to turn back towards the start line, the herder moves to baulk the turn. The trick is to ensure that the baulking is always legal.

Occasionally it will be possible to trap the opponent outside the approach line to one end or other of the line. If this can be done, the successful trapper can pick his own moment to come in on a sweeping approach, grazing past the committee vessel or the limit mark at the other end – known always as 'the pin' – and leaving the opponent no option but to follow dutifully along in his wake. Cudmore successfully did this in his classic last race against the swifter *Kiwi Magic*, but such obviously one-sided outcomes of the pre-start dance are rare.

As regards the pre-start manoevures themselves, there are text book gambits and replies, but because of the skill of the people involved in America's Cup now there are very few opportunities to play the sort of tricks one would do on a less skilled player, in the way in which Dennis Conner would have done ten years ago against the less skilled sailors who came from Europe or Australia in the late seventies and early eighties.

There are certain classic moves and counter-moves, but most boats now accept that they will probably hit the starting line in sync about the same time as the other boat. The fight is usually to be on the right- or left-hand side of the other boat, or for the bias of the line, or the right to go the way you want to go on the opening beat.

Probably the most important element of the pre-start tactic now is the ability to judge the other boat's performance. In this respect America's Cup is unlike say Congressional Cup or Royal Lymington Cup where you have boats of equal speed, performance and handling characteristics. In America's Cup you have to try and judge what the other boat's speed and performance is going to be.

For instance if you are more manoeuvrable but not as quick, you will opt to start near the opponent and force him to tack away. Then you have the initiative and can work the shifts to get ahead and keep him nailed down because you can tack quicker. If not you try and work the shifts and stay away from him to compensate for your lack of speed.

The start can be crucial, but more often it is neutral, and the two boats start even. With the skill of the present sailors and the fact that traditionally it is a 400-yard starting line (thus with plenty of room along it for two boats to cross without interfering with each other) you have a situation where it's really a boat speed race. If you have a quicker boat, that wins. It is only with equal boats that it becomes interesting.

CHAPTER TWELVE

Like chess – only more complicated

Yacht racing differs from all other forms of racing in one vital regard: the equal importance of position with speed. Motor races, horse races, downhill ski races, 100 metre sprints and Marathons are tests first and foremost of speed. Stamina, reliability, tactics and all other factors lie subservient to speed: ten out of ten dictionaries will define a race as 'a competitive trial of speed'.

In yacht racing, however, it is perfectly possible for a slower yacht to win a race against a faster yacht simply by continually being the better placed of the two in relation to the opponent, the next mark and most important of all the wind direction. Yet it is a fact that – simply because the wind cannot be seen by the eye nor captured by the television camera –all popular attempts to portray yacht racing have completely failed to capture or convey this equality of importance, treating it instead as some sort of arcane mystery too complex for the general public to understand. It seems no exaggeration to say that until a way is found to convey this importance, yacht racing can never become a popular or even interesting spectator sport, since such a large part of its very *raison d'ëtre* will be missed.

The importance of good positioning stems from the fundamental fact that sailing yachts can only sail at a given angle to the wind direction, rather than directly into it. Thus any destination that lies upwind of the yacht must be approached obliquely, by a series of zigs and zags which the yacht achieves by sailing close-hauled on one tack, then on the other. If the destination is directly upwind the length of the zigs will be the same as the length of the zags, but if the destination is displaced to one side or the other of the direct upward line the distance which must be sailed in the zig

Position

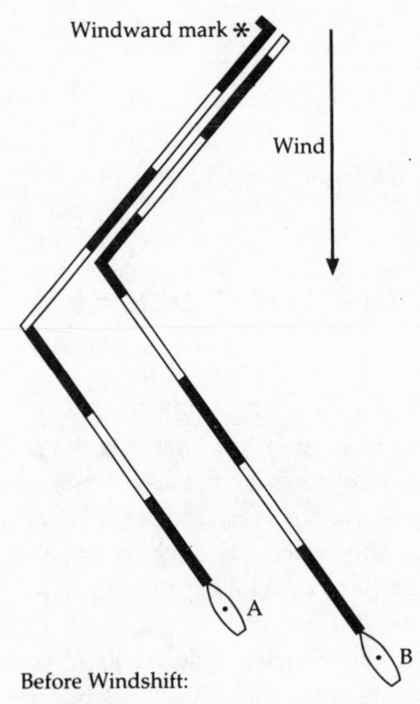

Before Windshift:

Sailing distance to mark for A is 6¾
Sailing distance to mark for B is 7¼
Therefore A is ahead of B

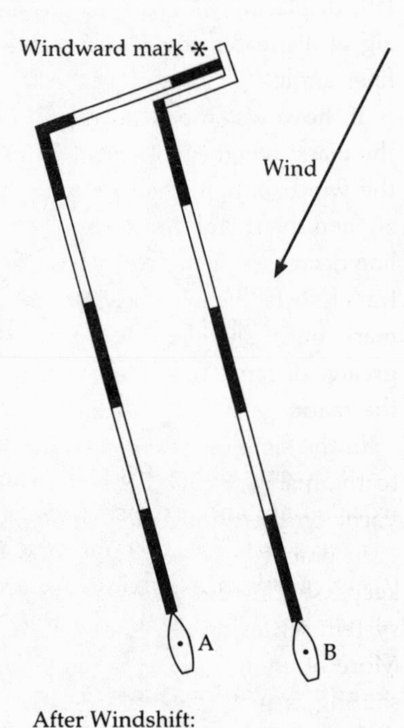

After Windshift:

Sailing distance to mark for A is 6½
Sailing distance to mark for B is 6
Now B is in front, although the two boats are still moving at same speed, and B cannot be said or seen to have 'passed' A

Yacht racing's unique ingredient: position. Being on the correct side of a windshift can take you from behind to in front – so a clever skipper can sometimes use his better knowledge of how the wind will shift to position his yacht. The better positioned skipper compensates for lack of speed by giving himself less distance to sail.

will be longer than the distance which must be sailed in the zag, or vice-versa.

If the wind direction remains the same during the time the yacht is zig-zagging its way towards the mark, it will not matter greatly which leg is sailed first, the zig or the zag: the total distance to be covered will be the same whether the yacht first zigs off left then zags back right, or whether she zags off right and zigs back left. The only difference will be in the angle of the zig and the zag to the direct line – called the rhumb-line –

between the yacht's starting position and the destination: a windshift to the left, displacing the mark to the right of the direct upwind line, will put the zig at a greater angle to the direction of the rhumb-line and the zag at a finer angle.

If, however, the wind direction changes again before the yacht reaches the mark, whether the yacht is on the zig or the zag matters a great deal. If the wind shifts further to the left, it will mean that the angle between the zig and the rhumb-line increases, while that between the zag and the rhumb-line decreases. If the yacht has already started up the zig, she now need not travel so far before she can turn on to the zag and head straight for the mark, but if she elected to go up the zag-leg first, she will have to travel a greater distance before she can turn on to the zig which will bring her into the mark.

In the simplest terms, a windshift to the left shortens the sailing distance to the mark for a yacht on the left of the rhumb-line, and increases it for a yacht on the right of the rhumb-line.

In practice, the wind rarely shifts only once, and for that matter rarely keeps shifting only in one direction. That can happen if a new weather system settles on the course during the race, bringing with it a new breeze. More often, however, the wind direction oscillates about a mean direction, shifting first a few degrees left, then swinging back to the mean, then shifting a few degrees right, then swinging back to the mean again. To anyone doing anything other than trying to put up a tent or sail a racing yacht to windward these small and periodic windshifts are barely noticeable, but in fact their pattern is well-documented and well understood by most meteorologists and some sailors.

The laws that govern the wind's behaviour are both complex and incompletely understood, so that predictions of the size and frequency of these shifts lies somewhere between being but an inexact science and a black art. It is an art, however, that sets the successful yacht race tactician apart from the unsuccessful tactician.

Each windshift alters the geometry of the yacht's zig-zag progress along the rhumb-line, serving first one side then the other of the rhumb line and making first the zig and then the zag the sailing direction which lies closest to the yacht's ultimate destination. By always taking the favoured line, by always being on the right zig or zag at the right time, by always being on the favoured side of each successive windshift, the skilfully positioned yacht can accomplish the trip between starting point and upwind mark in significantly less sailing distance than a yacht which either ignores the windshifts or which finds itself continually on the wrong side of them.

Lay-lines

The lay-line is the line along which the yacht needs to sail just to 'lay' the mark when beating to windward. This direction is determined by the position of the mark, the direction of the wind and by how close to the wind the yacht can sail: it may be different for each of the two yachts in the match race. Judging your yacht's lay-line is one of the most important skills of the helmsman or tactician. Once you have gone beyond the lay-line your only option is to tack for the mark and the extra distance you have sailed is wasted distance.

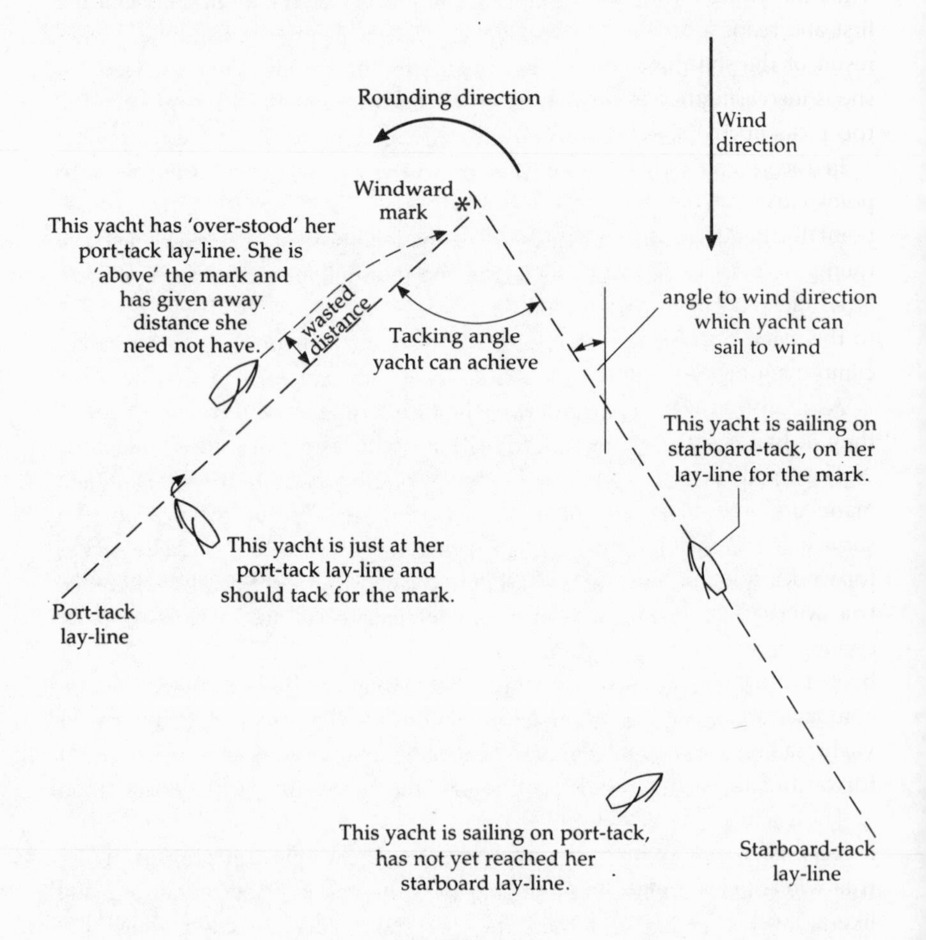

This 'playing the shifts' is half the art – quite literally – of upwind sailing and is the way in which a slower yacht can actually arrive at the upwind mark ahead of a faster but less well-navigated opponent.

Not only is position relative to the rhumb-line important; so too is position relative to the opponent. With the breeze shifting to the left, the yacht on the left of her opponent will be handed a number of advantages. If both yachts feel the effect of the windshift at the same time, the yacht on the left will have a shorter distance to sail to the mark than the yacht on the right, the advantage in distance being roughly equivalent to the lateral distance between the two yachts.

Most usually, however, a windshift moves across the course in a defined line, invisible to the eye but apparent as soon as it reaches and affects something in its path – such as a Twelve Metre sailing hard on the wind. Thus the yacht on the correct side of her opponent picks up the windshift first and reaps a double advantage: not only is she picking up distance as a result of the shift, but because her opponent is still sailing in the old wind, she is increasing her advantage with every yard she sails until the opponent too picks up the shift.

In the jargon of yacht racing, a wind shift which allows the yacht to point closer to the mark is called a lift, while a shift which forces her to point further away from the mark is called a header. As a simple rule of thumb, it pays to tack each time the wind heads, shifting over on to the lifted tack and gaining what benefit is to be had by sailing the better slant to the mark. Should the windshift be a lift, it generally pays to hold on, and climb even nearer the mark.

As if all that were not complicated enough, not all wind shifts are what they at first seem.

The wind the yacht feels blowing aross her deck and across her sails is made up of two components: the actual wind blowing across the sea's surface and the wind that is created merely as the result of the yacht's own forward motion. If the yacht could move forward without there being any true wind at all, the wind that would be felt on board would apparently be coming from dead ahead – as is the case with, say, a fast-travelling speed boat. In practice the wind felt on board, known as the apparent wind, is a combination of the forward-motion wind and the true wind and, for a yacht sailing close-hauled, it feels to come from somewhere just slightly forward of the real angle the true wind makes with the yacht.

The yacht's speed through the water, and thus the self-created wind that it feels, is of course directly related to the speed of the true wind. If the true wind speed begins to fall quickly the yacht, particularly a heavy yacht like a Twelve Metre, carries her momentum onward until her own speed falls in correspondence with the new true wind speed. For a brief time, she is travelling too fast for the wind she is experiencing. When that happens, the apparent wind felt on board briefly contains an unduly large component caused by the yacht's forward motion and it apparently moves forward – in other words it heads, and on board it feels as if the yacht has just sailed into a header. It is not a true heading shift, however, merely the temporary effect of a drop in the velocity of the true wind and it is known as a velocity header. The helmsman, assisted by the onboard instruments which read the direction of both the true and apparent wind, must be watchful for such an illusion, and not be tempted to tack on the deceptive velocity header, or he will lose even more speed as he finds himself tacking into a lull in the wind speed, without the former power in the breeze to help him accelerate out of the tack.

For a time after the start of the beat the yacht will not be able to point directly for the mark no matter which tack she sails on, but the further her zig or zag takes her away from the rhumb-line the nearer she will be to the point when all she has to do to sail directly towards the mark is go about and sail on the other tack and she will find herself pointing straight for the mark. That point is called the lay-line to the mark: literally the line along which the yacht can lay a close-hauled course that will just take her to the mark.

Lay-lines and rhumb lines

The rhumb line is simply the straight line between two marks

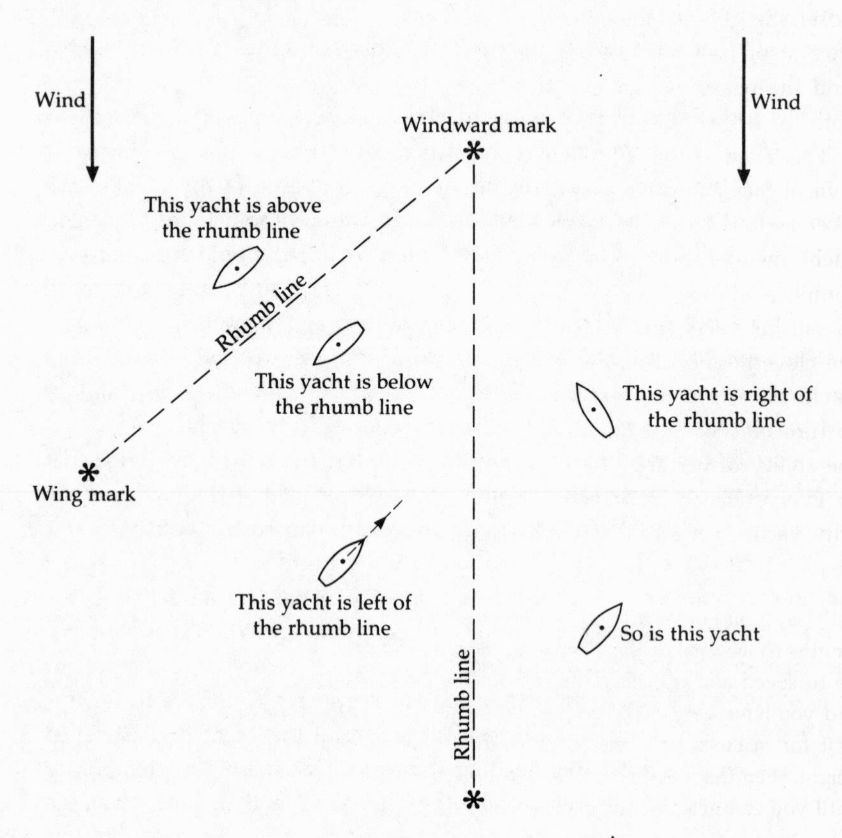

There are, of course, two lay-lines, one out to the right of the rhumb-line (the starboard-tack lay-line, along which the yacht can sail on starboard tack to arrive at – in the jargon, to fetch – the mark) and the port-tack lay-line, out to the left-hand side of the rhumb-line.

It can quickly be seen that the precise position of the lay-lines depends on several factors, the judgement of which is crucial to the tactics of sailing the upwind leg. The first is the direction of the wind, and it can just as quickly be seen that a shift in the wind direction will immediately alter the position of both the starboard-tack and port-tack lay-lines. The second is the pointing ability of the yacht: the closer the yacht can sail to the wind on each tack, the narrower will be the angle of her lay-lines radiating outwards from the mark.

It can also quickly be seen that the upwind area of 'the course' is thus in effect a narrowing cone, with its apex at the windward mark and its sides bounded by the two lay-lines. The nearer the yacht stays to the middle of that upwind arena, the greater the range of options she leaves open to herself to respond to wind shifts and the moves of her opponent. The closer she gets to one or other lay-line, the more her options reduce until, once at or past her lay-line, all she can do is tack and head for the mark. And the nearer she gets to the mark, the more the room for manoeuvre both for herself and for her opponent is reduced.

This, then, is the complex tactical battleground that is the upwind leg of a yacht race and the reason that positional play is as important to the yacht racer as it is to the chess player. There is much of the game of chess in yacht racing, and in match racing in particular. Add in to the already complicated mix the ingredients of boat-speed, the ability of the helmsman to sail his yacht quickly and cleanly through, round and over the waves, the cleverness of designer and sailmaker in producing a yacht that can sail as closely as possible to the wind's direction, the ability of the yacht herself to turn quickly through a tack without losing speed or slipping sideways, the ability of her crew to trim the sails to perfection, adjusting their shape to every nuance of the constantly changing breeze and we begin to see why yacht racing is such a fascinating sport.

Let's say you both come off the line together. You on the left and thus four boat lengths to leeward of the opponent. You start drag racing along, getting the boats up to speed and watching the opponent to assess how you're doing against him, and you have very quickly to indentify the relative performance of the boats.

If for instance you are going straight-line speed a bit quicker but with more height, then the judgement is can you get round his bow? So you just keep going until you can get around his bow, and then tack.

His normal response if he senses you will cross him would be to tack with you, leaving you up on his weather hip. He might sense a shift and tack off earlier, in which case you would immediately respond and go with him and then get into a tacking duel.

If he thinks your ability to cross him is marginal, then he may keep going and try to nail you down, because if you can't cross him you will have to tack underneath him again. With more speed on, he might be able to roll over you, or if he can't do that he would have you pinned under his bow and simply force you to sail out to and past the port-tack lay-line. Then all he has to do is tack on his own lay-line for the mark and that's that: there is no way you could get past him and he would arrive at the top mark first.

So to prevent that happening if you can't get across his bow and then tack and cover him, you tack under his bow and then you try to point higher, and squeeze up underneath him to give him an upwash effect off your own sails and so force him to tack off.

All this happens in the first fifteen minutes of the race, until the yachts reach the port-side lay-line. [With a tacking angle of 65 degrees and an upwind leg of 3.25 miles, the Twelve Metres have just two miles to sail until they reach the lay-line, sailing at between 8.2 and 8.5 knots.]

So what happens is you drag out from the starting line and within half a mile (in other words, just four minutes sailing time) you must make a decision. For the first half mile settle down, trim the boat, everything else: thereafter you have to match race.

If speed and height is even you track on until close to the lay-line, pick a shift and tack. The opponent will tack because he can't afford to get the other side of you. If that happens close to the lay-line you can tack back, force him out beyond the lay-line and close him out.

So he tacks under you when you tack. Now you both head towards the starboard lay-line. Sooner or later he will tack back and close with you, and eventually if you are still close together with no boat having a clear speed advantage you get into a tacking duel. Or you might get right across to the other lay-line, and get into your tacking duel there.

The tacking duel is beloved of the dramatists of Twelve Metre racing, and indeed a full-blooded one can be as enthralling for the spectators as it can be exhausting for the competitors.

The essential object of the tacking duel is for the boat ahead to cover the boat astern, by staying between it and the mark and by blanketing and disturbing the air reaching its sails. The object for the boat astern is to break through that cover, to get out into clear air and develop the speed to come back again, a little closer to the opponent – or to wear down the stamina of her opponent's crew so that they either break-off the tacking duel, leaving her to go off on her own and perhaps pick up a favourable wind shift or, better still, begin to fumble their own tacks, thus slowing down.

A tacking duel will only develop between two boats evenly matched in speed, or when the faster boat of an unevenly matched pair finds herself behind. If the faster boat is already ahead, there is nothing for her to gain and everything to lose by becoming involved in a tacking duel: provided she sails merely to keep in touch with her slower opponent, covering the possibility of the sort of unexpected change in the wind that can reverse a previously settled match, her clear air and superior speed will keep her out of trouble and there is no point risking a foul-up in repeated tacking which might spell disaster for her.

By definition, it takes two to make a tacking duel, as with the tango. The duel is initiated by the boat behind, but the duel only commences when the challenge is taken up by the boat ahead. If the boat ahead declines the gambit, there is no point in the boat behind throwing in unnecessary tacks which will serve merely to put her further behind.

Occasionally a situation will arise – as in fact happened between Dennis Conner's *Stars & Stripes* and Iain Murray's *Kookaburra* – where one boat will have a straight line speed superiority (in this case, *Stars & Stripes*) and the other will be more manoeuvrable and thus have an advantage in tacking. Should a duel develop between these two, the more manoeuvrable boat, quicker to turn and more eager to accelerate, can close up on and eventually get through the faster boat. Once ahead, she can use her better manoeuvrability and acceleration to harrass her opponent, keep her tightly covered and stay ahead on the upwind leg. If she is as fast or faster than her opponent downwind, she can then protect her lead and use the same covering tactics on the next beat and so on to the finish.

This is precisely what happened between *Stars & Stripes* and the New Zealand boat nicknamed *Kiwi Magic* in Race Three of the final of the Louis Vuitton Cup. It might have happened in the America's Cup also, except that Dennis Conner on all but one occasion repeatedly declined to be drawn by Murray into the duel. Conner being Conner, on the one occasion he did consent to a duel he won that, too.

The tacking duel has an especial place and fascination in Twelve Metre racing because of a design and handling peculiarity of the boat, the unique result of its size, its relative slowness in stays (through the tack itself, in other words) and its somewhat ponderous acceleration characteristics.

In smaller, lighter and more nimble boats the advantage in a tacking duel normally lies with the boat ahead. She sails always in clear air while the trailing boat sails into and suffers from disturbed air every time she crosses astern. In Twelve Metres there is a critical distance, anywhere between one and four boat lengths, where the positions are reversed and the advantage passes to the trailing boat.

Each time she crosses, the trailing boat finds herself being briefly lifted as she sails into the bent flow of air coming off the lead boat's sails just at the moment she sails into the smoothed water of the lead boat's wake. Properly exploited by a skilful Twelve Metre helmsman and sail trimmers, this phenomenon can be used to allow the boat to grab an extra few feet as she goes into her tack. Not many feet, perhaps ten or twelve. But six tacks gains sixty feet and sixty feet is one boat length, twelve tacks is two boat lengths and eighteen tacks is the three boat lengths she was behind.

There comes a point when the advantage can no longer be exploited because as she comes across on port tack the trailing boat must bear away to avoid her starboard-tack opponent by an amount greater than she can recover as she swoops across her stern, and although next time the pair tack she goes on to the right-of-way starboard tack, the port-tack opponent can still cross ahead. She can, however, use the phenomenon to close right up, at which point the lead boat slam-dunks her with a very close covering tack, blankets her completely and she slips back the crucial half-length.

If after the start you find that he is gaining you are on a hiding to nothing by simply sailing on to leeward of him, so you tack and hope you'll get close to him so that your bow is at his stern. So he lets you sail through with a slight lift on his backwind and he's allowing you an option to open up. On the other hand he might be sufficiently confident of his speed where he goes three or four boat lengths and tacks, hooking up on your hip to weather of you, just like he was on the other tack, and thus stays in the same wind. And just pounds you down.

Very often though what he will do is he will tack on you as you come through his wind shadow, forcing you to tack again and thus sending you off to the left again. Then what he will probably do is if he perceives that he is tacking at the same speed you are he will wait until he is up to speed and then he will tack and come back with you again.

So then you come back and you commence a tacking duel because you don't want to be pushed out of the left- or right-hand side of the course. One reason you do not want that to happen is that then you would have done two extra tacks to his tacks, and even with boats of equal speed a tack costs you between a quarter and half a boat length. The other reason is of course that you only want the two of you to get out to the lay-line when you are in front and can thus dictate the action.

If you find he sails a bit quicker but tacks slower than you do, then you've got some options, because every time you tack you're coming back at him. In those circumstances, the best he can do is slam-dunk you – and that's a good option. But he might not want with his superior speed to let you get to the top mark that close, particularly if he fears your higher speed on the next leg.

The slam-dunk is another Twelve Metre match racing manoeuvre beloved of the dramatists among us, albeit that not every commentator who uses the term knows precisely what it is supposed to mean. Indeed, the very term is not a sailing expression at all: it arrived in the America's Cup lexicon thanks to an American basketball writer who found himself suddenly sent by his newspaper to cover the yacht racing on a day, presumably, when the Harlem Globetrotters were out to lunch. Nonetheless it is an expression which graphically captures the aggressive finality of the manoeuvre it seeks to describe. The slam-dunk works as follows.

As the two boats come together to cross, the first relevant rule requires that the boat on starboard tack has right of way, so the port-tack boat must take avoiding action. The other rule that applies is that the starboard-tack boat must not take any action to baulk the other as she is keeping clear, and this prevents her tacking right in front of the port-tack boat.

Under the rules, a tack does not begin until the boat tacking is beyond head to wind. Up to head to wind she is luffing, but under the rules is still 'on a tack': in this case, on starboard tack and thus the other boat must still keep clear.

In practical terms the rules allow the starboard-tack yacht to sweep up head to wind while the port-tack boat is dipping her stern, but if she goes through the eye of the wind before the port-tack boat has set a track to clear her stern, she is breaking the rules.

The slam-dunk is particularly used in Twelve Metre racing because of yet another design peculiarity of the boat. In most boats as the bow is turned one way, the stern swings out the opposite way. Thus with the port-tack boat coming across to dip the starboard-tacker's stern if the starboard boat luffs too early the stern swings toward the port-tack boat, either forcing her to take further avoiding action or forcing a collision – both of which would be against the rules. Twelve Metres behave differently.

As long as the initial luff is not too pronounced, the turn in other words too violent, the whole boat lifts up to weather, tracking up on its keel rather than pivoting round it, and the stern actually lifts away from the port-tacker, opening the gap between the two boats rather than closing it.

The slam-dunk is used when the port-tack boat has got so close to the starboard-tack boat that only drastic, close and all-over cover, clamped on as tight as a saucepan lid, will keep the port-tacker at bay. If left too late, there is a chance that the trailing boat will break through to leeward of the leading boat as the latter gathers speed after completing her own tack. If that happens, and the trailing boat is the faster of the two boats, when she next comes back on starboard tack she will hold right of way and she will be close enough so that the lead boat, still on port tack, will be unable to cross ahead of her.

If the slam-dunk is timed correctly, the trailing boat cannot break through and, slowed by the turbulent air coming off the lead boat's sails, she slips back again. Then if she is not simply to fall further and further back she must tack to find clear air to sail in – and the tacking duel recommences.

When the tacking duel is sustained, the effect is for the two boats to stay locked in combat only a couple of lengths apart, and thus they arrive at the windward mark. Indeed, if the faster boat gets ahead but does not then break-off the duel and go on to sail her own race, the effect of her continued participation in the duel is to give the trailing boat an invisible tow to the windward mark, pulling her upwards every time the trailing boat sails into that convenient smooth wake and lifted air that the lead boat drags behind her.

In Fremantle it was noticeable that the Australian defenders, racing in their trials, used the tacking duel tactic a great deal more than did the challengers during their racing. This was possibly partly because the Australian boats were initially more evenly matched in terms of speed than were the more disparate challengers, but undoubtedly largely because the two principal and rival Australian defence syndicates had been allowed to enter two boats in the defender trials themselves.

When the two *Kookaburras* and the two *Australias* raced each other, they concentrated on crew battles and crew sharpening at the expense of boat speed and continually reached the first windward mark close together and this pattern continued even when an *Australia* raced a *Kookaburra*. The challengers, meanwhile, were a larger and more mixed bag, and seemed to be more intent on developing their individual boats. Before the America's Cup itself many Australian experts believed that their closer, tighter racing was going to produce a better match racing defence, but with hindsight it became plain that in spending so much time in tacking duels they had allowed themselves to be distracted from the principal thrust of their cause, which was to develop the fastest Twelve Metre.

CHAPTER THIRTEEN

And marched them down again

So you finally get to the top of the first windward leg and turn on to the run. If the boat behind is within a certain number of boat lengths – which will vary depending on the strength and direction of the wind, as well as on your own perception of your own strengths and weaknesses against the opponent, and in this case the important question is which of the two of you runs the faster – the boat ahead, assuming the wind to be true to the course, will gybe-set. The boat behind will either gybe-set or do a bear-away-set and then gybe over.

You gybe-set because what will tend to happen is that because you do not sail directly dead downwind (one, that's very slow; two, there is too much danger of doing a crash-gybe) you sail maybe twenty degrees up. If the boat ahead comes round the mark and does a bear-away set, that carries her high of the rhumb-line from the windward to the leeward mark and on to the outside of the course. Even if the following boat does a bear-away set also, she will naturally lie on the inside of the leading boat's track – and the inside is the vulnerable side. She will either begin to blanket the lead boat immediately, or if she does not do that she will blanket the lead boat when the lead boat gybes to come back on to course for the mark.

America's Cup courses are always laid so the marks are left to port. The yachts' final approach to the top mark is therefore on starboard tack and as she passes the mark she turns hard left, bearing away from the wind and setting course to go straight back downwind to the America's Cup buoy. The spinnaker will be set on the opposite side to the mainsail (for one thing, it cannot be made to work if set on the same side as the mainsail since that sail will blanket the flow of air into it, for another it is against the rules) and the crew have the choice of either simply bearing away and setting the kite, or first gybing.

The bear-away set is the slicker and easier of the two manoeuvres: the spinnaker pole can be set up on the starboard side while the yacht is still hard on the wind on her final approach to the buoy, and the hoist begun a few precious seconds earlier. In the gybe set, the yacht is gybed right around the windward mark, and the genoa must be shifted across before the pole can be raised. The latter is much the more complex manoeuvre, but its advantage is that it puts the yacht on the inside of the rhumb-line course to the leeward mark.

The inside position is vitally important, because under the rules if the two yachts are overlapped as they come into the final approach to the leeward mark – in other words if the trailing yacht manages even to get her bow level with the stern of the leading yacht and on the side that will be the inside of the turn – then the leading yacht must move over and give her room at the mark.

Running directly downwind is potentially the slowest point of sailing for the Twelve Metre. In effect, the yacht can merely bowl along like a piece of paper being blown by the breeze. For the sails to work aerodynamically, the air must flow not into them but across them. In light weather particularly, the difference in speed between sailing straight downwind and sailing obliquely across the wind is dramatic. As the wind increases in strength and the Twelve Metre begins to approach her theoretical maximum hull speed (the speed which the physical laws of hydrodynamics dictate she cannot exceed without being able to surf on the face of a wave, roughly equivalent to 1.4 times the square root of the waterline length in feet and for a Twelve Metre somewhere between ten and eleven knots) the difference is less marked and there is less advantage to be gained by reaching off, because the gain in speed does not match the extra distance which is covered.

The amount of aim-off that is used is called the gybing angle, which is the amount through which the Twelve Metre has to turn to get from her aim-off course on one side of the rhumb-line to the corresponding aim-off on the other side: a gybing angle of forty degrees, therefore, represents on aim-off of twenty degrees either side the rhumb-line.

Running downwind in the heaviest conditions you can gybe within a twenty degrees gybing angle – in other words sailing about ten degrees up from the straight downwind course, depending on the sea conditions as well. In light winds you might be gybing through eighty degrees – that would be down to Number Two Spinnaker conditions, perhaps. We rarely got down to Number One spinnakers because at Fremantle the race committee tended not to hold races in conditions much lighter than that, although in Newport a Number One spinnaker was quite often used and gybing angles could be as much as 120 degrees. Even gybing through eighty degrees is quite acute; you have to watch the other boat all the time.

Occasionally it would have been possible, with only a relatively small shift to the mean wind angle on the basic course line, to track almost straight to the bottom mark without gybing. Of course, any overall shift of more than ten degrees off the rhumb-line course is going to give a straight track to the mark, providing you can keep your air clear.

Positioning on the downwind legs is hardly less important than on the upwind legs. Just as the wind oscillates while the yachts are sailing upwind, so it continues as they go downwind, although because of the changes in apparent wind speed (the Twelve Metres' own speed through the water takes her away from the wind, and in a twelve-knot breeze a Twelve Metre sailing at eight knots will feel a breeze across her decks of only four, five or six knots, depending on how deeply downwind she is pointing) the changes are more difficult to detect. All the same, by monitoring these continuing windshifts and gybing in phase with them, the Twelve Metre can reduce the amount she wanders away from the rhumb-line and thus the extra distance she sails. Staying on the favoured gybe is no less important downwind than staying on the favoured tack while going upwind.

Apart from superior speed bestowed by differences of hull design, the tactical initiative downwind passes from the yacht ahead to the yacht behind. It is always easier to overtake going downwind than it is going up. The principal weapon at the disposal of the attacking yacht is again her wind shadow: the area of disturbed and turbulent air that spreads out downwind of her sails. In this case it is of course now in front of her rather than behind, so the trailing yacht will always try to sail so that her cone of disturbed air falls across the sails of the leading yacht, and the leading yacht must adjust her own tactics downwind to try always to keep clear of the yacht astern.

Going downwind there are any number of tactical options that open up. If the boat ahead, having protected the inside track by gybe-setting at the top mark, gybes back, the boat astern can try and roll over him to weather, or he can use his windshadow to let him get up to the other boat, dip inside and just park in to leeward of the lead boat's mainsail, establish the overlap and just wait for the mark to roll up.

In different conditions he might gybe across his stern and then reach out to one side and maybe be able to establish the overlap from there.

The defence of the lead boat is of course to keep gybing away from the trailing boat's wind shadow, but at the same time never letting the trailing boat get properly established on the inside of the course.

The techniques of steering downwind are similar to those of most racing boats. In the big winds and waves of Fremantle the Twelves behaved remarkably like dinghies. The basic technique is to steer straight down the wave face, trimming on the sails as the boat gathers speed down the wave front.

As the wave picks up the stern, you turn the bow to face straight down the wave. As the boat accelerates, you ooch the sails. As you go into the trough, you come up a little and sail her across the trough, then go down the next wave in the same way.

In lighter weather you mainly sail on speed. It doesn't pay to accelerate and decelerate, so if you get a slight lull you may lift a little to keep the speed on. The only time you would want to let your speed drop is if you get a settled drop in the wind strength. If the wind drops from, say, five knots to four knots true you might want to drop your speed from, say, 6.8 to 6.0. You might be prepared to decelerate to that extent.

You know the optimum speed of your boat in any given wind speed in two ways. First of all you get to know it in your mind, because you have the problem of wind sheer always to interpret, so its the weight of the wind rather than the windspeed at the top of the mast, but in *White Crusader* we also had a computer programme which threw up on a read-out display just below the speedo the speed we ought to be doing, a target boat speed as it were.

That speed is worked out by the on-board computer from the polar diagrams developed for the boat during all the months of sail testing and boat development, but even so it is still necessary to interpret that a bit in your mind to make due allowance for sea conditions and the like.

So you get to the first leeward mark. It is very hard to pass after this mark, because the boat ahead tracks around the mark and the boat even very close astern has to follow round in her wake. Then the second boat normally has to wait and settle down, waiting until she is clear of the residue of the quarter waves both boats have been generating coming down the run. If she tacked right at the mark, she would tack into her own quarter wave and have to pound through it.

So if the second boat can just hang in there for a little while it is better: if you are thirty seconds behind at the mark, you would try and hang in there for about a minute.

You tack when you get the chance, and he tacks himself, and is up on your weather hip and he's in a strong position.

Well, now that he's ahead of you once, the chances are that he's quicker than you. So then you track away for speed. If you don't tack quickly and you've got a slow boat, you've had it. It's all over unless something on his boat breaks, there is a dramatic change in the weather pattern which brings in a completely new wind or you get some other minor miracle which gets you back into the boat race.

On the other hand, if you have a quicker tacking boat you still have the option of fighting back. Then at least you get to the top mark close to him.

On the reach, you have your final chance to find a point of sailing on which you are faster. It is very hard to pass on a reach, but some boats were exceptional, like the Kiwis. *USA* was very quick on a reach but in general there were no significant place changes on the reaches.

The reach is an opportunity to produce any secret weapons in your sail armoury – although in an America's Cup summer not much stays secret for long if someone uses it and it is seen to work. The gennicker is an example.

Gennickers have been around for a long time, but they were very well developed by Tom Schnackenberg for *Australia III.* They are basically just an assymetrical spinnaker, longer on one luff than the other and cut so that they take up a shape best suited to close reaching. On a technicality they cannot be measured-in as spinnakers, because the rules require that spinnakers are symmetrical about their centreline, but they are measured-in to the boat's sail inventory as jibs. They work quite well but have a very limited use: they were all right close reaching but didn't work on a broad reach. They didn't seem to win many races, put it that way.

In fact, the gennicker possibly cost the New Zealanders one of their races against *Stars & Stripes* in the Louis Vuitton final. Trailing at the third mark, *Kiwi Magic* set a gennicker and, already shown to be a faster reaching boat than *Stars & Stripes* began to overhaul the American dramatically. A one minute twenty-one second deficit at the third mark was reduced to some seventeen seconds by the wing mark.

On the second reach, Conner defended firmly by sailing very high of the rhumb-line, taking *Kiwi Magic* deep into the triangle formed by the windmark mark, the wing mark and the leeward mark: so deep that the two boats had almost reached the direct windward-leeward axis of the course before Conner turned back downwind and headed for the leeward mark, running now very deep and almost square. The Kiwis bore away and their gennicker, so fast on the reach, set so badly on the run that they were forced to go for a spinnaker change. But they bungled the sail change, getting the two sails inextricably twisted and eventually had to lower both and sail the final quarter of a mile bare-headed. Conner pulled steadily away and was back to a lead of almost a full minute by the leeward mark.

What the reaches can do, however, is bring the boat astern up close to her opponent, and of course if the opponent makes a mistake – for example doesn't handle the shy-to-shy gybe at the wing mark well – allow her to get through. There were several instances in the racing where yachts astern got through their opponents at the gybe mark simply by better boat handling. The racing is a test of crewing skills as well as everything else.

Back at the leeward mark you have the same problem you had at the start of the second beat, but if you could stay in contact on the second beat you can do so again on this third beat.

The last run is the last chance to pass your opponent, so you can fight that out, get back up to him and go for the crucial inside overlap at the bottom mark. If you haven't passed him by then . . .

Sailing the boat that has the advantage – say like *Stars & Stripes* where you have a speed advantage but perhaps do not manoeuvre too well – the most important thing to do is break the line simultaneously with the other boat even if on the opposite tack, then as you sail out you can tack back to meet him, but only on a good heading so that you make the first crossing ahead of him.

As you approach him you make the decision: do you slam-dunk, or will you cross ahead of him and then tack and go up on his hip? If you decide to cross ahead and then tack, you time your tack depending on the heading: you might sail on for thirty seconds and tack if you feel you are in a lift. If you're in the lift, he's in the corresponding header and if he tacks back again he'll be slightly further behind you. If after you have tacked you are both in the lift, then you sail on and work out from him, either gaining height or moving ahead depending on just where your speed advantage lies.

But if after the tack you are both headed, then he tacks and comes back and he will be in the lift and will be closer to you. If he is working the shifts well and is timing his tacks to coincide with the oscillations, you don't have to get too many of those wrong or you are in trouble yourself, even in a quicker boat.

But because you have the confidence in your superior speed you sail conservatively, you don't have to mix it too closely. As he comes back to you on a good shift, you can tack safely undeneath him without going on to force the crossing situation and perhaps precipitate a tacking duel, which you don't want. You tack safely underneath him and now you will both be on the same lifting slant. Your speed will stop him gaining any more and when you tack again on the next header you will be on the inside of the subsequent lift and you are back up on his weather hip.

It is very easy to look very clever if you're in the quicker boat.

On the runs, you keep your air clear and hope he doesn't catch right up to you. If he does you have to work very hard to protect the inside overlap and as long as you lead round the third mark, you should be safe enough.

If he has got ahead of you at the turn, you must try and break through his cover. As soon as you've done that, your superior upwind speed should get the race back for you.

*

Ultimately, when everything is working in a Twelve Metre the racing becomes very stylised and, frankly, it becomes not very interesting to the general spectator. That's a problem from the popularity point of view of the sport and it will always be so in its present form, because the decisions have been 'pre-made' by the designers, by the sailmakers, by everyone else.

For instance, in many ways the actual racing between *Stars & Stripes* and *Kookaburra* in the actual America's Cup itself was almost irrelevant. *Stars & Stripes* was just quicker in all conditions and on all points of sailing, period. *Kookaburra* was just a second-level boat, like ourselves. It would have been much more interesting to watch *Kookaburra* race *White Crusader* – and this is why the present framework of the challenger and defender trial racing is so important. The most interesting racing – both to watch and I suppose to take part in – in Fremantle was the Louis Vuitton round robin racing, with next the earlier defender racing, although that was sometimes more like watching gang warfare than yacht racing.

Against the Kiwis, *Stars & Stripes* was quicker but she would tack slower and she was probably a bit slower downwind – in some conditions at least – therefore they had to be more careful.

For instance the day the Kiwis got ahead, first when *Stars & Stripes*' spinnaker fell down, letting the Kiwis get back at them, and then the Kiwis very fine edge of speed downwind allied to an error on *Stars & Stripes* part allowed them to gain the inside overlap and get in front at the bottom mark and they stayed ahead through 113 tacks. The Kiwis won that day because even though they were slower they were more manoeuvrable, were allowed to get ahead essentially by the faster boat making a mistake and, because they could tack quicker, they stayed ahead. *Stars & Stripes* tried to use her superior speed to break through but didn't have enough space to do it. The Kiwis sailed a very good race, held her off and won. It was a classic case where the only answer for the slower boat was to get ahead, which they did.

The result of course was that Conner realised he could not allow himself ever again to be trapped by the Kiwis, so at the subsequent starts he always stayed away from them. If they allowed him the leeward berth, he would just track away from them and sail round them, if they forced him to go to the right – as in the last race of the Louis Vuitton final – he just went off, picked up a shift, came back and was in front anyway.

The racing itself often isn't that attractive – what is attractive is the getting there. It's a bit like motor racing: a lot of motor races are rather boring. Just a few cars following each other round a track: once you're used to the high speed (which of course is not really very dramatically displayed by television) it's very boring unless something goes wrong – then it gets interesting again, like *Stars & Stripes* suddenly blowing out her genoa at the end of the third beat in the Louis Vuitton final.

What is really interesting in motor racing is the getting there and the organisation and how the teams position themselves against their competitors. It's a very complex sport – and there are strong comparisons to be drawn between it and yacht racing at the Louis Vuitton/America's Cup level. Yacht racing is only now developing a public profile: in some ways it is more sophisticated than motor racing: the actual sport – the designing, testing, sailing of the boats, the problems that the yacht race itself presents – is actually more complex, but in most ways the sport is not as sophisticated, particularly at the commercial and management level.

But the sailing of the Twelve Metres themselves, is richly rewarding. Probably of all sporting contests, yacht racing is the most complex. I certainly cannot think of any other contest that has quite so many variables that must each be individually mastered. It involves design, construction, tuning, physical effort, teamwork, individual excellence, athleticism, intellectual ability, psychology.

And in yacht racing, the racing of Twelve Metres for the America's Cup is the contest that requires the greatest and most committed input from every element of the equation. Only when you get everything right can you hope to win.

CHAPTER FOURTEEN

The time has come, the walrus said . . .

On Sunday, October 5th, 1986 the time for guessing finally ran out for the White Crusade, and the first real racing for the 1987 America's Cup began. The Louis Vuitton Cup regatta was the elimination series for the thirteen prospective challengers and was organised in a manner expressly designed 'to help the improving boat'. The *White Crusader* team set great store on their being 'the improving boat' around which the series had been designed.

There were to be three round robin heats, a semi-final and a final. In a round robin heat, racing is arranged to allow each boat to meet each other boat once in a single win-or-lose race, so that in a field of thirteen challengers, *White Crusader* would face twelve races, one each day, against a different opponent. For the first heat, there would be one point for a win and none for a loss; for the second, five points for a win; and in the third twelve points for a win. The top four boats on accumulated points would go into the semi-final and start again with zeroed score cards.

Many, including Britain's Chris Law, went on record with the thought that the first round robin would thus 'not really matter' and indeed this was probably the organisers' intention: with only a point per race at stake, losing a few early races should not have mattered. Ironically, when it came to getting into the semi-final and the chance to start afresh, single points – and especially the five-point units of the second round robin – were to matter a great deal.

White Crusader's first race was against one of the four American contenders: *USA*, the weirdest yacht ever to try for a place in the America's Cup. Such was the secrecy surrounding her that on that light October Sunday morning, with the Antipodean winter turning to Spring, none of her opponents had the faintest idea what she really looked like under water and rumours were rife.

USA, in fact, looked like no boat on earth. She had a recognisable Twelve Metre canoe body, complete with that pregnant whale look that all modern Twelves have, but instead of even an upside down winged keel, which would have surprised no one, she had no keel at all. Instead she had a slim vertical strut with suspended at its lower end a torpedo-shape lead bulb, already unflatteringly christened by her designers 'the Geek'.

Her rudder, right at the aft end of the waterline, was unusually deep and straight-sided but, most curious of all, she had a second rudder, a match of the one at the back, at the front – right at the forward end of the waterline. She was a Twelve Metre version of Long Gone John and his shoes with the:

heels on the front
and heels on behind
so's you couldn't tell which
way Long John gwined.

USA's unconventional appearance was reflected in her performance: she was not just an unknown quantity, she was an unknown quality. If her looks were so radically different, what was her 'performance profile' going to be? Racing her was going to be like racing no other Twelve Metre.

It was one of those days that started badly and got worse, and aboard *White Crusader* Cudmore fought a day-long battle with gremlins: gremlins who seemed determined to drive home the message 'you guys should have been out here and racing a year ago'. Fifteen minutes before the scheduled start time, as *White Crusader* wound-up her preliminary sail evaluating, a number three genoa split. During the pre-start manoeuvring, a runner winch spun uselessly out of control, its pawls clogged by an over-enthusiastic application of grease and then, just before the start itself, the rudder jammed and until it could be freed Cudmore had to steer *White Crusader* using only the trim tab, the slim rudder-like flap on the trailing edge of the keel and normally only used for fine tuning the handling of the Twelve.

The pre-start manoeuvres themselves were inconclusive. With all his problems Cudmore avoided the sort of in-fighting that goes on in match racing in smaller, more manoeuvrable and less exhausting boats and concentrated on getting cleanly off the line. The flamboyant, motor racing extrovert Tom Blackaller, with whom incidentally Cudmore is a great personal friend, did the same, not least because the handling characteristics of his strange craft were idiosyncratic, to say the least. As far as the British, and indeed most of the Challengers, were concerned the principal object of this series was to work the boats up for the races to come, rather than simply win one-point-a-time races for the sake of it.

Up the first beat, Cudmore worked *White Crusader* steadily out ahead of the curious Twelve, the British boat pointing as high as the American, footing as fast and making noticeably less leeway. She was a good half-minute in the lead, two-thirds the way toward the first mark, when the boom crashed on to the deck and the mainsail began to slide uncontrollably down the mast: the masthead lock on the main halyard had failed.

Instinctively, Law at the helm laid the boat off the wind by five degrees to keep speed on and the trimmers eased the genoa to give more power while Stanbridge, Haynes, Mason and the others set about repairing the damage.

With the halyard still attached to the sail there was no need for Stanbridge to go to the masthead, but even so it took almost four minutes before the mainsail was again properly re-hoisted and set. All the time, Blackaller and *USA* closed the gap relentlessly. There was nothing Cudmore could do to defend: he could only leave Law to nurse the boat along, wait for the sail to go back up and for the lads to sort out the wreckage. *USA* powered past and *White Crusader*, going again at last, went round the first mark thirteen seconds astern.

Clearly, there was no problem with upwind speed as long as the boat held together. The boat holding together was going to become quite a problem, although nobody knew it then.

On the run, *White Crusader*'s crew continued to tidy up the mess while Cudmore concentrated on holding on to Blackaller a bare two or three boat lengths away, but *White Crusader* rounded the leeward mark still thirteen seconds behind.

Now the afternoon sea breeze was starting to fill in, and the white British boat put her shoulder firmly into the task of taking her crew upwind. With every tack and with every windshift, Cudmore began to pick off the yards to Blackaller's transom. Half way up the beat *White Crusader* powered through the American boat's lee and, coming back on starboard, crossed ahead.

With clear air and the upper hand, Cudmore took control of the beat and *White Crusader* drew steadily away to lead by five clear lengths at the windward mark again.

Up went the pole, Law swung the wheel and the boat laid off on to the reach with the spinnaker already snaking towards the hounds. With a crack it opened, blossomed and filled and Cudmore turned to watch and see how the American would fare. To his dismay, he saw the cream-coloured Yankee boat pick up a wave, surf and settle again, perceptibly closer. Again it happened, and again. There was no doubt – the US boat was gaining, and gaining fast. Something was clearly radically wrong.

There is little on the reaching leg that the leading skipper can do to defend against an opponent in a faster boat. He can sail high of the rhumb line, preventing the opponent from getting up to windward and stealing his air, but apart from that this is a pure test of speed. The problem with going high is that sooner or later you have to come down again, and that means slowing down: you only go as high as is necessary to defend against the opponent, in other words as high as the opponent dictates, and Blackaller elected to stay low. He sensed already that his boat had the legs on the British Twelve.

By the wing mark, Blackaller had caught up all of his seventeen seconds and established an overlap to leeward of *White Crusader*, poking his bow in under the British stern in the crucial final approach to the buoy and claiming the right to take the inside route at the turn, a move that inevitably puts the inside boat ahead as the two come out of the turn.

Down the next reach Cudmore grimly tried to hold on to Blackaller's funny machine, but it was a painful process. Racing sailors have a saying: 'he's hurting us'. It is apposite.

The two big yachts, separated by maybe sixty or eighty feet, race along together, their white wakes sizzling past the cockpit and the steady roar of the quarter wave drumming in the helsman's ear. Aboard each, there is only silence as the two crews concentrate on the last tenth-of-a-knot of speed and the tacticians watch for the results of their crews' endeavours.

Both yachts are sailing at maybe nine or ten knots. Even between radically different Twelve Metres hull speeds are unlikely to vary by more than 0.1 or 0.2 knots, in other words a factor of a few per cent. Yet a few per cent is all that is needed: over the three-and-a-half hours of the full America's Cup race, a difference of less than 1% in upwind speed or 2% in downwind speed will translate into a sixty second lead at the finish. Sixty seconds may not sound much, but the barren waste of water that lies between the trailing boat and the line and which she must sail alone in those sixty seconds will be the farthest she has sailed that day. A one minute loss is the same as a crushing defeat.

For fifteen minutes the two Twelves will hang together, racing along in formation. Imperceptibly, with a slower rate of advance than the hands of a grandfather clock, the distance between the lead boat's stern and the trailing boat's bow begins to increase. After five minutes the lead boat has opened out another fifty feet, less than a boat's length; after another five, the distance has opened out a further fifty feet. From the trailing boat the slow, inexorable advance of the opponent's lead is like watching your own slow death. It hurts all right.

Little is said on board: the trimmers gaze fixedly at the spinnaker's curling edge, constantly easing and bringing on the sheet to keep the sail poised on a knife-edge of balance. With the sheet on too hard, the bellying balloon of the spinnaker is pulled out of shape and not presented to the fast-flowing air at best advantage. With the sheet eased too much, the sail is allowed to belly too freely; it swings imperceptibly round towards the bow of the boat – too far forward and into the wind – and its leading edge, the luff, starts to curl in temperamental warning. If the trimmer ignores the warning, the curl on the luff suddenly falls inwards on itself, collapsing the sail in an angry welter of flogging nylon. Then the sheet must be hauled hard, to pull the whole sail flat, recapture the air and start again, while the sail itself crackles and flogs, shaking like a flag.

The flogging spinnaker throws turbulent air into the back of the mainsail and shakes the slender mast like a willow wand. The mast crashes and bangs and the whole boat shakes; as the weight comes out of the spinnaker she swings upright, then as the weight comes back on she heels again, throwing the helm out of balance and making the helmsman fight for control. Up forward the spinnaker pole crashes against the forestay as the weight first comes off and then is flung back on to the guy. Lazy sheets and guys – no soft ropes, but hard slicing wires – snake and writhe and crewmen keep their heads down. A swipe from such a flailing line is like being hit by the branch of a falling tree.

USA pulled out a full fifty yards on *White Crusader*, giving Blackaller a lead of ten seconds at the bottom turn. He rounded neatly and *White Crusader* followed in the American boat's wake. Cudmore sailed the necessary 300 yards or so to clear the disturbed water of the two yachts' wakes and flung around on to port. *USA* tacked straight away to cover. Now it was Cudmore's turn to hurt Blackaller, and slowly, remorselessly, he began to grind back the fifty yard deficit. Again *White Crusader* crossed *USA*, forged steadily ahead and was forty-two seconds up at the windward mark.

It should have been more than enough. By the time the struggling American had reached the mark, Cudmore in *White Crusader* was round, had gybe-set and quickly settled down and was nearly 300 yards in front, well clear of Blackaller's dirty air.

But the race was far from over. Downwind, *USA*'s radical underwater configuration really came into its own. The odd-ball Geek keel was no longer, as it was upwind, constantly giving away precious yards by losing its grip on the water, while viewed from ahead its pencil-slim profile and the knife edge of the rudder foils presented much less drag than the conventional underbody of *White Crusader.* With the full-blowing Fremantle Doctor well established, the cream-coloured American boat fairly flew downwind and surfed easily past the despairing Brits.

Then disaster struck for the Americans. As Blackaller wound the wheel to start his 150 degree turn around the leeward mark, the complex hydraulic linkage to his forward rudder failed, the rudder slammed hard across and *USA* spun wildly out of control. In a match race, disaster for one is fortune for the other and with gleeful relief Cudmore grabbed the plate-presented opportunity with both hands. As the spinnaker landed neatly and safely on deck Law calmly steered *White Crusader* around the outside of the feverishly working Americans and hardened on to the wind for the final beat.

Blackaller's men had their problem quickly under control and *USA* swept round the mark in *White Crusader*'s wake, and the two set off up the beat. For Cudmore it was essential to keep Blackaller tightly covered, and the crews sweated through thirty-three punishing quick-fire tacks as *USA* tried to break free. She could not do it. Clearly in trouble against the Geek downwind, Ian Howlett's design was a match for her upwind, and the British crossed the finish line eleven seconds ahead of the Americans. What was all that about round one races not really mattering? It was, in truth, a hard earned point.

'If they're all going to be as hard to win as that,' remarked Cudmore in the crew room that evening as they stripped off their sweat-drenched, salt-stained clothing, 'they can keep their bloody Cup!'

The next afternoon was altogether the sort the British had hoped for in their planning sessions. *Canada II* was no slouch, and indeed was touted by several, including Conner, as a good bet for the semi-final. She had shown excellent speed against her trial horse, *True North,* during the very public blood-letting between the two Canadian syndicates before they had merged into one, and done well in the previous February's world championship.

In a convincing text-book job Cudmore and *White Crusader* summarily despatched her. Cudmore won the start, Law steered flawlessly and *White Crusader* showed enough upwind speed to lead comfortably at the first windward mark.

Rather less comfortingly, *Canada II* showed herself, like *USA,* to be quicker than *White Crusader* downwind. Although she never managed to pass the British boat she either held on to her or even gained on every downwind leg.

America II was a different proposition. The champions of the New York Yacht Club, her squad had been practising off Fremantle longer than anyone, including all the Australian defenders except Bond. Their boat was rumoured to be fast, their skipper John Kolius had in '83 scared Dennis Conner rigid while racing him with the old wonderhorse *Courageous*, their crew work was practised and slick and their budget looked to be second only to that of the National Aeronautics and Space Administration itself.

Cudmore once again won the start but when Law took over to take *White Crusader* up the first beat it soon became apparent that yesterday's comfortable edge was not going to apply across the whole Challenger board. *America II* was every bit as fast as *White Crusader*. The two boats came at each other again and again, separated only by yards as they crossed and counter-crossed; as each skipper tried to find a tactical handle on the other. Cudmore kept control of the important right-hand side of the course, thus always holding the right-of-way starboard tack as the two yachts tried for advantage no less than thirty-two times up that first beat.

As they neared the top mark, *White Crusader* was still to the right of the pair, *America II* to the left and the two boats were each on their own side of the rhumb-line, on opposite tacks. Kolius in *America II* was first to reach his layline, and as he tacked on to port to try for the mark, Cudmore called *White Crusader* into a tack. Law obeyed and the British boat swung around on to starboard just below her own layline and came back to attack the American one more time.

So high do Twelve Metres point compared to other yachts, so efficiently do they go upwind that laylines are notoriously difficult to judge, even with computer-assisted instrumentation. It is possible that Cudmore thought *White Crusader* might just squeeze up to the buoy, but what he really wanted to do was nail Kolius down on the wrong side of the approach line. With *White Crusader* on starboard Cudmore held right-of-way as the two boats came together, and it was up to Kolius to judge whether he could cross the British bow or whether he should take avoiding action.

If Kolius had to tack he would be under Cudmore's lee bow, unable to tack back again until Cudmore tacked: all Cudmore would have to do was have Law sail *White Crusader* to a comfortable approach angle to the mark, tack, and *America II* would have no option but to wait until the British had turned for the mark and then dutifully follow around. If Kolius bore away to take the British stern, Cudmore could have slam-dunked slap on top of him, nailing the Americans down on the other side and taking them over to the right-hand layline before turning for the buoy. Either way *America II* would have been firmly behind *White Crusader* at the mark.

Kolius did neither of those two things. He was by now the most experienced Twelve Metre skipper in Fremantle with the exception of Conner himself and he and his afterguard had been sailing *America II* for so long that they knew to within an inch what she could achieve. With stony stare the soft-spoken, blue-eyed Texan – the complete gunfighter model even down to the bushy, droopy moustache – laid his Twelve Metre across the advancing British course and *America II* slid across *White Crusader*'s bow with barely feet to spare. It was an ice-cool move, and the clinical detachment with which it had been executed showed both Law and Cudmore just what they were going to be up against in the weeks to come.

It was, Cudmore later admitted, a tactical error on his part. What he should have done was sail on to his own layline and tack. Then he would have been approaching the mark on starboard. With *White Crusader* already fetching the mark, there would have been no point in Kolius crossing ahead and carrying on, since to do so would have taken him beyond the layline to the mark. He would have been forced to tack just as he met the British boat. If he had tacked early, he would have had to squeeze for the mark and slow down, in which case *White Crusader* would have rolled past to windward, slowing him even further. If he had crossed *White Crusader* and tacked, Law would have been able to drive *White Crusader* off for the mark and take the inside berth at the turn.

Of course it is always easier to win boat races afterwards. People who win boat races at the time, when in the heat of battle there is no time to sit and plan the move carefully, are the people who make more correct instinctive judgements than do their opponents. All the same, the cost of missing the baptism of fire that had been the world championships, not to mention the 1983 America's Cup, was already beginning to show.

Now *America II* began to slide away from the British on the run, to lead by forty-three seconds at the bottom turn, and this became the pattern for the race. Cudmore could hold the American boat upwind, but there was clearly something desperately wrong going downhill.

If there was any doubt the next day's race against Dennis Conner removed it entirely. Yet again Cudmore won the start, but half way up the first beat the quickly freshening breeze required both boats to change headsails. The British crew ran into trouble with theirs, had to re-reave the sheet and in the few minutes that it took to sort the problem Cudmore, tactically paralysed, had to let Conner slip away and into a favoured slant of breeze.

When next they crossed Conner was ahead and immediately locked *White Crusader* in a tight cover. Again, *White Crusader* lost more ground downwind than she did going up and when Conner won by ninety seconds everyone in the White Horse compound knew that something dramatic had to be done with the downwind speed.

Nowhere was the message more keenly delivered than in the sail loft, where Angus Melrose had been overseeing design. Melrose had made a considerable reputation for himself during the Victory campaign and come out of that regarded as one of the best Twelve Metre sail designers in the world. Certainly, his fore-and-aft sails were good, but the spinnakers were just plain wrong: too small and the wrong shape. Ken Rose of Banks Sails, and an acknowledged master of the spinnaker was called in to assist.

The first round of racing finished with *White Crusader* 'in good shape' as the Cudmore public stance put it. After losing to Conner, she had gone on to win against all her other opponents except New Zealand, which surprised no one, and *Italia*, which surprised everyone.

The *Italia* match was the last of the round and was sailed in light weather, with *White Crusader* struggling for an edge upwind and still out-run on the downhill legs. Law had to come back to England in the interval between races and was indeed flying home that day, so Eddie Warden Owen took the wheel. Coming in to the bottom mark with the Italians having overtaken on the run, Cudmore was desperate for the inside berth so as to start the beat with the advantage and told Owen to go for the overlap. Owen went and took the inside at the turn, but the Italians protested that *White Crusader* had not established her overlap in time. The British won the race on the water, but later – to the aforementioned surprise of virtually everyone including, it was said, the Italians – found themselves thrown out in the protest room.

The loss dropped *White Crusader* from nine points for nine wins to eight points for eight wins, and left them equal fourth with *USA*.

Round Robin Two began well enough, with wins in quick succession against *Azzurra*, *Italia*, and *Canada II*, and then came a narrow loss against *America II*. The American boat was herself beginning to show signs of disappointing but was being kept alive by her crew work. She started the round robins as probably the best prepared and best raced boat of the whole Challenger camp, but she had little more left to give in the way of improvement while boats like *Stars & Stripes* and especially *USA* were able to make dramatic improvements. *White Crusader* also improved, but either she began too far down, or did not improve enough, and she was overtaken by some of the others.

USA was the real thorn in *White Crusader*'s side. The day after the loss against *America II* Cudmore came up against the radical American again. This time *White Crusader* was able to give him a real and positive edge. The breeze on the first beat was already piping at a good eighteen to twenty knots – the sort of day that would have brought worried frowns to the Newport race officers, but which in Fremantle was merely considered a good sailing day – and *White Crusader* reached the first mark over half-a-minute ahead.

Calling by the book, Cudmore gybe-set at the windward mark to protect the inside of the course and took *White Crusader* left. The British Twelve was well clear of the mark by about 150 yards as Blackaller followed round, but instead of gybe-setting and coming over to attack *White Crusader*, Blackaller took *USA* wide and set his spinnaker as he bore away, moving fast out to the right. Even though he held the inside of the course, Cudmore could not afford to let Blackaller diverge by too much and ordered a gybe aboard *White Crusader* so as to run parallel to the American.

White Crusader gybed fast, maybe too fast, and as the boom swung across hard the pulley block that takes the permanent backstay exploded under the shock load and the backstay – the wire which goes from the very stern of the boat to the tip of the mast and the only support that the top of the slender spar has – went slack, allowing the top of the mast to flick forward.

Accidents on boats, from aircraft carriers running aground to Twelve Metres breaking their masts, are almost always the result of a concurrence of tiny incidents giving a domino effect that ends in disaster. In this instance what happened was that the block came to bits, the backstay went suddenly slack and the mast tip flicked forward; it should have then been held by a preventer strop attached to the bottom of the backstay – but that failed too, and even more backstay ran out, leaving the mast tip completely unsupported.

Even so, the mast should have been stayed lower down by one of the two running backstays, but in the gybe, the working one, the port side runner, had been let go and the new runner, the starboard one, was still being wound on and the consequent slack was enough to allow the 60ft tube that is the mast to 'invert': that is to bend the wrong way. Masts are designed and built to bend backwards in an even curve, rather like a huge fishing rod. In normal sailing as the mast bends aft the middle section of the spar bows forwards, but when the mast itself bends forward too far the middle section bows backwards. The effect is rather like someone trying to bend their leg the wrong way – something has to give.

In this case it was the front wall of the tube itself, creasing and threatening to collapse inwards like a broken drinking straw, about twelve feet above the deck just above the spinnaker pole track, and that crease caused the side wall of the tube to start to collapse inwards. Although the mast did not break completely, the damage was enough to force *White Crusader* to pull out of the race there and then.

At the time, the official story was that the axle pin of that one little pulley block – a sheeve block, in nautical parlance – was to blame. It broke, the block exploded, the backstay ran out, the shock load was too much for the preventer and so on. That, true enough, is what happened – but what wasn't said at the time was that the preventer itself was wrongly rigged. Cudmore himself had detailed off the job of rigging the preventer to a crew member who should have known how to do it – but had neglected to check that it had been done properly.

The loss of the race was to prove crucial, for not only did *White Crusader* lose five points, *USA* gained five and instead of putting the two boats ten points apart in *White Crusader*'s favour it brought the two boats level on points. It also, when the rest of the Round Robin Two racing was totted-up, took *White Crusader* out of a safe third overall to a precarious fifth, level with *USA*.

All was not entirely gloom and despondency. When *White Crusader* met *Stars & Stripes* it was on a gentle, light-air day that was not at all to the American boat's liking. Conner had predicated his entire campaign on the statistically-probable heavy weather which would prevail off Fremantle in January and February, when the Louis Vuitton final and the America's Cup itself would be raced, and he was having real trouble with his boat every time the breeze dropped below twelve knots.

On this day the breeze never got above ten, was frequently less than six and with the time limit running out the race was officially shortened and stopped at the end of the third leg of the eight leg course. *White Crusader* was a comfortable 300 yards ahead and in the gentle evening light it took *Stars & Stripes* two-and-a-quarter minutes to reach the finish line after the British boat had crossed. The five points were valuable, and although Law in particular drew tremendous personal confidence from having outsailed 'The Legend' most in the team knew that those were five points that might not have been lifted had they met Conner in the sort of conditions in which they had lost to Blackaller.

Or the sort of conditions in which, two days later and having comfortably beaten the US-entered *Eagle*, they met *French Kiss*. *White Crusader* was the firm favourite to win this one – and would probably have done so on any day except one that blew a steady twenty-two knots, gusting twenty-six. *French Kiss* was exceptionally fast in heavy weather, and *White Crusader*, during the second round robin, was still desperately short of stability.

Stability itself was not the problem but rather the cure. The problem was that the boat herself was tender, and that she went out of balance when heavily heeled. The pregnant curve of her leeward belly which became more and more immersed as she heeled over, tried to force her into a turn, rounding-up into the wind, and this tendency had to be corrected by applying more and more rudder to keep the yacht tracking straight. A smaller degree of this weather helm, as it is called, is desirable in a yacht, but too much requires the rudder angle to be so great as to cause excessive drag, as if the yacht is trying to pull a half-open door along with her under water.

There are several ways to make the boat more stable or 'stiffer': from changing the shape of the keel and even the hull; to moving the entire rig of the boat, which is a more expedient measure and will thus inhibit the amount she will heel in the first place. All methods were under active consideration, and Ian Howlett was 'working on it', but the rules forbade changes to the boat during the course of each round robin series.

Even so, the French boat's win was as much down to a succession of British sailing and crewing errors as it was to simple French speed. Cudmore won the port end of the line, safely to leeward in clear air, and handed over to Law who immediately began to get the best out of the boat. After four minutes, he was able to cross ahead of the French and seemed to be in control until two-thirds the way up the first beat, when either the British numbers began to tumble or the French slipped into a higher gear. Either way, *French Kiss* began to close the gap and crossed ahead with a mile still to go to the windward mark, leaving her a comfortable but catchable forty-five seconds ahead at the turn.

Then came the sort of errors that are born of pressure. In the whirling frenzy of the mark rounding, going for a gybe-set, a flailing sheet caught Melvyn Coleman full across the chest and thrashed him clean over the side of the boat and into the water. As he went, Coleman grabbed a trailing line and Law abandoned the wheel to grab his clothing as the badly winded crewman was swept alongside the steering cockpit by the roaring quarter wave.

Cudmore took over the wheel, but it still took two or three minutes before Coleman could be got back on board, badly bruised, and bundled out of harm's way. The spinnaker was set, but with the crew now firmly rattled it was allowed to snag as it went aloft and a small tear occurred. The sail blossomed open, the small tear ripped wide open, and the sail had to come off again and be replaced.

By now *French Kiss* had more than doubled her lead to ninety-three seconds, but the gremlins had not finished with the British boat yet. As *White Crusader* rounded the bottom mark and tacked, her second Number Three headsail burst apart from leech to luff at about two-thirds height. In the sail loft, the spreader patches – which are supposed to protect the delicate fabric of the sail from chafe where it might rub against the ends of the spreaders (the horizontal struts which stick out from the mast and 'spread apart' the steel rigging rods which give the mast lateral support) – had been put on the sail a fraction too low, and the damaging spreader tips had been rubbing on the raw cloth itself until it eventually wore into a tiny hole, a hole that in seconds became a catastrophic split.

Quickly the headsail was changed and Cudmore pounded up the beat after his opponent, even gaining a few seconds, but on the reach he now had only a Code Three spinnaker in his armoury, the heavier Code Four having been ripped on the run.

Taking a risk, the Code Three was set but within a short time it blew out, leaving no more heavy spinnakers on board. With *French Kiss* already approaching the wing mark and now a good 500 yards in the lead it was decided that there was no point in risking another too-light spinnaker in what was fast becoming a fruitless pursuit and *White Crusader* did the rest of the leg and all the next in 'cruising mode', two-sail reaching under mainsail and genoa only.

It was five more crucial points – and again the loss was against just the wrong boat. Even counting the loss against *USA* when the mast had crumpled, *White Crusader* beating *French Kiss* would have left the British at least clear fourth after two rounds and *French Kiss* ten points further away.

But the tide was running against the British in another way. Having blitzed the first round robin with eleven wins and only one loss, Dennis Conner had come horribly unstuck in the second. He had lost his first two matches, one of them to Blackaller in *USA* (five more valuable points to one of *White Crusader*'s tightest rivals). Then in the light weather at the end of the series he had been in real trouble, lost two more, and gone tumbling down the rankings – but just as *French Kiss* got her weather for the crucial race against the British, so Conner and *Stars & Stripes* got their weather for the last race of the series against a crucial rival. *Stars & Stripes* beat *America II* and by doing so moved back up over the head of *White Crusader* into the top four again.

The British were now equal fifth, having in fact scored fourth-highest in the second round robin. Even more crucially they were two points down on the boat lying fourth – *French Kiss* – and she was just one point down on the third boat, *Stars & Stripes.* In some ways, it was still wide open – but now the British were on just the wrong side of the game. They had left themselves with it all to do in the final round robin. Who was it who said that those one-point races weren't going to matter?

CHAPTER FIFTEEN

That's it, folks

Immediately after the end of the second round robin, *White Crusader* went into the shed for yet more modifications, the accumulated aggregation of all the little things that had made themselves manifest. High on the list was another keel, with Howlett still working on the numbers for a further keel to be fitted before the start of the semi-finals, which the entire camp still saw as being well within their grasp. By this time, though, there was no one who did not fully appreciate the magnitude of the task. It was going to be no routine sailing job.

If taking off the foredeck, the keel and the stern are minor modifications, then the changes required to *White Crusader* were indeed minor. It was, true enough, just a matter of re-tuning the hull. The yacht had been designed and built in a manner specifically intended to allow such changes to be made, but the work load was heavy none the less.

The boat went back into the water with the British, in the words of Keith Wheatley writing in *The Times*, 'everybody's nap for the fourth berth in the semi-final'. New Zealand, unless the Americans succeeded in having her declared illegal because of alleged irregularities in her glassfibre construction, was clearly going to be top scorer. *America II* looked to be lying a comfortable second. There were then four boats for the two remaining places: *Stars & Stripes*, *USA*, *French Kiss* and *White Crusader*.

An America's Cup without Dennis Conner was as inconceivable to those who could remember more about him than The Man Who Lost The Cup in 1983, as it seemed possible to those who saw only *Stars & Stripes* struggling with light weather and ragged crew work. That left the screw-ball American boat with the two rudders and no keel, the French and the British.

Not even the French had expected they would be doing this well, this far into the regatta. As Bruno Troublé, once the Baron Bich's annointed Twelve Metre helsman and now press officer for the Louis Vuitton Cup, had once put it in his distinctive Gallic cadence: 'yew put elevon Amerikons on a Twelve Meeter, yew 'ave a Twelve Meeter crrew; yew put elevon Frrenchman on a Twelve Meeter, yew 'ave eleven Frrenchman.' But in Marc Pajot, the French had a world-class helmsman and in *French Kiss* Pajot had a remarkably quick Twelve Metre, especially in a breeze.

That left *White Crusader*. Cudmore's reputation was as one of the very best skippers in the world, and the Howlett design, now that her downwind problems appeared to have been eased if not completely cured, was recognised as being a good middle-of-the-road boat and particularly good upwind in medium air.

Before the beginning of each round robin heat, the draw was made to decide which boats should meet on which day of racing and for this heat *White Crusader*'s draw of opponents was well-balanced with, if anything, the softer targets grouped towards the early part of the series. She met and disposed of *Eagle* on day one, *Italia* on day three and *Azzurra* on day four.

The races no one expected her to win were not until later in the programme, with the New Zealanders in the all-conquering *Kiwi Magic* on day eight and Conner and *Stars & Stripes* on the last day of racing. Her crucial matches were scattered through the schedule: the French on day two, *USA* on day five, *America II* on day seven, with 'easy' matches either side. It should have been perfect.

Things began to go wrong early, against the French. To begin with the Gods decreed that yet again it should blow old boots. This was fair enough. The Fremantle weather pattern must be one of the most predictable of any sailing venue in the world, and everyone knew it would probably blow harder and harder on more and more days as the West Australian summer advanced. No one expected a light weather America's Cup and no one had designed a boat for it – but the White Crusaders must well have felt that handing their French opponent her sort of weather twice in a row was a case of the Gods being unnecessarily testing.

Cudmore, as was usual, had both *White Crusader* and her opponent where he wanted them at the start with *White Crusader* at the port end to leeward but in clear air and already going at full chat as he handed the wheel over to Law. Law settled quickly and the British boat began to work out steadily ahead until Cudmore judged he could get round the Frenchman's bow. Law tacked and the two boats converged, with *White Crusader* crossing ahead of *French Kiss* by a comfortable couple of lengths.

The French began an easy going tacking duel, taking their time and picking their moments and their waves with care. By a quarter way up the beat, it was obvious the French were closing the gap, the pale grey Briand design with her distinctive turned-up bow looking happier in the big Australian seas than the Howlett boat, despite the modifications to her bow to give more freeboard forward. Half way up the beat, *French Kiss* crossed ahead of *White Crusader*, but after another ten minutes the British boat was back in front.

So it went, nip and tuck, with the French boat looking to be moving easier in the seas and sailing faster but with Law tacking the British boat quicker and more smoothly, and Cudmore always managing to keep her between the opponent and the mark. *White Crusader* raced in to the top mark a bare eighteen seconds in the lead.

At the top of the wind range, Cudmore called a gybe-set and laid firm hold of the inside of the course, but it was a decision that was at the time strongly objected to both by Law and by mainsheet trimmer Mike McIntyre. It was asking too much of boat, gear and crew, they said, to go for such an aggressive move with the Fremantle Doctor pulling the tops off the waves in twenty-five knots of breeze and the savage gusts hitting thirty-two and thirty-four knots, right on the limit for Twelve Metre racing.

Cudmore drives his boats and his crews hard. Even if he did not say it at the time, his view would have been that if they can't do what is tactically required, they're not going to win the America's Cup and they shouldn't be here. Tactically, the gybe-set was the only option with an acknowledged faster downwind opponent following close behind – so the gybe-set it had to be.

Sure enough, things went wrong. The set was excrutiatingly slow and the spinnaker, when at last it was up, was twisted. They got it sorted but by this time *French Kiss*, following around into a safer bear-away set which had gone cleanly, had surfed up to almost alongside.

Cudmore did not hide his displeasure. Despite being legendary, Cudmore's vitriolic harangues are not something of which he is particularly proud. They are, he says, 'just one of those things'.

To most of the crews who sail the world's regettas with him, these Cudmore outbursts are something to be shrugged off, if even listened to. Virtually everything in racing, as Cudmore himself is fond of saying, has its downside and the upside of racing with Cudmore is that you win a great deal more often than you lose.

There was no doubt that day that *French Kiss* was the faster of the two yachts downwind, and both Cudmore and Law felt that in the conditions she had an edge upwind as well. If *White Crusader* followed *French Kiss* round the bottom mark there was no doubt in Cudmore's mind at least that the race would be irretrievably lost: they would never get past her on the beat and on the two following reaches she would just fly away from them, all contact gone. As they closed the bottom mark Cudmore told Law to get across the French boat's wake and grab the inside berth.

Law picked up a wave and slanted *White Crusader* across the stern of *French Kiss* in a high speed sleigh ride. The Twelve Metre gathered speed so fast that the mainsail, suddenly weightless, swung inboard catching McIntyre the trimmer unawares, and he had barely begun to take in the slack on the mainsheet when *White Crusader* reached the other side of the wake and buried her bow in the French yacht's quarter wave, solid water pouring across the foredeck back to the mast and slewing the twenty ton yacht almost to a standstill.

The full weight of the wind went back into the mainsail with a slam and flicked the mainboom out again where it crashed against its preventers all standing. The two preventers were attached to the boom at the same point but were intentionally of different length, so that in the event of just such a crash the shorter would break first, taking the sting out of the blow and allowing the second preventer to save the boom from crashing against the shroud. But unnoticed by either the shore crew or the sailing crew, the longer wire had ridden over the shorter wire and the two were effectively the same length and, worse, doubly strong. When the crash came the preventers held solid and under a point/shock load it was never designed to take, the main boom snapped like a cocktail stick. The race really was lost then.

Afterwards the public blame was laid, like an abandoned Christmas babe, at the door of the unfortunate makers of the unfortunate boom. In private and particularly by Mike McIntyre and Chris Law, Ian Howlett and Angus Melrose, Cudmore was blamed for reckless tactics in calling the move.

If the *French Kiss* match left people saying 'if only . . .', that against *USA* left them speechless. *USA* crossed the starting line fractionally ahead of *White Crusader* but with the British boat already in the lifting wind shift. Then the wind went back left and *USA* tacked on to port. *White Crusader* came back from the right hand side and *USA* crossed ahead. Half a dozen times the pair crossed, with *USA* always ahead but with *White Crusader* gaining until *USA* tacked so close on top of *White Crusader* that Law was able to squeeze up under the American's bow, luff sharply and suddenly and almost literally push the American off his weather side. *USA* tacked away, only to be ahead again when next they crossed, and then again, with *USA* coming this time from the right.

Again Blackaller slam-dunked on top of *White Crusader* and this time the American rolled the British boat. Law drove off to leeward, tacked smartly on to starboard and shaved the American transom by a coat or two of paint. It was heart-stopping stuff.

When the pair crossed again, the British were ahead and Cudmore moved out to the right in search of clear air. It was apparent by now that the two Twelves were sailing very differently, the twin-ruddered, keel-less boat having to foot off for speed before she could develop the necessary lift from her curious configuration and the conventional Howlett design pointing higher but not moving so fast through the water.

In such circumstances, both skippers try to sail their own race rather than in-fight, and when Cudmore came back again the British lead had opened. By the top mark *White Crusader* was a comfortable forty-four seconds ahead, but on the run it was clear that *USA* was a much faster boat offwind. She more than halved *White Crusader*'s lead before the bottom mark was reached but on the next beat Cudmore was again able to use the Howlett design's upwind legs and opened out again, to be fifty-five seconds up as the reaches began.

USA took six seconds out of *White Crusader* on the first reach, and a further eleven seconds on the second, but the British began the third beat still with a comfortable majority of thirty-eight seconds.

Then came a turning point in the race. With the breeze following its usual pattern of building in strength as the afternoon wore on, both boats changed down headsails, *White Crusader* going for a new and little used Number Four. There should have been no problem, even though the sail had been looked at and found to be slightly flatter – thus less powerfully – cut than the previous Number Four which it replaced. But instead of continuing to build as usual, the breeze began to lighten again and for such conditions the new Number Four was entirely the wrong sail. Both Law and Cudmore were taken by surprise.

Worse, in sailing their own race they allowed Blackaller to go substantially to the left where he found a useful heading shift. *USA* tacked on to port as the lift began to move from left to right across the course and reached *White Crusader.* There seemed no point in tacking to cover Blackaller now and Cudmore hung on, and on, and on . . .

Still the wind stayed left, putting *USA* on the inside of the substantial lift and at one stage it even began to look, if Cudmore tacked on to starboard to try to get back over to the left side of the course, as if he might even be forced to cross astern of *USA.*

At last the long-delayed oscillation occurred and Cudmore gratefully tacked on the first suggestion of a header to get back across and cover Blackaller, but now the American was most decidedly back in the boat race.

White Crusader led around the top mark by 22 seconds, which was a bare two seconds more than the Americans had taken out of her on the first run.

Sure enough, by two-thirds of the way down the run *USA* was firmly on to *White Crusader*'s air, and only clever defensive sailing by Cudmore prevented the American from gaining an inside overlap. Blackaller pushed for the inside until the last moment, then gybed and tried to get past outside. Cudmore gybed and the two Twelve Metres approached the mark abreast, *USA* on the outside, and both with spinnakers still flying and the foredeck crews in hyper-active mode.

At this point there was a fatal breakdown in communication aboard *White Crusader*. Cudmore was standing in his customary place just behind Law and, his whirling brain running through the permutations of possible moves, reminded Law that he still had luffing rights over *USA*. There was no obligation under the rules for *White Crusader* to round the adjacent buoy closely, neatly or even at all: she could, if her afterguard so wished it, sail Blackaller off into the distance away from the buoy and give herself even more room and ample breathing space before turning back. It would not matter when she turned, as long as she did so still ahead of the American: the timing of the turn was completely in the hands of Law, as *White Crusader*'s helmsman.

Whatever way Cudmore chose to convey this information to Law, the latter heard it as a command to luff given by the skipper and he swung the wheel, luffing the boat sharply *away* from the mark just as the spinnaker was coming down.

The result was shambles. Law spun the wheel the other way and *White Crusader* swung back into her turn with the spinnaker still coming down in a heap on the deck and the half-raised genoa better than half-wrapped round the headstay. It had to be cleared and the sail was still going up, the spinnaker still coming down, as *White Crusader* rounded up. The grinders were still pounding their whirling windmill handles, and the trimmer was still hauling line off the spinning sheet drum, when the genoa filled with a bang and the sheet parted at the rope-to-wire splice which was still eighteen inches short of the drum and safety.

White Crusader came on up on to the wind with the genoa flagging and had to tack immediately, practically at a standstill in the water.

USA meanwhile, with more room from being on the outside, rounded less dramatically, hardened on and gathered speed and in her own time tacked back on to starboard, now up on *White Crusader*'s weather side but astern – what sailors call the weather hip. *White Crusader* tacked on to port and had to dip *USA*'s stern.

There seemed nothing between the two Twelve Metres in terms of upwind speed, while Blackaller, ahead, could call the beat as he wanted and Cudmore had to respond. Blackaller declined to become involved in a tacking duel but instead went for the breeze, and that left Cudmore's only hopes of passing dependent on either *White Crusader* having the speed to sail right round *USA* or of Blackaller getting his windshifts wrong.

Twice it looked as if Cudmore had pulled Blackaller back, but each time the American astutely covered until, himself going left, he offered Cudmore the option of either continuing to follow or of taking *White Crusader* off to the right.

With the two Twelves so closely matched in speed, Cudmore went hunting for a shift and looked to have found it, but Blackaller came back and realised that this time, he would not cross *White Crusader.* He tacked for the left-hand pin of the finishing line, and in a hold-your-breath finish the two Twelve Metres raced neck-and-neck for the line, *White Crusader* going for the right-hand end, *USA* for the left. *USA*'s bow crossed the line forty feet – three seconds – in front.

Now *White Crusader* was in deep trouble, and deeper trouble came when two days later she raced *America II.* It was Cudmore's last chance to get his boat back into the top four and the semi-final, and when he did not do it he blamed no one but himself.

The race was to all intents and purposes over before it began. With the weather unsettled, *White Crusader* tried various headsails in the hour-and-a-half before the start, and Cudmore left his call to the last minute before deciding on which one to use.

As the ten-minute cannon boomed out, *White Crusader* rounded the pin-end buoy and sailed into the racing area with her headsail still on deck and only her mainsail set. It was not a particularly unusual move, but at the other end of the line Kolius brought *America II* to battle with her genoa already set and drawing, and reached fast across from the committee boat end towards Cudmore to engage *White Crusader* early. Cudmore ran *White Crusader* off deep to keep her out of harm's way while the lads on the foredeck got the sail ready and up.

He ran her off just a fraction too deep. With the sail half hoisted the wind caught the back of it, flicked it through the foretriangle and pulled the bolt rope out of the headstay groove – the slim channel up the aft edge of the shaped aluminium aerofoil which fits over the forestay and which holds the forward edge of the genoa.

The sail had to be brought down and the hoisting operation begun again. There was a further delay and by the time Cudmore was able to bring *White Crusader* on to the wind, he had run out of time to get back to the line. Kolius jumped on to Cudmore's weather bow and covered him all the way up to the line; both boats were over half-a-minute late and *America II* already held a twelve second lead.

The two boats were evenly matched in speed upwind, and Kolius in clear air pulled out a thirty second lead by the top mark. *America II* took another three seconds out of *White Crusader* downwind but Cudmore pulled back to only twenty-five seconds astern at the end of the next beat. On the next reach the American pulled out another four seconds and at the bottom mark his lead was thirty seconds.

Cudmore caught up on the next beat to be only thirteen seconds astern at the start of the final run, and it looked for a brief moment as if the British might be back in the boat race.

As Law swung the yacht through the sharp turn of the gybe-set and the spinnaker blossomed out, *White Crusader* put her nose into a wave and began to slew round out of control and into a broach, burying the foredeck under tons of water. Paul Stanbridge and another crewman were almost swept away with the forestay buried for over two feet of its height and with green water all the way back to the mast and beyond. Law had to use full rudder and trim tab to bring the wallowing Twelve Metre back under control and the genoa was swept off the foredeck and had to be quickly cut free. Then, just as everything seemed to be coming back under control, the clip on the end of the spinnaker halyard let go and the spinnaker fell down. That was more or less that. *America II* was off the hook and eventually won by one minute and forty-seven seconds.

Now only miracles would get *White Crusader* into the semi-final, and in the 'impossible' match against the New Zealanders, beaten only once in thirty-seven races, the miracle lasted three hours and fifteen minutes.

Cudmore stitched Dickson into an escape-proof bag at the start, closing the New Zealander out at the committee boat end and leaving *Kiwi Magic* to do a complete circle while *White Crusader* got away with an eight second lead. The Kiwis tried everything to get past, but between them Law and Cudmore handled *White Crusader* superbly, alternating between loose cover when they sensed they were in the favoured wind slant and tight blanketting when they wanted to force *Kiwi Magic* off to one side or the other. *White Crusader* fetched the top mark fifteen seconds up.

On the reach the much faster New Zealand boat quickly rolled up on *White Crusader*, and Cudmore defended by taking *White Crusader* higher and higher from the rhumb line to prevent Dickson overtaking until the two boats were so high of the mark that they were 400 yards directly upwind of it. Cudmore turned downwind and gybed to block out the inside berth, *Kiwi Magic* followed and gybed to try and get across, and Cudmore had Law luff *White Crusader* hard, taking the Kiwis by surprise as they completed their gybe. *Kiwi Magic*, already having trouble with her spinnaker pole, spun up into the wind with the foredeck a shambles and *White Crusader* bore away. In the melée the Kiwis had broken a pole-end fitting and the result was that Cudmore had given *White Crusader* a thirty-eight second breathing space that grew to forty-one seconds by the bottom mark.

Kiwi Magic halved *White Crusader*'s lead on the next beat and eradicated it on the run, but again Cudmore defended the inside berth at the mark and *White Crusader* rounded with *Kiwi Magic* hard on her transom. Between them Law and Cudmore held off the inevitable until only a couple of hundred yards from the finish line, when a slam-dunk finally went wrong. With Law steering from the windward wheel, the practice for the slam-dunk was for Cudmore to take the leeward wheel where he could watch the approaching opponent and then tack the boat at just the right moment. It had worked again and again, but sooner or later there had to be a slip, and it came in the final stages of the final beat. Watching for a 'flat' between the waves in which to begin the turn, Cudmore left the tack a second or two late and the faster *Kiwi Magic* was left with the yard or two breathing space that was all that she needed.

Dickson drove his boat off for full speed and then squeezed hard: he broke through *White Crusader*'s lee then began to work up under her lee bow until the British boat had to tack away to avoid the turbulent upwash from the New Zealander's sails. *White Crusader* tacked and *Kiwi Magic tacked, now up on White Crusader*'s weather hip. With her superior speed and height she climbed away from *White Crusader* and crossed the line six seconds ahead.

It had been an all-but faultlessly sailed race against a faster opponent, but even had *White Crusader* won she would still have had to have beaten *Stars & Stripes*, by now fully on song and going away, to amass enough points to get past *USA* and *French Kiss* and into the semi-final.

In the final points tally, *White Crusader* lay sixth, behind *French Kiss, USA* and *America II* with *French Kiss* and *USA* in the semi-final, and with *America II* and thus the New York Yacht Club, for the first time in history, out of the America's Cup.

The margins of defeat were tantalisingy narrow. *White Crusader* had 115 points, *America II* 128, *French Kiss* 129 and *USA* had 139. With twelve points for a win, *White Crusader* beating only *America II* would still have left her two points short of the semi-final, but with the net twenty-four point difference to the scores beating only *French Kiss* would have given her the place. Had she beaten only *USA*, both boats would have tied on 127, and *America II* on 128 would have taken the semi-final place.

CHAPTER SIXTEEN

The people you meet

It would be quite wrong to think of the White Horse Challenge, as it was eventually called, as just my campaig ı. We eventually had about seventy-five people working together on it, and each one made a significant contribution. They had to, or we couldn't have afforded to keep them! It is safe to say that there was no one, absolutely no one, who was involved who wasn't contributing.

In contrast to the *Victory* campaign, we only had a couple of people who had to be given their Plane Tickets Home, as the euphemism has it – I'm not talking about people brought in temporarily to do a specific job who were not in the first place taken on for the whole campaign. One of those left of his own volition – found he just didn't like it – and the other fell off a wall and broke his leg.

There were four executive directors – Phil Crebbin. David Arnold, Spud Spedding and myself – and we worked together in Perth, each with our own responsibilities. I just didn't get involved in buying houses, dealing with Customs – that sort of thing.

In some ways it would be more accurate to describe the sailing campaign, as it finally evolved, as the joint effort of Phil Crebbin and myself: I was sailing director, and skipper of the yachts; Phil was technical director. The Twelve Metres were in a very real sense his, and the technical direction – in both senses of the word – was very much his.

Phil Crebbin is probably the keenest mind in British sailing. With a good degree from Cambridge in computer studies, he's analytical and he's thorough. Like all sailors with a drive to win he has a powerful ego, but allied to that he is something of an introvert, and that's a difficult mixture for himself, but an easy one for the rest of us because it makes him easy to get along with.

His great strength is that he brought a very organised mind to the sport, plus experience of being involved with *Victory* and having been involved in the business of yachting. He ran a mast-making business for some years.

His specific job as technical director was to control the design programme, to control the testing programme and to control procurement. This involved building the boats: Dave Arnold did the legal and contractual side, Phil did the technical side. The planning and purchasing of the equipment, the decisions about the equipment – they were more or less all his.

He was also involved in the development of the computer program with Graeme Wynne to ensure we had the program we wanted within the very tight budget constraints the campaign was forced to work under.

So inputting together, he and I worked very closely together, he being the primary person at this stage. When we became operational, I ran the sailing programme, he backed me up in that as I had backed him up on the technical programme.

On the technical side, Phil made the decisions and I would advise; on the sailing side I made the decisions and he would advise. It was not just a matter of my deferring to his judgement on the technical side, it was more than that. Phil actually ran the technical side, and made the decisions, from deciding which models to run to deciding which instruments to buy. He was part of the design decision group, and largely shaped the pattern which the design work would take. His other major contribution was handling the procurement side of things when we simply didn't have any money. He knew exactly what we would have to buy, what we could do without. There wasn't a penny of what little money we had that was wasted, or spent on kit that we didn't actually need.

From a sailing point of view, Phil is one of the top yacht racers in Britain, yet like many he hasn't gone full time into it and therefore suffers from the constant problem of being a part-time sailor in a world that is now inhabited increasingly by full-time sailors.

He is probably the most brilliant sailor in the country and allied to his analytical brain this gives great potential. At some stage he may wish to test that potential at the highest level but then he'll have to face the problems of handling the pressure of winning, having certainly the talent to win.

His Olympic record of having won several races but yet not getting a medal is one of the problems he will have to address if he wants to get back into racing at the very highest level, and in a comfortable partnership he could achieve it.

I've always felt that he and I together could achieve that. Unfortunately, due to personal circumstances – domestic and business problems and ambitions – while he had first option to race the boat, which we would of course have jointly skippered, he chose not to do so. Then when I'd invited other people into the programme I couldn't, when Phil became available, in fairness ditch those people. Perhaps I should have been more ruthless, and broken the promises I had made to the others, but they had given a lot just on trust, and I didn't want to break that trust.

In the boat he is very cool, very decisive. Certainly when I'm on board he's the relaxed one. He tends to make a succession of good decisions, doesn't psyche-out, doesn't do anything wrong: just sails awfully well consistently. Really he is a lesson to others. I think when we sail together I perhaps help stiffen his resolve, and he keeps me under control.

From a campaign point of view, Phil is the sort of person who likes to come to the boat well-organised, race, and at the end of the day go away and prepare for the next race. He doesn't take readily to the rough and tumble of all the other thousand and one things required to keep a long-term programme like this running at a high level: protests, organising changes to sails, to the boat, meeting the press and so on. If all that can be taken off his shoulders then he can be very, very strong.

On the race course, he thinks very quickly and he responds very quickly, as I do. He can both think with me and at the same time think independently, which is quite a trick, so we tend to arrive at good decisions between us. It's a relationship that can work very well. It is one that can be got to work with other people but in retrospect maybe I was over-ambitious in expecting or hoping that it would work with Chris [Law] who is perhaps more driven than Phil but doesn't have the same intellect.

Spud Spedding – his real name is Andrew but I've never heard anyone call him that – was the shore boss and quite simply kept the programme and the boats running. Spud is archetypal Englishman. His motivation, I always think, is whimsy – and yet he will work endlessly. He is one of these people who is difficult if not impossible to explain to an American or an Australian, or to anyone who sees things and people in two-dimensional terms. Spud will do incredible work but doesn't appear to be motivated by the reasons that other people are motivated by – so why does he do it? In that sense he's complex.

His method, certainly, has been influenced by the Royal Navy and allied to that is this tremendous memory. He is great with people, has a tremendous sense of humour, and a great knowledge and sense of right and wrong, of behaviour – of all the good things so it culminates in a classic example of, well, of a good upbringing.

He handled the operational side and was a complete confidante of the other executive directors, but he would himself deal with all the logistics, customs, the shore-side operations. He had his own team of people and he ran them in his own way, in a different style to the style I adopted with the sailors yet there was no problem between them.

His professional background and experience is impressive: North Sea diver, farmer, author, long-distance short-handed sailor of great experience, a very skilled seaman. He originally joined the *Victory* programme as navigator, then moved to operations, joined us as co-director. He is very important of course to the physical structure of the syndicate: I always say that if the whole BACC programme went into hold, were put on ice as it were and the personnel slimmed down to the minimum, Spud would be the last one left on the payroll. Everybody else could be done without if the programme went dormant: Spud could only go if it were being closed down completely.

The other executive director was David Arnold: Master mariner as well as a successful businessman. As a Reservist he was actually invited to navigate Britain's first nuclear submarine. He subsequently navigated ocean racing yachts – and has won the Admiral's Cup three times. He is bluff, genial, hard-working, blunt. His role of chief executive put him under the major burden of handling the club, and the contractual side of the challenge. It was he who did all the very clever business and property deals when we first went to Fremantle.

Graham Walker was campaign president, but not an executive director. He is above all a racing enthusiast, a very private person. He came in to support the Royal Thames and in a way found himself lumbered by them, but unlike so many others he didn't shrink from what had to be done to keep the challenge rolling. He never wanted to take a public role – and throughout most people managed to respect his privacy. Certainly, I shall.

When it comes to racing a Twelve Metre you need a whole variety of people – eleven very considerable individuals who have to coalesce together into a team, but who need very different skills. Sometimes, the skills overlap, but sometimes it is enough for an individual to be extremely good at just one job because that is actually the only job you want him to do. If you look at our final crew, you'll see what I mean.

Paul Stanbridge is a *bowman* – straightforward, pure and simple. It's partly a physical thing – he is not big enough for any other role on the boat – more importantly a psychological outlook, a mental attitude. That's all Paul wants to do, and he does it brilliantly, simply because he gets such a big kick out of doing it. He's not ambitious to go to the back of the boat – he's just a bowman and when he's finished being on the bow of a boat he will rejoin the serious world – probably. I think Paul's got a degree, he's certainly intelligent, qualified, which means he's also a great guy to have. This is his role. He's nerveless, He'll go up a mast in a maxi in the Southern Ocean or up the mast in a Twelve Metre when its blowing twenty-five knots – he loves it.

Then you get someone like Timmy Haynes, who became our rigging specialist. He actually joined us thinking he might go on the bow, and indeed he wasn't precluded from that – but his talents were better employed elsewhere. Timmy is a true professional, and he is amazing about work: he only had thirty-six hours sleep one week. Eventually he would end up sleeping in the car with the passenger door open for a couple of hours and just keep working on into the night. You can only do that for a limited time and he did it for us. A *very* special guy. And of course he found the whole programme enormously valuable from his own professional point of view: to be given the opportunity to spend a year doing nothing but working on Twelve Metre rigs, the most sophisticated and specialised in the game – more specialised even than the big multihull rigs – that was a great experience.

Guy Baron on the other hand is like neither of those two – he was not a full-time sailor, and he's not a full-time adventure freak either. In fact when he came to us he'd been working as a tree surgeon. So he was one of the less experienced people, but with such a lovely attitude and he's come out of it all very highly thought of as a person, super to have around. He also worked around the clock for us. Why should you want a tree surgeon in a Twelve Metre campaign? Well, at least you know he's not afraid of heights.

Melvyn Coleman came in to the programme as a boat pro, a man to find himself a job and, if he could do it, to stay at it. A nice bloke, I wouldn't have said very experienced . . . well, very anything really, except very stroppily determined. He was not very fit to begin with either, but during the programme he got to be one of the best. He became fit and capable and dedicated, and very much in full control. He was straight mast man. Some people might wonder how anybody could spend his life just concentrating on that job but Mel did it and did it brilliantly. He worked out all the operations, every last detail: how many elastic bands on the port leg of a spinnaker, how to put this clip on, this rope goes here, 'I'll put my foot here . . .' Just like a dancer he studied the choreography of that one act and spent nine months doing it and at the end of it he was very, very good. You have to have people like that in something as big, as complex, as a Twelve Metre campaign. They don't all have to be people like myself with the mind going simultaneously in a hundred directions.

Indeed, for such a job, a guy can be a bit too clever. We had others who came in to do that very job and in some ways I might have thought them better suited: more powerful, somewhat more experienced technically. You know what found them out? That questionnaire thing, when it came back in. Three or four people in that area in two boats and they are all pointing at one guy. That's where you can use group psychology constructively, what I call peer-group selection – which is a very fancy title for a manager using not just his own common sense but the common sense of the people who are on the ground, doing the job.

Another great individual we had with us was Mark Preston, nicknamed Dennis, as in Menace. Mark has a big knife and likes to use it – not on people, fortunately – but on goods. Mark lost two front teeth in one of the races and really didn't want to get them fixed; he was very content with broken teeth. It suited his image.

There's not an ounce of malice in Mark, but by God he's absolutely hopeless to take to parties. He's always the first to chuck the plates. He married a very nice girl, and they make a very straightforward couple. His father is a fisherman from Salcombe and he's a fisherman as well; he goes out and lays the lobster pots; does a bit of netting, a bit of drinking; plays a bit of rugby: a super guy.

Of course, not everyone involved in the programme came from sailing or in fact needed to be a dedicated full-time sailor or top performer in yacht racing. Clive Roberts came in from rowing. He's very aggressive, very dedicated, a top oarsman at world level, but perhaps a little too individualistic to fit into the sort of long-term work pattern that is required for sustained Twelve Metre effort. It's a team game on and off the water, with a lot of work required off the water – not just fitness but all the other things that go with a huge and complex sailing programme. Mind you, Clive's job on board, his job with the programme, was fairly narrowly defined, leaving him not much place to go, really. He was in a job which just required strength and he didn't quite have it. Clive was perhaps one of the iffy ones.

Jabba, on the other hand, who came in from the *Daily Mail* Winch Winder competition was classic able seaman, navy – Royal, US or Merchant; does it matter which navy? He is a senior rating sort of guy. He worked out all the short cuts – a natural non-worker, but a great charmer, and not afraid to work if there's no alternative. Jabba was a guy we had to take the old whip to a little bit, but in fact he was especially keen on fitness, and he finally got fit and did the job right. In the end he turned out to be pure gold – but in a programme that has to be as self-disciplined, as self-motivated really, as the Twelve Metre thing a couple of guys like that left to do what comes naturally could ruin the whole work ethic.

A good contrast to someone like that is Sean Campbell; much more dedicated, much more hard working directly, but in some ways maybe a bit depressive, even a bit of a whinger. Again, one who is very keen on fitness. He did his job absolutely thoroughly and was very aggressive for success. Sean was very disappointed with the lack of success at the back of the boat. He feels that the back of the boat – us, me: whatever group you like to blame – let him down: 'I did my job, you guys screwed up.' Well, that's OK. Certainly I would use Sean again – but he mightn't come with me!

One person who really has to be singled out when it comes to talking of the sort of personalities you need to run a big Twelve Metre programme is Chris Mason, who is just an absolute tower of strength.

Chris Mason joined the *Victory* programme as a sailmaker and overlapped a little bit into the sailing, but as he developed he got more and more into it and finished up as mainsheet trimmer on *Victory* and was very highly spoken of. He subsequently became the boat professional on Admiral's Cup campaigns and then came back to join us when we got up and running.

With his experience of the first campaign, his very positive attitude to sailing, he was very valuable and quickly became a mainstay of the programme. He is a wonderful seaman, but as well is a good communicator and became something of a coalescent for the rest of the crew. It's having people like that in his group that has enabled Dennis Conner to stay on top. Some of his Chris Masons are now into their fourth campaign and this is what supports Conner, not just simply his own talent.

Some of our sailors, Mike McIntyre, Gerry Richards and of course Chris Law, came from the Olympic classes primarily. The Olympic classes have a different requirement. They have a requirement for dedication but it is a delicate dedication: it's perfection. The sail must be within a centimetre in setting, everything about the programme must all be very carefully laid out – a bit like a doctor's tray, scalpel, forceps, monkey wrench. Our Olympians certainly found a problem with the hours the boat pros worked and thus with all the implications that such a problem led to. The compatibility was a little bit difficult.

In a more fully-funded programme in the future one would more completely separate the maintenance of the boats and the sailing of the boats, so that the sailing crews become more like test pilots or battle crews. As soon as the boat gets back in after the day's sailing or racing, the crew should be able to get off and walk away from it, and the maintenance team swarm all over it. If you could do that, it would take a great deal of pressure and work load off the sailors. Of course, we didn't have that sort of money and so when the sailors came ashore they had to roll their sleeves up. The boat pros didn't mind that because it's the sort of life they are used to, but one or two of the Olympians seemed to find it a problem. Nonetheless, they made a big contribution.

Mike McIntyre, for example, was really a management man – a super guy, hard working, ran the fitness programme – terrific. But what I'm getting at is best explained by recalling that he came down to Fremantle with his wife; they brought their own china and everything else – settled in properly and set up home. Care and precision, everything sorted out, everything – including the work programme – in its proper place.

The real full-on, full-time, fully committed sailors don't work that way. A girlfriend is to reduce the time you spend looking after yourself, not to spend time with. So there was that definite difference in approach.

There was no problem with lack of respect or anything like that. Make no mistake, these guys are really good sailors – really understand what they are doing and what they are trying to achieve. It was just a certain lack of compatibility of style between Gerry, Mike and Chris and the rest of the guys in the campaign. The Olympic class sailors are all dedicated in their own way, but there is a difference between being dedicated and totally, utterly involved. There is dedication to the results, but perhaps it is because they don't come from backgrounds that say you use every working hour to achieve them. They come from a background that says you use the time involved, the time you devote to your sailing, efficiently and to maximum effect and you think very hard about making sure that effect really is maximised. There is a difference. You go out in your Soling, say, and you have a race; then you fiddle a little bit with it and you go in. Then you talk, think and plan in the bar; then you sleep well and you are rested and you do a little bit of fitness training, and then you turn your mind to another problem and you deal with that in the same, super-effective, super-efficient manner. But this idea of a slog of twelve or fourteen hours a day, talk about it all day and roll it through, seven days a week for eight or twelve months . . .

Of course one of Chris's proud achievements for many years has been that he can achieve the sort of results that the full-time dedicated sailors can achieve *and* he can run a wife and a family and bring up two children and take them to school in the morning *and* he can be the director of a very successful business. In fact that's probably the trouble. If he did only one thing he would be capable of being a really world class top sailor, but as a gifted amateur, which is what he is, the fact is he bumped his limits in this programme.

In the case of Mike the job he was doing was within his capabilities easily, but it took him a long time to adapt to the mores of operating within a big crew. That's hardly surprising – he sails a Finn, [the Olympic single-handed dinghy]. Mike tried hard; very, very hard, and I'd invite him back – if he'd come – if we were doing this sort of thing again. But even when he was racing, he's a canny, tough Scotsman; he would be minding his job. Whereas Chris Mason seemed to have eyes in the back of his head if something went wrong – he would dive across the boat if a stray line was going into the genoa block, something like that – the eyes of a professional. The seaman's eye.

The Olympic sailors just didn't have that. It's not a carp, nor a complaint about them, or anything like that. It is just the reflection of a difference in style. They brought in their own strengths and those were very valuable.

Running a Twelve Metre is very much like running a maxi except you do it all the time and it is much more intense. But you've got to be totally absorbed with the idea, and you've just got to love boats. If you don't really love boats you can't really do what the workaholics were doing. So many of the Olympic sailors, in general terms, don't love boats. Some of them do not actually like boats very much; do not care for them or about them. What they love is beating other people. They love winning.

Absolutely typical of the sort of people I mean when I think about people who love boats are Lou Varney and Michel Meader. Michel of course stayed with the campaign right through as the port trimmer. Lou came down for a while but he had too much else on back in England with his rig consultancy business and his other racing. Of course, like Michel, Lou and I are old friends, and that helps a lot. It could even have been that because of that there was a measure of unfairness felt by some of the others in the campaign – and if that's the case, I must accept the blame. The others knew how to run the thing, but Lou and Michel had a certain licence because they brought such enormous experience. Perhaps I was a little less tough on them than the others.

They both in fact have been more than just dedicated; they were both thoughtful, mature. You can't put a price on that, on guys who will go that extra half-mile for you, not so much without being asked but in fact without you even knowing that the half-mile is there and has to be covered.

The best people for an America's Cup campaign are those that encompass both types of outlook, both the dedicated sailor's total absorption with boats and the Olympic sailor's dedication to perfection and to results. Some dedicated sailors just lack that final two per cent of racing talent, while some of the pure results-seekers never become more than Olympic sailors sailing Twelve Metres. Some, like Dennis Conner, are absolutely obsessed by their boats and can still handle the fund-raising, the public deal and everything else.

Eddie Warden Owen in many ways has all the qualities that are needed. He has spent all his life, since he was a kid, in boats: building them, repairing them, sailing them, making sails for them and everything else. And he has the grounding in sailing the Olympic classes as well. In much the same way I have both the background of having spent a boyhood and youth just sailing, sailing, sailing and the background of Olympic participation, though I don't talk about my trip to the Olympics very much.

What Eddie hadn't quite come to grips with this time around in Fremantle was that he hadn't built his self-confidence sufficiently, and in this game you have to have self-confidence. He could never quite believe that he was the best guy for the job, whereas Chris *always* believes that he is the best guy. Chris came down to Fremantle and there was absolutely no doubt in his mind that he would steer the British America's Cup Twelve Metre. He didn't view his role as being in any way competing with Eddie for the wheel because as far as he was concerned there was no contest. As far as he was concerned, no one acting rationally could have done anything else but give him the wheel.

I had to make the decision who would steer the boat and instead of Eddie going for it, shoving Chris aside and saying 'Oi – push off' he seemed to let himself be psyched into a position where he accepted that Chris was number one.

Look at what has happened since Fremantle. Eddie just breezes off and wins the Congressional Cup at his first attempt. It took me seven years to win that thing, and I was the first non-American ever to win it. Next year Eddie waltzes in and makes it look like non-Americans win it all the time.

I think Eddie may at last have taught himself that lesson that no one else can teach you, that you have to learn for yourself. You have to say to yourself 'Hey – I can do this. I'm just as good as these guys I've read about, and who keep telling me how good they are. In fact, I'm better.' Chris convinces himself that he is the best guy and then is terribly disappointed in himself when he turns out not to be and then he drives himself harder and perhaps wins again, whereas Eddie, with more natural talent, isn't sure that he is the best guy, thus he isn't *that* disappointed when he turns out not to be.

In Fremantle Eddie really was not taking the role of helmsman, but, with the benefit of hindsight, I think he probably would have had the talent and he and I might have got on better in the back of the boat, as we were able to do before in *Phoenix*, with who knows what difference to the results. Chris on the other hand was raring to take it and yet, because he hadn't committed his life to sailing, was in the very close circumstances found wanting.

Yet there is no question: I must accept the responsibility and thus a large share of the blame for what happened when it came to the final racing. My job was to make Chris comfortable with winning – not just with being good, he's pretty comfortable with his own views on that already – but with winning in those tight corners, in those no-way-out moments when you've just two, big boats close together and all you have is split-second decision-making situations. I failed. That's why we blew getting into the semi-finals. It's wrong to say we blew the event – we didn't. *White Crusader* wouldn't have beaten *Stars & Stripes*. After it was all over the *Stars & Stripes* camp reckoned their boat was five minutes quicker round an America's Cup course than *White Crusader*, four minutes quicker than *Kookaburra* and three minutes quicker than the Kiwis.

We should have got into the semi-final. Then, with a soft draw we just might have got into the final – but no way would we have got any further. Yet we didn't make it into the semi-final, and one reason – a large part of the reason anyway, for there were others such as the lack of crewing practice – was that we couldn't bring the back of the boat together.

There is now this well-recognised phenomenon in sports psychology which Laurie Hayden calls in John Bertrand's book 'the comfort zone'. Many people are just not comfortable with winning the biggest events. Chris is one: he storms the work-up regattas, then blows the big one. He did it first with the Olympic trials, then when he got comfortable with winning those he did it with the Olympics themselves. Phil is a little bit the same. You can tell this by their series results: they start well then fade out. Win the first two races, slip in the third and fourth so that by the end of the week they have only a narrow points lead, then lose the last one.

I tend to do the opposite, start badly and then come good – and that in itself is evidence that I too have a comfort zone, I need to get comfortable. It's always hard to be truly objective about yourself, of course, but my perception of my own performance is that I'm comfortable enough with winning big events – it's the context I need to get comfortable with. I'm a person who gets uncomfortable if things do not go the way I had envisaged, start to take me by surprise – I did here – which is the reason I often don't win things first time around. But I go back and bash away at it. Then I get comfortable. Then I win it. The Congressional Cup is an example of that.

On the other side of things take Lymington, and the Royal Lymington Cup – I just go on winning it, sometimes from completely outside situations.

Lawrie Smith is very good in this respect. And getting better, particularly with all the practice he's been getting. He's a good helmsman – but I don't think he's a skipper. He has a disruptive influence – a bit like Ian Botham. He's a charming, anarchical character. He doesn't unsettle the crew, but he unsettles the back-up group.

It's important to maintain a balance, a dispassionate balance, when it comes to sailing together in these major enterprises; to work together toward winning. It is something the Americans are very good at and have been good at for a long time, and something the British are not good at at all. Just look at the number of top sailors the Americans can bring together in a Twelve Metre, all of whom are prepared to take the longer view, to accept whatever the structure is and get on with beating everybody else. The British can never seem to do that – individuals always seem to want to have the thing completely to themselves. And as if the sailors stabbing each other in the back wasn't bad enough, you get everybody else from the designers to the journalists all pitching in, all pushing their own favourite candidate. It's almost a case of if they didn't pick him, then they want him off the boat altogether. The *Victory* business was a classic instance.

Funnily enough I have no personal animosity toward Lawrie, despite what happened in the *Victory* campaign. Chris I did find difficult to get along with on a personal level, and that translated itself somewhat into the boat. Chris has said quite openly that he found me difficult to get along with on a personal level also: I'm not his sort of guy. Again, though, it's not a matter of dislike. We worked quite well together, because I have great respect for his ability to get the best speed out of the boat on the day, and by the third round robin we were working very well together. The problem is, when you look around in British sailing, who is there that can be seen to be really talented on the international scene who is not of our generation. They have all 'equivocated' when it has come to going out and getting on to the international circuit. This I suppose is easy for me to say now. I just went out and did it, just went to regattas – many of them I helped to organise. I climbed into the system and I suppose in a way I blocked access, for there is not that much room for that many top sailors in each country. Even in America, there aren't really *that* many top sailors, considering the size of the country and the number of sailors and boats there are.

In effect, there is a missing generation of British international sailors, guys in their late twenties who are already pushing those of us in our thirties and early forties to move over and make room. We can still beat them, and beat them comfortably – and there is no point in us moving over until there is someone who can take our place and do better.

It's up to the so-called younger generation of British sailors to win in their own classes as they go. The British racing sailor who is closest to it is Jo Richards, who won a Bronze medal at Los Angeles (in fact, Britain's only Olympic yachting medal). He actually focused on an area, developed it, spent his life at it and achieved – bang. Now he's a guy it would be good to see to come into the system. This is one of the areas I have no easy answers for.

I think for our next generation of top international sailors we have to look to the very young sailors who are still in their teens – still sailing with the Youth Squad, that sort of thing. They should be coming into the next campaigns at a low level, be key figures in the campaign after that, be ready to take charge of the campaign after that. That has always been the American pattern: it is how they all came up, including Conner. He began his America's Cup involvement with a relatively minor role aboard *Mariner* in 1973. Until Britain develops that sort of attitude among its sailors it will always fall short of the really big league.

*

Another question we have to look at is whether the skipper of the Twelve Metre should also be the helmsman. Of course, we all have to look at Dennis [Conner] and when you look there that's a tough one. He just happens to be one of the best skippers – in a campaign sense – in the world and he also just happens to be maybe the best Twelve Metre helmsman in the world. He is really very, very good just at steering a Twelve Metre. He is the skipper more off the boat than on it in a sense: on the boat there is a very mature decision-making group whose input is very important. Dennis doesn't dominate, or maybe I should say domineer, on the boat.

People glibly talk about Dennis having done ten thousand hours behind the wheel of a Twelve Metre, but just stop and think what that really means. Ten thousand hours: eighty thousand miles, must be nearly two-thirds of it upwind. That's three times round the world. Chay Blyth sails around the world once against the prevailing winds and look at the fuss: Dennis Conner has done it three times, short-tacking a Twelve Metre!

Maybe I *should* steer. Most of the time I don't do enough helming but in the Congressional Cup, for example, I can sail as fast as anyone in the world. As well as being an intuitive helmsman, I now know enough about how the boats are put together to be able to connect all my senses to the whole boat, so if she's not going right I can feel it and know why. I can tune the boat from the wheel. I'm not exceptional, though, but would be in the top group – say the top eight or ten.

But so much of helming is trim-related. This is where Eddie Warden Owen is so good. Chris – not so much so. He would be less aware of the problem, and thus would not go and look for the solution. Chris has tremendous feel for the boat in the water. I began to reach the necessary level in the *Victory* programme. One day I suddenly realised I'd been day-dreaming – the way you sometimes do in a car on the motorway – and I looked down at the speedo and I was bang-on. Not even a tenth off it. I got to the stage I could turn the speedo off and still sail the boat at exactly the same speed. Not many people can do that.

I don't especially want to steer. Perhaps I should.

It's important too not to get too far removed from the fact that it can all still be fun. If it stopped being fun, I would stop doing it. That's one of the reasons I do it, though, because it is fun and a large part of the fun is the people you meet. We had one guy with us on the programme who could show you really why it still can be a bit of fun.

Craig Nutter was an unusual case. The family name is *completely* appropriate: Craig is an absolute nutter. We'd heard about him, he'd been bowman on *Courageous*. I said to him to come in and see me and he arrived at the door in a bright green coat, and carrying a big thick Filofax that even running a large empire wouldn't require. 'Hi I'm Craig Nutter' and he fell over the telephone line.

I was talking to somebody and I said 'Hang on a sec Craig, good to see you, just give me one moment'. The phone rang; he picked it up straight away and said 'Hello'. Then he looked around the office and said 'Who are we?'. We talked a bit then he left, as full of beans as when he came in, storming out the door – and forgetting his Filofax.

Twenty seconds later he was back: *'Forgot my Filofax'*. Out. If he ever happens to write 'How Not To Do An Interview' it'll be a winner. He did every single thing wrong.

So there we are, looking for a dedicated, single-minded bowman for Britain's Challenge for the America's Cup, a man who has to judge the line, who has to be very steady in action, a man who will call spinnaker gybes in twenty knots of breeze with the boats racing along neck and neck, a man who will have to outperform the best, the very best bowmen in the world and this apparition comes in the door. His hair falling out, overweight, not very fit, wearing this ill-fitting green coat that had come from Carnaby Street probably ten years ago. But he became very disciplined. Yet the first thing he did when this discipline came off was he went and crashed his motorbike! He hurt his arm.

Craig is my sort of guy. He has a whiplash brain. I don't know how bright he is but he is either very bright or very perceptive or both. If you listen to him he has two personalities – one is himself and one is a person who stands on his shoulder and discusses him and he is constantly running a conversation between the two. Constantly. 'Hey man ... this isn't what I want in life ... this is stange ... I'm under pressure ... I'm feeling depressed ... No, no – you're having a great time ... this is the most exciting thing in the world we're doing here ...' A fascinating character.

Mind you, Craig could be a bit volatile for the programme. We were so desperate for a strong, nerveless, experienced bowman – that was my original perception of one of our major weaknesses – that in fact we ended up with four good bowmen. There is no malice in Craig but he will naturally lead guys astray. He is one of these demonic people, he lives twenty hours a day. He came down to Fremantle and it was motorbikes, girls, on the drink *and* do his job. He could do it, that wasn't the problem, but it leads a lot of people astray. Craig certainly has this ability to live all night and all day.

Part of the problem is not to be disruptive of people who perform best on routine, steadiness and stability. On the other hand Craig inputs some of those magic elements of initiative, lateral thinking and excitement. He hypes everybody up to his speed, which is good. Not only does a Twelve Metre programme need workaholics but the work rate has to go up, that is terribly important.

In fact I suspect that what we achieved with our group eventually was the highest output of virtually any programme, because we were so short of people, and doing so much. So the guys worked endlessly but their work output began to improve, and that is the tougher one.

Eventually, we did with Craig what you would do with any trouble-maker: you fire them or you promote them. We promoted Craig. We said: 'Craig, OK, you're in charge of the boat. The first job you do is go down in the morning to make sure she's put in the water.'

The first few days he made a couple of mistakes which really were not his fault, but he was in charge so he got the stick. They were irritations rather than serious mismanagement: we didn't have a proper fender round the dock and one night the boat was not properly secured, it blew a bit and the paintwork got damaged. Craig is very conscientious and proud, and he was really angry with himself; in the end his personality changed in the twelve months he was with the campaign.

A major turning point in his life will have been this programme. He is one of the successes of the programme in human terms and he's one of the people I will always have a warm spot for.

These are some of the people drawn together in the pursuit of a great endeavour, ambition and dream. They were as fine a group of people with which I would ever want to campaign.

CHAPTER SEVENTEEN

Where to now?

White Crusader sailed thirty-four races in the Louis Vuitton Cup. She won twenty-one and lost thirteen (by comparison *Stars & Stripes* won twenty-seven and lost seven in the same series) and now she was out of the America's Cup. For Graham Walker, BACC, and for Harold Cudmore it was not, however, the end.

Walker, with the backing of White Horse Whisky, quickly made it plain that the company would continue to campaign for a British win in the America's Cup and announced his next challenge and the syndicate's entry in the forthcoming Twelve Metre world championship to be held in June (1987) in Porto Cervo, Sardinia. Phillip Crebbin would continue to be BACC's Technical Director and skipper in Sardinia and as far as Walker was concerned, Cudmore was still one of the best in the business and was still 'central to the thinking' of the syndicate's plans.

Most of those plans centred around the question of how much it was going to cost simply to stay in the game. The America's Cup was now a mega-spending operation: in the pursuit of designing and building the fastest Twelve Metre in the world no stone could be left unturned and as Iain Murray, *Kookaburra*'s laconic skipper-manager phrased it at a press conference 'turning over stones costs a whole heap of money'. The first thing that had to be decided was how much had this America's Cup cost the successful participants, and from that, work out what Britain would need to do in the future.

One of the lessons that came clearly out of the 1987 racing was that the biggest budget was devoted to defending the Cup. In addition to the Australian dollars spend by Bond and the two smaller Australian syndicate, Parry's Taskforce syndicate had an admitted budget of $A25 million with the suggestion in many quarters that it may have been nearer $A35 million. They had a hundred people on the payroll for the last year to thirteen months, excluding wives, girlfriends and assorted volunteer helpers.

Taskforce had three *Kookaburras* and a fully equipped yard facility with the capability of taking a boat at a time into the yard and virtually rebuilding her. In one case they took fifteen feet off the back of the boat, the whole transom and right up into the afterbody to change the whole designed shape of the hull. As they were doing that they were racing their other two boats, full tilt. Certainly they spent $A4–5 million on sails alone.

So that is one path, designing at full scale instead of making little tweaks on a model. That system is hard to beat as long as you have the design capability, and the funds.

Dennis Conner had been operating for a long time, although there is reason to believe he did not spend anything like the money that has been talked about. Certainly his Sail America Foundation spent about £10 million. They had *Liberty* and they put a new hull under the deck of *Spirit of America* then they built *Stars and Stripes 85*, the radical *Stars & Stripes 86* and then *Stars and Stripes 87*. That's a boat a year plus a rebuilt boat. Effectively they had four new boats, plus the bench-mark boat.

The Kiwis built two sister ships. Their strength was in three successful international designers even though they had not, apart from Lawrie Davison, touched Twelve Metres before, plus a tremendous reservoir of skills in rigs, in sails, and in crewing. They also hired in the best foreign knowledge to train their crews, including their French coach Laurence Esquire.

The Kiwis raced the two boats while the designers designed a third. Probably no one really admits how much they spent, but the Kiwis were into $NZ23 million, and allowing for their lower cost base they got a lot more for their $23 million than would be the case just converting New Zealand currency straight into, say, US currency for comparative purposes.

While Dennis Conner spent carefully, having such an enormous fund of experience. *Kookaburra* spent the most, but they had most to learn.

America II established a bureaucracy and thus lost sight of the essentials of what they were trying to achieve. They had a young, inexperienced decision group outweighed by an experienced bureaucratic group who didn't understand the requirements of the sailing. Although they had $US15 million, which is probably a bit more than *Stars & Stripes* they didn't devote that in the right direction to achieve the results.

So you therefore have to have sufficient money to do the programme you judge necessary. Our budget of £5 million included launching a public company and all the attendant legal fees, and the high cost of the legal dealings with the Royal

Thames. This ate into our operating costs to a sufficient degree to materally affect the outcome of the sailing, at least in terms of getting into the semi-final. We didn't have enough money to run a fully two-design campaign and in that respect we were either over-ambitious or forced to become over-extended, depending on how you wish to view it.

Next time, money will have to play a bigger part in the planning, based on what we learned here. We simply didn't have enough people: specialist areas were not covered correctly and we knew that – things like coaching, medicine and fitness training. A successful campaign, such as the New Zealanders' or *Stars & Stripes* or the *Kookaburras*, needs professional people in all these areas. It should have its own in-house sports medicine specialist, for example. We were very lucky in that Tina Amy, the wife of one of our team, was a trained physiotherapist, so we did have a physio this time, almost as a bonus. She did a tremendous job but she lacked facilities and we did not have any more money to provide her with better. We should have had our own fitness centre, instead of having to use a commercial one in the town.

With proper funding you can have things like your own helicopter, as the Kiwis had. In a sense it's not worth the money (which is why we didn't have one) but if you do have the money it is a benefit, for everything from weather spotting to transport. That is the sort of benefit in kind that can often come from a major corporate sponsor who places equipment he already has at the campaign's disposal, equipment that the campaign itself cannot really justify expenditure on. Or it can come from a wealthy patron who wants to get involved, be part of the campaign almost for the fun of it: that would be his ticket to the parties and the social side of things. You also want these additional people to assist ashore, to take the load off the racing crew. For the non-racing promotional and social events.

There is a danger that the programme could become too big and sloppy, but you can guard against this. Warren Jones has shown that a tight-knit, small programme is not as efficient as a slightly less tight but bigger and more powerful programme.

You have to decide the programme you want to do, and get the money to do it, rather than get as much money as possible and fit the programme into it. It is an old lesson of the America's Cup, and again it has been re-proved.

Time can equate inversely to money to a degree. You can spend more time on the water and thus less money, like Dennis Conner did. The New Zealanders were short of time because they went in later, and spent enormous sums of money to bring themselves up to standard. On the other hand *America II* had a lot of time, and money, but didn't have the correct decision input to use the time correctly, so that's another area too.

What we have to do over the next couple of years is stay with the programme, develop it step by step and use the abilities we have to ensure those steps are worthy steps. Once we decide the steps we want to make we must make sure we have the money or just accept we can't win the America's Cup, rather than go in with a jolly good British effort which is half-timed and half-funded.

Last time, the British misjudged the seriousness of some of their competitors. We judged ourselves against *Australia III*, *America II* and *Kookaburra*, to which we were as technically capable. What happened was that people like Dennis Conner achieved a higher standard.

One message that *has* emerged, yet again, from this America's Cup is that continuity of effort is the only way to garner any sort of success, indeed any sort of serious involvement, in the America's Cup of the future. The enormous design and development programme which the nature of the competition now dictates can only be achieved by a continuing effort. If the White Crusade proved anything, it proved that leaving a sixteen month gap between the end of one America's Cup campaign and the start of the next, along with a two-and-half-year gap between the securing of the necessary funding, is a sure-fire way not to win. Too little and too late; the Great British malaise.

Happily, there has now emerged a concurrence of need between the competitive requirements and the commercial possibilities of this unique phenomenon. So much money has to be tied up that it simply cannot be looked upon even by the largest and most profligate of spenders as one-off shot. A return, preferably a continuing return, simply has to be shown and the investment, to show that return, has to be spread over more than a mere three months of concentrated racing in just one venue. The gamble must be extended to give the game's participants more than just the one cast of the dice that is the single, three-yearly frenetic series of yacht races that lead up to the America's Cup itself.

The Twelve Metre syndicate of the future will have to have the capability of producing at least one new boat a year, simply to keep the design momentum going, and the only way to support such expenditure will be to provide something for those boats to do in the years when there is no America's Cup. There is only one thing Twelve Metres can do. Race.

Even as the Fremantle circus was winding up, Cudmore himself was asked by the International Twelve Metre Owners' Association to investigate a proposal for an organised programme of races and regattas which would support the continuing development requirements of the America's Cup design effort and provide a continuing publicity and promotional return to repay the necessary investment.

The new Twelve Metre circuit will probably be one regatta a year, primarily because it is very expensive to set such programmes up, to get people to the events and so on. Allied to the main annual regatta, wherever it is held, there will almost certainly be a Mediterranean circuit and this might well be a less serious affair, with the Twelves being towed between the various Mediterranean bases already established: the Palma base, a French base, an Italian base and so on. Each of these bases already has the necessary specialised facilities.

Take Sête, for example, the *French Kiss* base. They have two or three hoists. The circus would make a deal about using them along with the harbours and the sail loft facilities. The French yacht would allow the circus to use her facilities for a week to turn up there and would herself in return go to Sardina, use the Sardinia facilities, go to Palma, use the Spanish facilities.

The distances are small enough to tow the Twelve Metres from one place to another – even sail them if you pick your weather. Twelve Metres are not especially seaworthy but with a couple of people on each boat, all the hatches and deck openings sealed for passage making and a couple of genoas and trysails in case it was necessary to cast off the tow for any reason, it could be done. The boats may not be seamanlike in racing trim, but that's no reason for the sailors not to be seamanlike.

With the Mediterranean circuit as the secondary, lower-level infrastructure of racing events, all the syndicates would up camp and move to wherever the 'Worlds' were.

I envisage for the 'Worlds' a regatta of eight weeks, in which there would be twenty races and probably three events in the one full series. The main event would be the world championship, which is in two parts: the elimination series which is fleet racing, then the match racing tournament for the four, six or even eight top boats in the fleet racing.

There would be some sort of preliminary event as a warm-up and in between the two there would be a fun event. What I propose is two-boat team racing. Sounds crazy, but think of the fun and the interest. Imagine four Twelve Metres fighting to the death, with the match race skills already developed in the class. Great drama!

It would of course be necessary to think very carefully about the rules for this latter event – perhaps even say 'any collisions, both boats disqualified – match declared void', something like that. Even that requires great thought, because you can't have any rule that makes it worthwhile the trailing team to break to retrieve a losing situation. The trouble with contact between Twelve Metres is not so much the hulls as the rigs. Touch these rigs together and you just rip them out and do a lot of expensive damage.

To fund a Twelve Metre circuit, the boats' owners would meet the cost of operating the yachts themselves, but be able to go to the regattas for free. So there should be sufficient funding from the organisers of the regattas, plus the add-on from the syndicates own sponsorship, to pay the bills. The cost of an America's

Cup campaign would be additional to that so there would have to be major sponsorship for that as well, either separate or as an add-on for one major sponsor.

So for the regattas, you'd pay your crews and operating costs as though you were practising, but the world championship venue would pick up the cost of getting and staying there: air fares, transport for the boats, accommodation for the crews: everything. And of course, the Twelve Metres use the base facilities for free.

The venue itself makes the money to pay for this through the economic impact of such a two-month event. For example, if the event went to somewhere in the United States, the economic impact might be, say, $50 million to the area. So the class is saying to the State: 'devote 10 per cent of that to bringing the event there in the first place, $5 million to buy that regatta so each of the syndicates can go to the regatta for free, just having to pay their own operating costs.'

What the class is looking for is not so much just a larger 'event sponsor' but the benefit of the economic impact of the regatta to be put partially back into the class, up front, in return for that benefit. Then the event sponsor – such as Louis Vuitton – would be putting up the prize money and attendance money, which gives a reason for the good teams to attend. The winner of the regatta then gets, say, a million dollars and makes a profit (which he can put to his America's Cup campaign). The last yacht gets lots of valuable experience and at least his expenses are covered.

The next commercial tier consists of the teams' own in-house sponsors, who get a big add-on by their presence at the regatta.

The sponsors themselves need to look very carefully at what they think their money will bring them: it is easy – as this America's Cup all too readily demonstrated – for a sponsor to get very little. Several big Australian corporate sponsors paid a lot of money to the Royal Perth Yacht Club and got precious little out of it.

The same applies to the sponsors of the Twelve Metre syndicates. Up to now, the Twelve Metre sponsor has got very little out of it unless he organises it correctly for himself. In our own case White Horse, although coming in late, devoted a substantial group of people to promoting their association, with a proper advertising campaign around the spirit itself, so they used pictures of the boat and the whole association with the sport very wisely. In their case of course the brand is a world-wide name and they had a press centre both in Fremantle and in London, pumping out information and getting true widespread coverage. It was a total marketing operation.

What White Horse did was an object lesson for any potential sponsor. They were far and away the most successful sponsor in Fremantle for the amount of expenditure.

The sponsor has to realise that, with the best will in the world, the sailors to whom he gives the money are going to use it to buy sails and masts and pay designers, not sell whisky or airline seats or whatever. That is his job, and the sponsor needs to think in terms of spending the same again promoting the product. So £1 million to Twelve Metre means £1 million in promotion, simple as that.

This is what happens in motor racing: the people who build the motor cars don't go around promoting the sponsors' products. What the syndicates must do is to ensure that the promotional facilities are there, and that the drivers are available between races for set performances and personal appearances on behalf of the sponsor.

As to the future, the America's Cup is at another cross-roads. In one sense it is potentially one of the most powerful promotional events in the commercial sporting league. It has everything that advertising copy-writers need; big money, glamorous yachts, exclusivity, glittering social scene. The Australians when they got their hands on it decided to use the America's Cup to promote and display to the world the best picture possible of themselves. So you had a State, a town and to some extent a club motivated towards the good of the America's Cup; rather than the narrower line of keeping it by hook or by crook, and allowing the Cup to develop a public image incidental to that, which is what the New York Yacht Club had done.

Now because of what the Australians achieved with their investment in television time, the winners have acquired an asset from which, in the short term, they should make some nice money. But if they do not move on from what the Australians did – go back instead to a narrower, New York Yacht Club type of role – then the America's Cup may not expand. So much momentum was created in Australia, however, that in all probability the next event, being in America, will be very big indeed.

Because it was in Australia in 1987 it was very hard to get British companies to fund a campaign, and that should be much easier with the event now in America. In television terms British interest was minimal. Very few people in Britain had grasped what was happening. Even if they had, the structure of sport awareness, in particular of media awareness of sport presentation, is such that if it doesn't involve a ball or have four legs and a jockey on its back, it is very hard to get a sport on to British television.

In Britain of the four television channels, two do not carry advertising, and two are very much constrained in how they use it. The promoter of a new sport is thus equally constrained. In Australia, for example, if a promoter comes up with a new event, television there will – assuming they like the idea at all – will cover the event for free in return for free access and co-operative facilities. In return, the station will offer support to the event promoter of, say, so many slots of advertising. The promoter then approaches the sponsor and says: 'here is the event. We have three hours of television and in the lead up we have twenty thirty-second slots. The package costs $1 million – are you interested?'

In England, you go to the television station and you might get them to say 'yes, we will cover that' and the promoter says 'this is my sponsor' and the television station will immediately explain why it can give the sponsor either very little or – if it is the BBC – absolutely no air time at all. The best that can be hoped for is a certain bending of the rules: a shot of a spinnaker with the sponsor's logo, a strategically placed advertising hoarding or bill board near a goal post.

In Britain, sailing cannot go commercial until television changes its outlook. In Australia and in America, the outlook has already changed. Those countries, along with New Zealand and next time Japan will have no trouble mounting effective America's Cup campaigns. In Britain, it needs a big change in a large number of attitudes, not all of them directly connected to the immediate needs of sailing Twelve Metres, before we will ever win the cup.

That Britain has the talent to win the America's Cup is unarguable; that it has the will, even the culture, debatable. In Olympic sailing, Britain is a repeated medal winner; in offshore racing a recurrent world champion. British yacht designers drawing yachts to rules other than the Twelve Metre's International Rule are acknowledged among the best in the world; British yacht builders building one-off offshore racing yachts and Olympic class dinghies likewise. Yet yacht racing's ultimate competition is traditionally regarded, even by a large section of the yacht racing fraternity itself, as an irrelevance: shortly after the finish of the '87 America's Cup, a letter appeared in the country's principal yacht racing magazine from one of the country's principal yachting photographers accusing it of being precisely that.

On the broader front, newspapers continue to treat yacht racing as a minority, fringe sport. Only two national dailies regularly carry yacht racing, and even then not on a daily basis. Television generally declines to treat it as a legitimate sport at all, but is still hung up on its spectacle and the fact that a few of its participants are very rich, wear white hats and drink pink gin. There was virtually no BBC Sports coverage of the 1986/87 America's Cup – only documentary coverage – and even the single, half-hour per week, Channel 4 coverage devoted only seven minutes per show to the racing, leaving the rest of the time for 'Interesting Stories'.

After the '87 Cup, Cudmore put the realistic cost of mounting a worthwhile 1991 challenge at £20 million. Who in Britain would put up such money, why and for what? The last part of the question is the easiest to answer: conservative estimates put the value of hosting the 1990/91 Cup at two billion dollars US. Put like that, winning and then hosting an America's Cup would be as valuable to the British economy as a year's supply of North Sea Oil – and in drilling for oil, £20 million does not go very far.

And there is another reason. The America's Cup was made in London, and raced for in Britain only once: in the year in which was held the Exhibition intended to mark British excellence and pre-eminence in every field of endeavour. It was lost. Surely it is time Britain had it back?